D1585306

KEY TO OPERATIONS
○ RETAIL
● DISTRIBUTION
□ AGRICULTURE
■ HOSPITALITY
△ ASSET MANAGEMENT
▲ FOOD PROCESSING

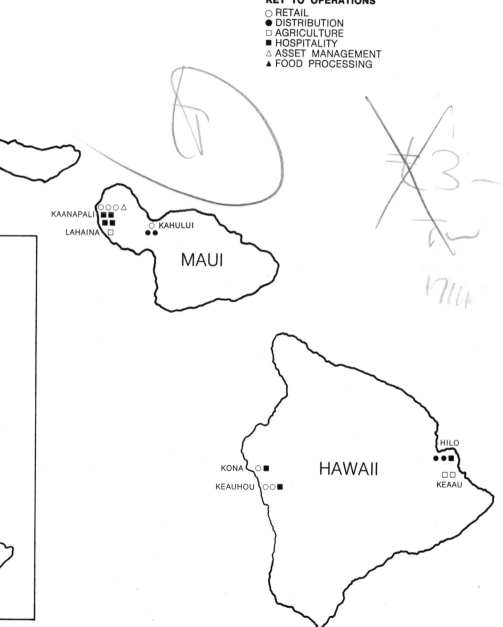

Dynasty
in
the
Pacific

Dynasty
in
the
Pacific

Frederick Simpich, Jr.

McGraw-Hill Book Company

New York   St. Louis   San Francisco   Düsseldorf   Johannesburg
Kuala Lumpur   London   Mexico   Montreal   New Delhi
Panama   Paris   São Paulo   Singapore
Sydney   Tokyo   Toronto

Library of Congress Cataloging in Publication Data

Simpich, Frederick, Jr.
  Dynasty in the Pacific.

  Bibliography: p.
  1. Amfac, inc. I. Title.
HD9503.S54   381   74-11387
ISBN 0-07-057450-2
ISBN 0-07-057451-0 (pbk)

1234567890 BPBP 73210987654

This book is dedicated to those people who over a period of 125 years have contributed to the development of Amfac, Inc., from a small mercantile store on the waterfront of Honolulu to a diversified consumer service company spanning much of the United States and with growing interests in other parts of the great Pacific basin.

Contents

Preface

Books about business tend to be boring, saccharine, or just flagrant flackery. This may be due in part to the subject matter—it is hard to find fun in proceedings before the Securities and Exchange Commission or romance in running a railroad—but it also may be due to the fact that it is a rare management that is willing to have an outsider dramatize its mistakes and indulge in an occasional chuckle at the expense of its corporate dignity.

In the case of the vast enterprise that is the subject of this corporate biography no such limitations apply, and that is well for, in the course of its colorful history, it has survived gunfire from the opium wars in China to Pearl Harbor. Its establishments range from the depths of the Grand Canyon to the top of Tokyo's Ginza. The very diversity of its business is spectacular, trading as it does in everything from silks to sugar, transformers to toupees, and the diversity of its mistakes ranges from a half century of effort to build a coffee industry in Hawaii to bad timing in getting into mass merchandising.

Nevertheless, its management opened wide all the resources sought by a nosy chronicler. Directors' minutes, personal correspondence files, and guarded corporate plans were made readily available to me. Furthermore, the policy of all levels of management was one of complete disclosure.

This is not necessarily surprising. I number some members of the Board and its Chairman among my close personal friends. As part of the tightly knit Hawaiian business community for nearly 40 years, I have shared many experiences with them and their associates. In the 1930s I sat on a committee with a man who is now a Senior Vice President, and we helped draft the first Unemployment Compensation Law for the then Territory. In the 1940s I sat with another executive, now also a Senior Vice President, on the industry committees that negotiated strike settlements for the Islands' sugar and waterfront industries with Harry Bridges and his militant International Longshoremen's and Warehousemen's Union. More recently, we have had experiences in common in the development of housing outside Honolulu and second-home resorts in California.

While these associations helped me to understand the company's affairs and gave me ready access to the history and workings of the organization, they also introduced the dangers of excessive intimacy. This required the establishment of ground rules in regard to the preparation of the manuscript. They were simple: management review would be confined to the correction of any errors in fact or breaches of confidence; the adjectives, emphasis, incidents, and organization of the narrative were to remain my affair. So if this account of the history and activities of multifaceted Amfac, Hawaii's largest business, fails to entertain as well as inform, it can be only my fault.

Frederick Simpich, Jr.

Acknowledgments

M y gratitude runs high to many but first, of course, to the Amfac people who helped. I cannot name all of them by any means, but it was Senior Vice President C. E. S. Burns, Jr., who first suggested the book; Vice Chairman E. Laurence Gay who steered it through the company and corrected it for fact; and Vice President Wallace S. Willis who helped unearth obscure corporate data and old photographs essential to the final product.

Nor can I overlook those who helped in other ways, from the six group chairmen and their executive and operating people, who taught me what makes the mare go, to others further down the corporate ladder. I am grateful to June M. Boranian for her help in obtaining maps and pictures, to Mildred Read for editing and proofreading, and to Lori Busby, all of Willis' staff. Then there were Charleen Ikeda of the Corporate Secretary's Office, guardian of the vaults, who gave me access to them for hours at a time, and Edna Bechert, now retired, the first woman to be made an officer of the company and the most knowledgeable of all about the history of corporate headquarters. Finally, I wish to thank the staff of the Communications Center, who spent more time than the White House in rerunning and transcribing tapes.

Others outside the company helped as well. My wife hunted and pecked her way through the second draft of the manuscript. For the most part, the rest were librarians and archivists. Principal among these was Agnes Conrad, Archivist for the State. Also there was the staff of the Hawaiian Room in the Honolulu Public Library, as well as that of the nearby Hawaiian Historical Society. To a lesser degree the stacks of the Hawaiian Sugar Planters' Association, the University of Hawaii, and the public libraries on the Island of Maui were employed. The California Historical Society in San Francisco and the Library of Congress were consulted. A morning in the British Museum in London was also productive. Sophie Cluff, who has spent years preparing for a library and museum on Kauai, was good enough to read and make constructive suggestions on sections relating to that Island. As usual, my agent, Julian Bach, Jr., of New York, contributed sage editorial advice that came up with the best possible union of text and publisher.

The photographs used in this book were selected from the Amfac collection, built up over many years. Few of the photographs indicate a source, but I believe they came from such files as the Hawaii State Archives, the Bishop Museum, the Hawaii State Library, the Hawaiian Sugar Planters' Association, and the U.S. Navy.

1

Introducing Amfac

The history of the Pacific can be told from many different points of view but none better than in terms of the great trading firms that have long dominated it. For it was they who fashioned the Pacific's destiny after the Portuguese, spurred on by the vision of Henry the Navigator, first opened it to Europeans. Seeking to traffic in the spices of the Indies, the Portuguese were to prove better explorers than traders. It was to be the Dutch who set the pattern for commerce in the Pacific. Driving the Portuguese from their colonies, they set up a network of forts and warehouses that ranged from Sumatra to Macao. Operated in fact by the Dutch East India Company, organized in 1602, these facilities were to control Western trade in the area for the ensuing 160 years.

Paradoxically, even as Englishmen were losing the Revolutionary War in America, their fleet was badgering the Dutch from Ceylon to the islands of Indonesia, finally driving them from the seven seas. At the same time, their leading explorer of the day, Captain James Cook, was discovering the Hawaiian Islands, an event of major importance to this account.

As the British East India Company, with its "ships of azure," moved into the Far East, it took over the forts and warehouses, political influence, and commerce of the Hollanders. It was to monopolize trade with the Orient for two centuries, the keystone to its arch of outposts being its warehouse at Whampoa down river from Canton. Only after the settlement of the opium wars and the cession to Great Britain of Hong Kong in 1841 and Kowloon in 1860 did the center of England's trade begin to shift to the Crown Colonies with their better access to the Middle Kingdom (China).

The wealth being derived by the British in the Far East in the first half of the nineteenth century was not unnoticed by the cities of Germany and Scandinavia. Traders from Hamburg and Bremen began to explore the commercial aspects of the Pacific. They were led by a flamboyant merchant prince named Johan Cezar VI Godeffroy, whose fleet of barques, flying a pennant emblazoned with a white falcon, ranged from Europe to Valparaíso, Australia, and the islands of Samoa and Palau. There were less spectacular but dogged ones, too, such as Bremen's Heinrich Hackfeld, who, starting out with but a single vessel, found means to catch crumbs from the table of the British East India Company in the entrepôts of Whampoa and the godowns of Hong Kong.

So dominant did the European traders become that their organizations frequently survived the military and diplomatic disasters of their nations. The Dutch were to outlast the British in Java, and while the China monopoly of the British company began to decline after the American Civil War and the onslaught of Americans relying on the speed of their clipper ships, it was to endure in many respects until World

War II. In fact, English chartered ventures, like the British North Borneo Company, survived until 1964, and such private companies as Jardine-Matheson, founded in 1832, continue to thrive in the area as never before, despite the dissolution of the Empire.

Witness, also, the endurance of Japan's exploiters of its pre-Pearl Harbor "Coprosperity Sphere." Firms like Mitsui and Mitsubishi rose phoenixlike from the ashes of Tokyo and Hiroshima to reestablish themselves as major factors in the worldwide commerce of the Pacific.

Somewhat similarly Hawaii's Amfac, founded by Heinrich Hackfeld in 1849 from profits grubbed along the China coast, survived a World War I take-over of German interests to emerge as one of the great Pacific trading houses of the 1970s. Listed on the New York Stock Exchange, Amfac's sales would place it Number 264 in Forbes' rankings of American corporations.

How this 125-year-old enterprise survived the vicissitudes of a half dozen wars in the Pacific, a revolution and five changes of government in Hawaii, as well as economic depressions and failures in many of its undertakings, is the thrust of this narrative. First, however, there should be a summary of its history and what it has become today. Thus, as personalities and events emerge in succeeding chapters, the reader will identify the seeds that are to mature as major stands in this forest of enterprise.

Herr Hackfeld

Heinrich Hackfeld was as German as knackwurst. When he determined to settle in Honolulu in 1849, the ship he bought was the 156-ton *Wilhelmine,* which was built in the Bremen yards, and the $8,394.50 worth of goods he loaded aboard her was purchased from Bremen sources with money he borrowed from private bankers in Bremen. He brought many Germans to Hawaii, most of them relatives, and became a South Seas patriarch, passing the mantle, along with the executive role in H. Hackfeld & Co., to a brother-in-law, J. C. Pflueger; a nephew-in-law, Paul Isenberg; a nephew, J. F. Hackfeld; and, in time, assorted kin and Bremen neighbors with "old country" names like Hagens and Glade.

Hackfeld's venture prospered from the outset. His decision to settle in Hawaii was influenced by the business boom in the Islands, induced by the 300 to 400 whaling ships and their crews that wintered there. When he set up shop on October 1, 1849, he was to prosper, as well, from the trade generated by the California gold rush. Everybody in San Francisco (but for an enterprising French family whose firm his successors were to buy 123 years later) was too busy digging gold or running saloons to bother with merchandise. They even sent their laundry to Honolulu. The sea captain turned merchant was quick to add shovels, tarpaulins, tents, and soap to his inventory.

Sugar production was expanding in Hawaii, stimulated by the demand of the forty-niners. While Hackfeld knew nothing of agriculture, the men starting the little plantations knew nothing of purchasing and shipping, insurance and selling, all of which had to be second nature if one were to survive as a China trader. Within 4 years Hackfeld had become a "factor," in effect a business manager, for the oldest of the fledgling plantations to survive, and two more were to seek him out in 1855. His first store, having become more a transshipment operation in the industrial goods of the day than the retail grocery and dry-goods establishment he originally visualized, expanded to a second "upper store" removed from the waterfront. A nephew, B. F. Ehlers, was installed as assistant manager. Thus began the retail activity of Amfac, which today has retail sales of $276 million a year in stores extending from Texas to Japan.

Hackfeld began importing building materials with the gold rush and enlarged his trade in such commodities by bringing in lumber for Hawaiian use in 1851. From these beginnings the Distribution Group has emerged with over 120,000 different items in inventory, ranging from bidets and bedpans to batteries and boilers.

Hackfeld and his successors in the German partnership made great personal fortunes, and the assets of the partnership itself grew from year to year. When H. Hackfeld & Co. was incorporated in 1897, its holdings totaled $3,856,561.91 and the capital contributed by the erstwhile partners was $2,252,941.82, represented by 7,000 shares of common and 3,000 shares of preferred stock, each with a par value of $100. H. Hackfeld & Co. assumed leadership in the business community, and when the United States entered World War I the assistant manager of the company was also President of the Chamber of Commerce. The year before, Manager George Rodiek had been head of the Hawaiian Sugar Planters' Association, something akin to being the Grand Lama of Hawaii in those days, but 4 years and the Alien Property Custodian were to change all that. By 1919 Hackfeld's "Huns," as they were then regarded, had largely returned to Bremen.

"The Yanks Are Coming"

The German managers encountered all manner of difficulty in operating the company even before the United States entered World War I. The British forbade them to use code in communicating with the owners in Bremen. German ships for which Hackfeld acted as agent were interned in Honolulu harbor. There were difficulties in getting proxies from German stockholders to vote at shareholders meetings, and the community, dominated by a strong British-Scotch-Irish ethnic coalition, turned militant where anything German was concerned. When the United States entered the war and George Rodiek was convicted by a federal court in San Francisco of conspiring with other Germans to stimulate a revolution against British rule in India, it became abundantly clear that all enemy interests in the firm would be taken over. There were many in the Hawaiian business community who were well aware of the inherent value of the Hackfeld properties and eager to participate, beyond the demands of patriotism, in their liquidation.

The solution finally evolved by the Alien Property Custodian was a transfer of the assets to six Hawaiian firms in comparable lines of business, that is, sugar, shipping, and merchandising, as well as to the Wilcox and Dillingham families, long associated with many Hackfeld endeavors. Thus it was that Alexander & Baldwin, C. Brewer, and Castle & Cooke, and the Matson Line affiliate, joined by the Dillingham and Wilcox interests, purchased the assets of the company and installed the President of one of the local banks as operating head of the enterprise. They renamed it, with warlike fervor, American Factors, Ltd., and Ehlers' "upper store," with a blare of trumpets, became Liberty House.

Years of heated litigation followed. Essentially the German interests claimed they were undervalued. The government and the new owners claimed with equal passion that the $7.5 million paid for the properties represented its full worth. The federal court in Hawaii sustained the German contention, but it was reversed in what proved to be one of the longest civil proceedings ever to come before the Ninth Circuit Court in San Francisco. Lacking a constitutional issue, there was no success in an appeal to the Supreme Court, but individuals continued to protest. As late as 1934 Rodiek, as trustee for the J. F. Hackfeld Estate, tried again but was denied the claim, as he was unable to prove the American citizenship of the heirs at the time of the take-over.

The Caretaker Years

The company had lost all its vessels during the war and never was to resume shipping operations to any major degree. This is probably due to the fact that some of its new owners controlled the Matson Line, which itself had become a shareholder. Thus they prospered from the fact that American Factors shipped more down-bound freight than any other Island concern. In effect, the new owners viewed the role of the management of "Factors" as custodial. Innovation was reserved for their own companies. Nevertheless, the decade following World War I was a good one for Hawaii and American Factors. Sugar and merchandising, insurance and other collateral activities prospered. Even the Great Depression following the stock-market crash of 1929 was felt less in the Islands than on the mainland. As a consequence of the Depression, however, legislation was adopted regulating the production of domestic sugar and the importation of foreign-grown sugar. It was the long battle of Hawaiian interests before the Roosevelt administration and the Seventy-Fourth and Seventy-Fifth Congresses that first brought a personality long associated with the company to the attention of most Islanders.

H. Alexander Walker was a hard-working *kamaaina* who had been brought into American Factors (generally referred to as Amfac) from the Hawaiian Sugar Planters' Association in 1927 and succeeded to the Presidency in 1933. His knowledge of sugar, his persuasive manner, and his ability to circulate in

Washington society were major factors in the Hawaiian legislative triumph at the time. Passage of the Sugar Act followed a lobbying donnybrook where many politically potent heads, such as those of the sugar-beet states and the Eastern refiners, were bloodied. These interests had wanted Hawaiian sugar treated as "offshore" (along with foreign countries) rather than as "domestic" and, so, American. Walker was prominent in gaining Congressional recognition of Hawaii as an "integral" part of the United States. While he was influential in Hawaiian affairs during the 1930s and a strong link between the community and the military government that followed Pearl Harbor, Amfac long remained hobbled by the very fact that it was controlled by its competitors.

Had World War II not intervened, it is likely that the Justice Department would have been aroused by labor and political complaints of interlocking directorates and the "Matson monopoly" and taken action to force the other members of the so-called "Big Five" sugar factors to divest themselves of their interests in Amfac. Two of them, C. Brewer and Castle & Cooke, were not insensitive to this threat and jumped the gun by selling out by the war's end.

"Twenty Tedious Years"

This phrase, coined by Homer, finds current application in reporting Amfac's postwar problems. With the Castle & Cooke and Brewer interests sold, Walker might have been free to move the company forward to a destiny independent of others in the Big Five; but those, Walker among them, who had anticipated major labor problems following the end of military government were proved absolutely right in that expectation. In 1946 Harry Bridges and his belligerent International Longshoremen's and Warehousemen's Union (ILWU) moved first on sugar and struck the plantations—all of them—for 6 months. The issues were not of organization but of wages, perquisites such as housing and medical care, industry-wide bargaining, and, most important to the labor leader, union solidarity items, notably the closed shop, seniority, posting of vacancies, and appointment of shop stewards. The employers took an awful pasting. Kekaha, one of Amfac's irrigated plantations, saw tons of cane worth over $400,000 wither and die. At the other extreme Puna (formerly named Olaa), on the wet mountain slopes of the Big Island of Hawaii, did not have to irrigate. Its labor costs, however, were proportionately much higher than those of the other plantation companies in the "Amfac group" since it alone harvested its cane by hand. Already deeply in debt to "Factors," it glumly had to accept the ILWU contract that increased its basic wage rates by 70 percent.

Pineapple, in which the company's interest was small, was next to be struck, then sugar again in 1948; but the most damaging encounter came in 1949, when Bridges turned his attention back to his old haunt, the waterfront. The 9-month strike closed all ports in the Islands. According to Walker, it proved more costly to "Factors" than Pearl Harbor, with losses in merchandise compounding those from unshipped sugar and pineapple.

When Walker retired as President in 1950, the labor picture had stabilized and his company was organized to treat industrial relations problems in a progressive fashion. A depression that had threatened the Island economy even in nonstrike periods of the late 1940s had passed, and the buildup for the Korean war and the beginnings of the tourist boom promised prosperity for the merchandising arm and appreciation in the values of Amfac land. But the man chosen to succeed Walker showed no disposition to advance the affairs of the company.

Poor judgment in managing personal matters led to his replacement within 2 years. An extremely able successor found his wife could not adjust to living in Honolulu. So he resigned a year later before he could do much for the enterprise. In turn, he was succeeded by a long-time company executive who brought a fast mind and broad experience to the job, but his administration was marked by basic conflicts with some members of his Board.

Amfac did not lose all momentum in this decade of executive turnover. It became mortgage loan correspondent for John Hancock in the early 1950s, thus paving the way for its current, large-scale involvement in financing and the servicing of mortgages. It had its first experience in subdividing land at Lihue on Kauai, which led to the establishment of that community as the hub of commercial activity on the Island. Problems ranging from insurance claims for volcano-ignited cane fires at Puna to a growing concern over the unprofitability of wholesaling groceries were disposed of. The expansion of coffee plantings on the Island of Hawaii was continued, while the sale of ethical drugs was abandoned.

In 1959 the company chose as its next President a man with an unlikely background and age factor, a long-time head of the Insurance Department. But 62-year-old C. Hutton ("Conch") Smith, an inveterate golfer, had the energy and the knowledge of the company's people for the job. He rapidly restored internal harmony even as troubles were brewing among the stockholders. They were not of his making. When Castle & Cooke and C. Brewer sold out, influence on the Board passed to G. P. Wilcox and Walter Dillingham, engineers of the Alien Property take-over in 1919. They were aging by the time Smith became President and were overdue for retirement. This coming void in influence and the absence of any dominant shareholders were evident to many, and there were several responsible attempts to assemble a controlling interest. Ultimately, there arrived two opportunists, one, Harry Weinberg, out to profit from the company, the other, H. Leslie Hoffman, out to run it as well.

They came on the scene about the time Smith retired after 5 years' stewardship, in which the company's expansion in the retail field and land and resort development had their beginnings. Determined to take things easier on becoming Chairman of the Board, Smith turned matters over to Harold C Eichelberger, a Stanford "Phi Bete" whose first job on graduation was as an errand boy in the company's San Francisco office. Eichelberger, certainly one of the most respected citizens of Hawaii and a dogged worker, presided as the stock of the company was listed, tried to familiarize the financial community with it, and continued expansion along some of the lines begun by Smith. Cautious and sometimes brooding, he did not bring the gung-ho leadership to the situation Weinberg and Hoffman demanded. He stoutly maintained loyalties to executives in whom the militant Directors had no confidence.

When Weinberg failed in an attempt to pack the Board and sold out his interest in the company, Hoffman and Chairman Smith emerged to dominate its affairs. They felt that the qualities needed to get it moving again were possessed by 45-year-old Henry A. Walker, Jr., son of a former President. Neither of the Walkers was a Director at the time of the decision which elevated the son to the Executive Vice-Presidency. Two years later, in 1967, Smith bowed out as Chairman to advance Eichelberger to that position and the junior Walker became President and Chief Executive Officer. Supported by a Wall Street lawyer and financial officer named E. Laurence Gay, whom he and Eichelberger had hired the year before, Walker set about getting Amfac off the ground.

The New Broom

There ensued a whirlwind reorganization and reorientation of the company that has left little but the abbreviated name— by then officially changed to Amfac—to resemble the company the senior Walker had headed. Of the 18 principal officers today, only 6 were employed by the company at that time. In 1964 Amfac's sales were $120,927,000; in 1973 they were $950,123,000. In this 125th year following its founding, they will exceed $1 billion.

So the 125-year story of the Hackfeld dynasty is, for 118 of them, one of evolution and, for the last 7, one of revolution. It is no longer sugar and merchandising in Hawaii that characterizes Amfac. It is a business of managing men and money, whatever and wherever.

The junior Walker sees the company first of all as people. It is mule wranglers leading tourist parties down the gorges of the Grand Canyon, and it is designers transforming store windows into treasure troves at Christmas. It is waitresses, the "Harvey Girls" of other days, moving from marble tables in defunct railroad stations to vibrant airport restaurants, shedding black cotton stockings for pantyhose. It is irrigation-ditch tenders riding wooden rafts for 7 stygian miles tunneled through a Hawaiian mountain. It is dark-skinned youths in loincloths lighting torches and blowing conch shells to praise the sun as it sets on Hawaiian beaches. It is laboratory technicians experimenting with extruded onion rings and cattle buyers spending hours in wooden grandstands bidding in animals for Amfac feed lots in Colorado. It is vendors of health needs filling the prescription counters of Western drugstores and chic fashion buyers attending showings in New York's garment district and the silk factories of Kowloon. It is also MBA's mulling millions in financing Honolulu condominiums and mainland townhouses, and it is property analysts ranging selected California counties in search of developable land.

There are few trades or professions foreign to Amfac people. Walker could, if he chose, call forth a marimba player or a magician, an actuary or an apothecary. Of the 22,000 employees less than 200 are at corporate headquarters. Some of the employment is seasonal, but on the average retail sales involve 6,060 Amfac people and hotels 5,650.

The goods Amfac makes or sells would fill a mail-order catalog and require an appendix for such items as shiploads of sugar and molasses, wool and wheat by the ton, tract homes and townhouses by the hundreds, quiche lorraine and cherries jubilee by the barrel, and frozen french fries and apple turnovers by the carload. Add to these debentures, mortgages, and investment opportunities ranging from savings accounts to ownership to feed-lot cattle, all in multimillion-dollar dimensions.

To help manage these matters, Walker brought in Gilbert E. Cox, a lawyer long associated with the affairs of the company, as Executive Vice President and gave him the added title of Chief Operating Officer. In 1974 Walker became Chairman and Chief Executive Officer, Cox advanced to the Presidency, and Gay became Vice Chairman and Chief Finance and Administrative Officer. Cox, Gay, Executive Vice President John L. Baxter, Jr., Senior Vice President John P. Richardson, Senior Vice President and Controller T. R. d'Arcambal, and Vice President–Finance Richard Hagberg are members of the Operations and Financial Review Committee. This group is the pet cock that controls the flow of the company's resources. This, in turn, gives its members the authority over future plans and budgets.

Reporting to Cox are six senior group chairmen, who, in turn, direct the affairs of one or more relatively autonomous subsidiaries. Retail, for example, embraces the Liberty House,

Joseph Magnin, and Rhodes chains. The Food Group includes Portland-based Lamb-Weston, a processor of frozen potatoes and onions, and Wilhelm Foods of Denver, both purveyors in bulk to the burgeoning fast-food restaurant business. Recently acquired, Pacific Pearl Seafoods (formerly called Ivar Wendt, Inc.) is a small, Alaska-based packer of frozen and canned crab and shrimp which Amfac hopes to build into a major factor in the seafood industry.

Hospitality is the name given the group operating primarily in the restaurant and hotel fields. This includes the legendary Fred Harvey operation in the continental United States. Hospitality also includes 6 Fred Harvey operated airport hotels and some 10 resort establishments in Hawaii operated by Island Holidays.

The Agriculture Group is concerned with the sugar plantations that make Amfac one of the largest sugar producers in the free world. Also operating under Agriculture is Amfac's land development venture in Australia, where grain, cattle, and wool are produced.

In Hawaii the Asset Management Group is concentrating on the production of housing and commercial facilities on the Islands and the operation of the destination resort Amfac has created at Kaanapali Beach on the Island of Maui. On the mainland it develops planned communities and seeks opportunities in land purchases in California. Under a thrift plan the Group accepts savings deposits in Hawaii and does an active business in servicing mortgages and joint venture development of condominiums. On the mainland, through acquisition of Metropolitan Mortgage Corp. of Los Angeles and Commonwealth, Inc., which does business throughout the Northwest, northern California, and the Mountain States, Amfac has come to service $880 million in mortgages, ranking it about twenty-sixth in that business in the United States.

The final group, Distribution, is growing fast in pharmaceuticals and electrical wholesaling in the western United States, where acquisitions have spanned the territory from Wisconsin to Los Angeles and Alaska. In Hawaii, in addition to comparable services, Amfac continues in the wholesaling of building materials.

Presiding over the administrative details of this complex are two Senior Vice Presidents: one in Honolulu and one in San Francisco. Empowered to speak for the company, if necessary, there is seldom the need, as one of the two principals is usually on hand in their constant commute between the two cities. Walker, for example, makes up to a dozen trips from Honolulu to the mainland each year and maintains apartments in San Francisco and New York. This mobility is characteristic of a company which spent over $3,170,000 on travel in 1973.

Mobility is a requisite not only in managing people but in keeping an eye on assets—the product of 125 years of parlaying land and sugar into more land and more sugar along with the collaterals of vertical integration such as merchandising, shipping, and insurance. Today the land assets alone represent ownership of 85,000 acres and control, through lease, of as many more in the United States. This is five times the area of the District of Columbia and one-third the size of Delaware. Amfac grows enough sugar in Hawaii to feed 4 million Americans or 100 million Asians. Sugar employs five factories generating enough power to light a city of 50,000 and enough irrigation water to serve all the domestic needs of Manhattan.

Continuing with the scale of Amfac assets, on any one day its inventories will have cost over $100 million, its float (uncanceled checks in the mails or the hands of others) will total $4 million, and hundreds of its people will be in the air flying somewhere. At the peak of the travel season Amfac will serve more than 60,000 meals and 40,000 drinks and provide lodging for 10,000 people in a day. It is guardian of over $35 million of savings for over 10,000 depositors, and it services over $750 million in mortgages while leasing to others everything from pizza cookers to airplanes, pickup trucks to bulldozers. Its potato production would feed all of Ireland and Boston too.

To see how all this came to pass, let us return to the China trader, Captain Heinrich Hackfeld.

2

The China Trader

The 160-ton brig *Express,* 73 days out of Valparaíso and bound for Canton under the command of Bremen's Captain Heinrich Hackfeld, found herself in trouble south of Formosa on an October day in 1845, when she was caught up in a gale which was driving her helplessly before it. To anyone who has watched sullen seas arise from these normally benign waters, the scene is clear: the rain driving parallel to the deck, the wind screeching madly through the rigging, and the little craft, with sails furled, tossed and driven by the unrelenting tempest.

In the ship's hold that day were 160 tons of dyewood and $80,000 in specie to be exchanged in Canton, Hackfeld wrote, for "waren, stichereiem, spiegel, farbe, kleidungsstucke und munze"—that is, merchandise, embroidery, mirrors, paint, clothing, and coins.

Darkness before Dawn

Hackfeld was then a stocky 30-year-old and a seasoned trader as well as mariner. He was also, by all accounts, a determined young man, square of head, body, and jaw. Throughout his career he evidenced an obsession to get things done fast. He was never able to abide having matters taken out of his hands, so the roaring gale that determined his course must have concerned him not only for his cargo and his crew but for the very indignity of being helpless before it.

Late that night the *Express,* still driven by the storm, came to a bone-shattering, crunching halt that sent men sprawling and the cargo shifting. During the remaining darkness, Hackfeld and his crew could feel the ship breaking up beneath them and, if other evidence was needed, there was the sloshing of water rising in the hold to prove it.

With daylight the storm, but not the seas, subsided. Hackfeld was able to evaluate his situation. The ship would become a bundle of floating timbers before the day was out. It was aground on the center of a submerged reef that joined three high islands like the strand of a necklace and was but several hundred yards from the largest of them, where human figures and the smoke of cooking fires could be seen. Hackfeld remained with the ship and sent his sailing master and some of the crew members to recruit labor and some means of lightering the dyewood and specie ashore. It was well, too, to find out just where they were. While the landing party discharged its mission, he directed men overboard with ropes and chains to secure the remains of the vessel to the reef and so reduce the pounding and delay its disintegration.

On the shore party's return, he learned that these were the Batan Islands, 400 miles north of Manila, that there was native labor to portage the cargo, and that two Spanish priests, living in a missionary compound, were available to serve as translators. Equally good was the news that there was a sheltered harbor on the far side of the mountain. So it was that Hackfeld got his cargo and crew ashore, every stick, dollar, and man of it. With the help of natives, he transported the goods 13 miles through the steaming heat of the rain forest and over the mountain to the harbor's edge.

In the ensuing weeks, while residing in the mission, Hackfeld, in the best tradition of the shipwrecked, drove his crew to build and rig a raft sufficiently seaworthy to carry them and the all-important cargo to Manila. Then, in support of the belief that some element of luck attaches to any success story, when they were about to embark on the highly speculative voyage to Luzon, there sailed into the harbor a British man-of-war of 36 guns. It was H.M.S. *Samarang,* under Sir Edward Belcher, bound on a surveying trip. In the custom of seafarers, Sir Edward offered Hackfeld's crew and cargo passage to Manila. There Captain Hackfeld found means to transport the dye-wood and specie to its destination. On February 17, 1846, 203 days after he left Valparaíso, Hackfeld arrived at Whampoa, 13 miles down river from Canton, to deliver his cargo to the warehouses of the Co Hong, the Manchu-appointed monopolists of China's foreign trade.

China Hand

The Canton that Hackfeld encountered was still dominated by restraints on trade with foreigners, reflecting the belief of those who ruled the Middle Kingdom that anyone from elsewhere in the world was a barbarian. They traded with them only because they hungered for the foreign devils' bullion. Hackfeld, like all the others, was required to anchor and work his cargoes at Whampoa, never being allowed to approach Canton proper. He could trade only through the Co Hong, who controlled all commerce inbound and out. So established was their position that it was not unusual for them to exchange as much as $4 million worth of goods in one transaction. In payment for the monopoly, the Manchus expected the traders to sell tea and opium to the Europeans for gold and silver specie to the best advantage of the kingdom.

The big foreign traders were the British and the Scots, and the small ones, the Hanseatic types like Hackfeld, were compelled to follow their pattern. In doing so his conservative, somewhat humorless, Lutheran soul must have found some amusement at the contrast between his appearance, with his dumpy figure, derby hat, and muttonchops, and that of the Co Hong seated across the table, with their slender elegance and brocaded robes, hair in queues, wispy beards, and fingernails, 2 inches long, guarded by jewel-encrusted shields.

In the course of his trading Hackfeld, like all the other Europeans, was confined to the walled foreign quarter. There he was free to walk only in a square where soothsayers, letter writers, and mongrel dogs were his companions. The British East India Company maintained a gardened mansion within the walls but that was only for Englishmen and Scotsmen. It was a lonely life for Hackfeld, because as a foreigner he was denied the right to have his family with him or even to mix with the Chinese. He once sought to boat for pleasure among the floating towns of the river people and the anchored merchantmen, but that too was refused him.

Thus his familiarity with Canton was less than that with many other ports shown by his log as frequently visited. The list would make a travel agent drool today. There was Archangel and Messina, Gibraltar and Menton, Mazatlán and the Beatty Islands, Cape St. Lucas and Maracaibo, Livorno and the Rio Grande. Still his acquaintanceship with Whampoa and what he learned of Canton and the surrounding Kwangtung province was to provide an unexpected dividend when he later became involved in the labor-short Hawaiian sugar industry. Within 7 years he was to be sending recruiters with letters of introduction to his acquaintances among the Co Hong asking help in inducing indentured labor from the surrounding districts such as Pao On, Toi'shan, and Chungshan to come and work in Hawaiian fields.

While Canton eluded him, he was well acquainted with the 40-mile triangle formed by the estuary of the Pearl River with Whampoa at its apex, Macao at one base point, and the Boague Straits that mark the entrance to Hong Kong's passages at the other. It required more than seamanship to get safely through these waters. In that day pirates still lurked there. Not all were Asiatics, for Western adventurers sailing craft called lorchas, European hulls rigged like junks, often found piracy more profitable than trade. Standard items of Hackfeld's gear included cutlasses, muskets, powder, and shot. In his time, even as the missionaries in Hawaii began to disprove the phrase that "There is no God west of Cape Horn," few along the China coast had ever heard of Him.

Bremen Beckons

It was again luck that guided the lonely Hackfeld a half world away from home into contact with hard-bitten Captain John Dominis from Hawaii, who knew these waters even better than he did. Dominis offered the Bremen-bound, seagoing hitch-hiker passage to Honolulu aboard the *Swallow*. Hackfeld was to learn much from Dominis, who was more than a seaman. He was, in fact, a member of a family that was distinguished on Oahu. His son was to become its Governor and marry the last of the native monarchy, serving as consort to Queen Liliuokalani.

During Hackfeld's brief stay in Honolulu, before proceeding to Bremen by way of Tahiti, the canny captain was given a tantalizing introduction to business opportunities in Hawaii by Dominis and some of the Germans already residing there. The whaling fleet was then at sea, but Hackfeld had been in Honolulu in winter months when its harbor was so crowded that you could walk across it by stepping from the deck of one whaler to another. From Dominis he learned that the previous year nearly 500 of the malodorous ships with their riotous crews had wintered there; and 600 were expected in 1846. On all sides there was optimism as to the growth of the fleet and thus the increased demand for ship chandlery and provisions as well as merchandise for the free-spending crews. While the German colony continued small, several of Hackfeld's acquaintances had become established in Island trade, H. A. Widemann and G. F. Wunderberg among them, both from Hildesheim.

Their success encouraged Hackfeld to believe that should he settle in Hawaii he would do well also. Bremen, like others of the Hanseatic cities, soon would have a trade agreement with the Hawaiian monarchy providing most-favored-nation clauses. Repeated power plays by the principal European nations to gain political, and so commercial, dominance of the little kingdom had failed. By contrast with the China coast, the British, represented principally by Starkey & Janion (later succeeded by T. H. Davies), were far from dominant in the economy. The French, who once threatened the sovereignty of the Islands and rather arrogantly refused to sign a trade treaty with the monarchy, were actually represented by only 12 resident nationals and some Catholic priests.

It was the Americans who were in a position to control the fledgling trade in Hawaii. They were present in the greatest numbers and the missionaries among them had the confidence of the government. The whalers, who provided the principal financial support of the community, were of American registry, but the Yankees were so divided among themselves they could not form a cohesive force on most issues. The missionary element was at constant odds with the traders, the ships' crews, and the derelicts attracted by the South Seas. Hackfeld, with no political ax to grind, was encouraged by this division and the fact that there was no government-directed monopoly and no "squeeze."

Along with whaling, there was much talk of the possibilities in the growth of sugarcane. Hackfeld had voyaged to the East Indies and West Indies and knew that trade in sugar was booming, generated by the growing demand in Europe and along the Atlantic seaboard. He could not see why Hawaii should not share in it. This had to be a little naïve, however, because sugarcane, which was found wild in the Islands when they were discovered 68 years before, had been experimented with unsuccessfully throughout the intervening decades. Poor molasses and worse rum had been the usual result. There was one plantation, which had survived bankruptcies and ownership changes for 10 years, that was making a palatable, if unduly brown, sugar for table consumption. That plantation, Koloa on Kauai, was to figure in his future.

Another factor Hackfeld found favorable was Hawaii's liberal constitution guaranteeing citizens privileges still being contested in Europe. There was a related consideration that inclined him to establish himself in the Islands. This concerned ownership of land. If, for different motives, the foreign colony agreed on one point, this was that some system of Western land tenure was essential to the economic development of the kingdom. The ruler, in the days before discovery, "owned" all the land he could police. This tradition continued into the

1840s. As a matter of favor he allowed tenancy to chiefs and commoners, but it was at his pleasure and he could remove them summarily.

Led by Gerrit P. Judd, a missionary doctor who had become the principal advisor to the King just before Hackfeld arrived with Dominis, the monarchy adopted a system allocating ownership of land between the King and those enjoying its occupancy. Under the plan devised by Dr. Judd, the land was divided, one-third to the government, one-third to the King to hold in perpetuity as private property, and one-third to his chiefs as their personal holdings. Provision was made for commoners to obtain title to the parcels they occupied. Judd's interest was prompted by his desire as Finance Minister to provide a means for an extravagant government to generate income by leasing its only real asset. The power to tax had already exhausted a very meager base.

Judd was also prompted by a philosophy, more common today than at that time, to secure for the little man the right to own the land he tills. To protect the lavish-living Hawaiians from dissipating their only wealth, Judd's program provided that land could not be sold to foreigners. Those coming from abroad could lease it for no more than 50 years and then only if they had, as he had, become citizens of the kingdom. Even as Hackfeld walked the waterfront seeking a berth and cargo space for the next leg of his voyage home, a Board of Land Commissioners was hearing claims and making awards under what came to be known as the Great Mahele, or division. In the warehouses and taverns along the waterfront the traders and merchants were saying, "Now the missionaries can't stop them. The Kanakas will get so far in debt they'll have to sell the land."

In summarizing all this, Hackfeld found Hawaii in the spring of 1846 offering profitable prospects in the burgeoning whaling trade and the infant sugar business. He saw the Great Mahele as putting money in the hands of the Hawaiians and so creating a retail market. He saw in it, also, the probability that before too long foreigners could own land. The government, while autocratic, was guided by democratically minded Westerners like Judd. There certainly were no Manchus about and no monopolies like those that existed along the China coast. Nevertheless Bremen beckoned. Hackfeld had been separated for a long time from an ailing wife. He had his cargo of "waren and spiegel" to sell there and he must buy another ship.

The long return to Europe, 6 months via Tahiti, gave him plenty of time to think about a move to Hawaii. There were, first of all, the difficulties in removing his frail wife from the civilized precincts of Bremen to this remote, still rowdy spot, with its tropical climate. There was the problem of financing a business to be conducted in an area of American influence (unlike Samoa and Guam, where Germans were dominant), and there was some doubt that he could give up the sea and the adventurous trading life he knew so well for the humdrum existence of being a merchant. It was to take 1½ years to resolve these questions—a long, deliberate time for the hard-charging Hackfeld.

In the 1840s Bremen was a bustling trading center, where sardines, cheeses, coffee, and cigars scented docks also laden with whaleboat oars, Rhine wine, barrels of pork, and casks of brandy. So busy had the city of 50,000 become that a new harbor, the great Bremerhaven of today, was then being opened to shipping.

Like Lübeck and Hamburg, Bremen was dominated by a merchant class: burgher families such as the Hackfelds with strong social and commercial ties. Private banking was the rule. In fact, government-sponsored banking was practiced only in

Prussia at the time. "Vertical integration," as we call it today, was also the rule. There were no antitrust laws, so a trader like Hackfeld took his profit from the markup on his merchandise, on the freight charged for shipping it, and on the agent's commission for buying it, insuring it, and negotiating its shipment. Then there was interest to be collected for advancing the purchase price and perhaps an added management fee for the time and trouble involved in arranging the whole transaction.

Hawaii Calls

While the Hanseatic traders prospered and enjoyed the benefits of peace, most of the rest of Europe was at war or in revolt. It may have been the uncertain future of Bremen in a unified Germany that was the governing factor in Hackfeld's decision to return to Hawaii and settle there. In any case, for 18 months after he returned home he debated the decision. In this period he resumed his trader existence, reporting far-ranging transactions with Hong Kong and Valparaíso, Canton and Tahiti, Guayaquil and Mazatlán. Then on February 1, 1848, he cast the die and bought the brig *Wilhelmine,* of 156 tons, complete with masts, spars, rigging, and one set of sails, for $7,000. After sailing her on two voyages to the Caribbean, he loaded her with $8,394.50 worth of inventory, his wife, and her younger brother, J. C. Pflueger, and departed for the great adventure in Hawaii on November 28, 1848.

Among the crew were some Kanakas, as Hawaiians had been quick to establish themselves as able seamen and by then ranged the seven seas. Also listed on the manifest was B. F. Ehlers, one of Hackfeld's many nephews who were to share in his Island enterprises. Ehlers was to remain in Hawaii and, succeeded by his son, run the retail arm as Hackfeld's activities proliferated. On the voyage the ship was under the command of H. Schriever, for the *Wilhelmine* was to return to Europe for more merchandise once Hackfeld had gauged the demand in a Hawaii he had not seen for 3 years.

On the 238th day out, with stops at Hamburg, Lisbon, Valdivia in Chile, and Tahiti, the Hackfeld party arrived in Honolulu. They lost no time in setting up shop. Once again Hackfeld's good judgment was reinforced by good luck, for he found Honolulu booming. Besides the whaling trade, the California gold rush had generated a demand for sugar, which sold for 20 cents a pound. The need was less for the cloth goods that made up a quarter of his inventory, or for the "steel pens, copy paper, oil sheets, bedsteads, lead pencils, and looking glasses—$750.26" that was 10 percent of it, than for more robust stuff. Picks, boots, shovels, and tarpaulins were to be the next *Wilhelmine* cargo and the "hot" items in his first years as a Honolulu merchant.

Though Hawaii is often humid and muggy in late September and unpaved roads can be ankle deep in dust at that season, Hackfeld lost no time in getting going. In 4 days he had arranged to rent half the space in a store operated by one C. S. Barstow, discharged his cargo, and put it on display. He opened for business on October 1, 1849, and so founded a dynasty which also provided the occasion for the publication of this account of the ensuing 125 years.

Brother-in-law J. C. Pflueger, Hackfeld's only employee, in the early days slept in the store on a cot which he raised to the rafters during business hours by a system of pulleys. He entertained himself during the lonely evenings by playing a violin. The evidence is that the young boy, 18 at the time, minded the store while Hackfeld was the planner, buyer, financier, and ship chandler. Whatever the exact division of their duties, they did well from the outset, taking over all of Barstow's space within 6 weeks and establishing a second "upper store" within a year. Strong family man Hackfeld saw to it that there was a place for nephew Ehlers as assistant manager of the new establishment. Ehlers and Pflueger were only the first of a score of relatives and friends that the captain and his associates were to bring over from Germany.

Honolulu appears to have met all of Hackfeld's expectations, for the speed with which he became established as a merchant was matched only by the speed with which he became a leading citizen. By the time he took Pflueger in as his first partner and changed the name to H. Hackfeld & Co. in 1853, he had become a founder of the Chamber of Commerce, consul for Germany and Norway, and a confidant of royalty. True, there were only 1,000 Caucasian residents there at the time, and the once-dominant missionary group had disbanded when their support was cut off by New England evangelical sources and they became preoccupied with their own survival. This made room for the tradesmen, whose scruples were once in question, to assume positions of influence in community affairs.

Sweet Sugar

The greatest event of 1853 for Hackfeld was his appointment as business agent for Koloa, the first sugar plantation to endure. The history of Koloa over the preceding 18 years had been a reflection of the difficulties encountered not only by the fledgling sugar industry but by any business in the kingdom at the time. It reflected, as well, the character of many of the traders who had made their way to the Hawaiian Islands in the early days of their Europeanization.

Koloa had been founded in 1835 on land leased from the King, with the reluctant approval of the Kauai chiefs, by three young Americans, owners of Ladd & Co. While it struggled along, the three partners got grandiose ideas. In a fashion reminiscent of Harman Blennerhassett's and Aaron Burr's negotiations for a kingdom beyond the Alleghenies, they made a secret deal with the King for development rights to all the land in the Islands not yet under cultivation. They formed a stock company, and one of them proceeded to the United States and Europe seeking to sell these rights. He finally made a deal in Brussels for the establishment of a Belgian company to take over the arrangement with the King for $200,000. However, over a year before the European emissary returned to Honolulu, Ladd & Co. was bankrupt and in debt to the government and private creditors for more than $100,000.

The partners then sued the government, claiming that the bankruptcy had imperiled their ability to sell their rights and that there was a breach of contract in general. That the Ladd & Co. partners may have been akin to rogues is not to be doubted. It developed that while they had already sold one-half of their rights to New York interests, they were engaged in selling all of them to the Belgians. Nevertheless, the litigation divided the community into two factions, those who were owed money by Ladd & Co. supporting the partners and the rest siding with the Crown. Representing the King was the ubiquitous Dr. Judd, of the Treasury Board, as the Finance Ministry was then styled.

When the suit failed, a creditors' committee, created to handle the affairs of Ladd & Co., had the problem of disposing of Koloa. The plantation was bid in by Dr. Robert Wood, a prosperous Honolulu druggist, who, like Judd, was active in the business affairs of the community. Wood was to develop a penchant for investment in sugar. This inclination and his friendship with Hackfeld were to launch the captain in the business that has provided the resources which turned his modest enterprise into the Amfac of today.

Wood, impressed with the urbane, hard-driving Hackfeld,

sensed in him the combination of experience and business skills required to straighten out the affairs of Koloa. Hackfeld found in Wood a source of capital to introduce him to the capital-devouring sugar business. On July 5, 1853, there ensued some major changes in Hackfeld's firm. The lower store was moved from the Barstow building to a new structure nearby on Queen Street built for it by Dr. Wood. The doctor named Hackfeld agent for Koloa and transferred the representation of Russian commercial affairs in Hawaii to him. On that day, sensing that other major matters were to preoccupy him, Hackfeld admitted young Pflueger to the firm.

While Hackfeld was wrestling with the affairs of Koloa and soliciting the agency for its neighbor, Lihue, the partnership continued to traffic around the world in any commodity in which it sensed a profit. One entry for November 14, 1853, is quoted verbatim from Pflueger's accounts:

> Box of specie shipped to Wm Pustau & Co., Hong Kong for sale
> a/c HH&Co., containing
>
> | | |
> |---|---:|
> | Amount in slugs | $3,000.00 |
> | 22 Dubloons | 352.00 |
> | California Coin | 135.00 |
> | 2 L | 9.50 |
> | 1 gold ring | 30.50 |
> | Spanish & Mexican Dollars | 333.00 |
> | Spanish & Mexican Quarters | 140.00 |
> | | $4,000.00 |

For some years there was an entry carried as an asset: "Various Adventures from Boston, China and to Manila—$9,933.07." There is no further record of what that was all about.

By 1855 when Captain Hackfeld embarked on a 2-year trip to Europe to organize a larger purchasing and shipping structure there, John Hackfeld, a nephew, had come out from Bremen. Other Pfluegers had also entered his employ. H. C.

was attending to affairs in Bremen and G. F. was shortly dispatched to establish a store at Koloa. Most importantly, the partnership was representing a second Wood sugar venture, the East Maui Plantation.

Their assets at the time totaled $93,711.08, of which half was employed in the merchandising end of the business (including two residences on Fort Street where the partners lived). The balance was reflected in advances to various debtors, including Charles Brewer of Boston in the amount of $8,234.23 and the Hong Kong agent, Pustau, in the amount of $4,269.32. There was another item of $25,954.58 owed Hackfeld.

In the first year of the captain's absence Pflueger increased the net capital by 42 percent, and by 1859, when the enterprise entered its tenth year, net capital had grown to $109,387.63 from an apparent investment of less than $20,000 in the *Wilhelmine* and the opening inventory. Of this original sum, it is not clear how much was borrowed from the bankers in Bremen, but even the earliest partnership accounts show $25,000 to $30,000 due the founder. The amount was to rise to $45,606.07 by the time he returned to Bremen to retire in 1861. When he sold out his interest in 1886, the figure had grown to $95,053.33. In addition, he was paid $178,562 for his then two-sevenths share in the firm.

Hackfeld, ably assisted by Pflueger and subsequent partners, deserves full marks for the establishment of Amfac and, for that matter, the sugar-oriented economy that was to dominate Hawaii for more than a century. Perhaps his greatest contribution, however, was to come quite by chance, when he helped to introduce to the Islands a personality that was to influence their commercial destiny, as well as that of Hackfeld & Co., until this day. This man was Paul Isenberg.

3

Paulo

By the early 1850s a number of Germans had arrived in Hawaii seeking to pattern their fortunes after Hackfeld's. Among them were some people, like Stapenhorst, whose names have disappeared, and others like Hoffschlaeger and Schaefer, whose descendants are listed in the phone book today. One firm, Hoffschlaeger and Stapenhorst, had a partner in Hannover, a Hoffschlaeger brother, whom they asked to recruit a young agriculturist. They hoped to bring to the little Pacific kingdom the most modern farming practices of Europe. So it was that the small German colony of Honolulu, Hackfeld among them, turned out on October 14, 1858, to meet the brig *Harburg*, its master, Captain Gaefenheim, and his supercargo, agriculturist Paul I. Isenberg. The latter was in the undistinguished company of three pairs of sheep which he had tended on the 186-day voyage from Bremen.

The 21-year-old Isenberg was tall and heavy-boned, a huge

man but not fat. His fair-complexioned face was framed by neatly trimmed hair, parted to the right, and a short cropped beard that he allowed to grow longer through the years. Somber and handsome, he was to attract many a covert female glance before his marriage. Hoffschlaeger, on the other hand, was not impressed and wrote his brother, "I shipped your 250 pounds of Isenberg to Kauai today."

Isenberg carried himself proudly. He could trace his family back to 1575 and find that in generation after generation they were seamen and shipowners, men of substance in their day. His grandfather owned a fleet of vessels that carried grain and merchandise down the Weser River to Bremen. His father was a thrifty Lutheran pastor in Dransfeld, where Paul was born in 1837. When he tired of school his father urged him to learn a trade, and he apprenticed himself, at 16, to a farmer. Rising at 4 in the morning, he worked until nightfall drove him from the fields. He then became the manager of a large estate near Heide and ran it for 2 years. He brought to the Islands the European experience Hoffschlaeger wanted.

Isenberg was sent to Kauai in the care of Valdemar Knudsen, a Scandinavian whose lands were to figure in Amfac's future, to learn Hawaiian and earn his keep. After a brief stint as a laborer at the Lihue Plantation, he became a butcher at $30 a month (plus board and room) on a Stapenhorst ranch run by a Scotsman, Duncan McBryde. The product of the young butcher's effort was salted meat for sale to the whalers. He and McBryde became fast friends. When the latter elected to get married, Stapenhorst replaced him. He had a rule that only bachelors could run the ranch. Thus Isenberg succeeded to the manager's job in a matter of months.

The young German was proud of the responsibility and realized that joining the ranks of management, however modest his role, was a great opportunity. At the same time he was miserably lonely in the alien tropics amid a missionary-circum-scribed society. After attending a Sunday church service delivered in Hawaiian, he wrote, "To read a newspaper or a so-called 'worldly' book on a Sunday is regarded as a very great sin."

Such society as there was on the Island centered about traditional holidays, particularly an annual Fourth of July party staged by W. H. Rice, who managed Lihue. On that occasion his guests would ride horseback to the Wailua River, their infants carried in calabashes strung like saddlebags from the backs of horses. Dismounting, the group would sail up the shady, lazy river, disembark, pick mountain apples, and picnic ashore at the home of a friend. Isenberg was first a guest on such an occasion in 1859. A report of the affair by Rice's daughter, Maria, might have come straight out of Louisa May Alcott. She wrote, and there is a hint of prophecy in her phrases:

> Once I was sitting in an armchair when the sail gave a great lurch . . . we were uncommonly far in, for Mr. Isenberg and a native were pushing, when Mr. Isenberg's powerful arm pushed the pole in so far that it could not be pulled out and we sailed away from it. . . . We girls, under the guardianship of Mr. Isenberg, reached the house first and made ourselves at home. . . . As we passed through the dining room only one-half the door was open . . . Mr. Isenberg sprang forward to open the other. . . . Mr. Isenberg, too, brought out a German diary book, and I made him quite angry by laughing at the pictures of women.

Rice was in poor health, and within a year Isenberg returned to Lihue as the *luna* (foreman) in charge of the fields. The young man was influenced to take the job not only by amorous considerations but by a personal conviction that sugar must be irrigated to be grown successfully on Kauai. This was a belief that Rice shared. In fact, over the opposition of some of his stockholders, he had put irrigation to the test by beginning the first ditch in the Islands in 1856. It was Isenberg's task to enlarge it and the fields it served, and in doing so he won the admiration of the lethargic Hawaiians, who called him Paulo. Wherever there was danger, it was Paulo who placed the charges and lit the fuse. His vigor was such that he wore out three horses a day, often working a day shift in the fields and another at night in the mill.

By the time Isenberg became *luna*, Hackfeld was already serving Lihue as agent, Rice having been favorably impressed by the captain's representation of Koloa. On Rice's death in 1862, Isenberg succeeded him as manager; thus began the first direct association of burly Paul and the Hackfeld partners.

Isenberg and Maria Rice had been married on October 16, 1861. While Rice then owned 6 of the 14 shares of Lihue, for which he had paid up to $1,500 a share, there is no reason to believe that the ex-missionary left any substantial fortune to be divided among his five children. Rather it seems that Isenberg, starting at $30 a month, began to save from his first day's work on Kauai. When he was raised to $100 a month as manager, he began to accumulate wealth. By 1865, when George N. Wilcox started a plantation on neighboring Grove Farm, Isenberg personally supplemented the advances being made by H. Hackfeld & Co. and loaned Wilcox $1,000 to help build an irrigation ditch.

By 1871 Isenberg had prospered to such an extent that when Dr. Wood elected to retire to the mainland and offered to sell Koloa to Isenberg, he, joined by two Hackfeld partners, was able to take half of it. They paid $35,000 for the plantation, which produced 400 tons that year.

The Dynasty Emerges

While Isenberg was building up Lihue, J. C. Pflueger was doing the same for Hackfeld & Co., and the founder of the company, back in Bremen, was providing purchasing and shipping services for his Honolulu partners. In 1864 Hackfeld & Co. had built its net capital to over $250,000 and showed advances to Dr. Wood and the new East Maui Plantation of $14,233.01, while Koloa enjoyed a credit balance of $4,127.42. There was $31,469.34 in merchandise in Petropavlovski, Russia, and $2,398.24 due the Russian American Company in Sitka, Alaska; these amounts were the outgrowth of the Russian representation assigned Hackfeld by Dr. Wood over a decade before and were based on trapping seals for fur.

Pflueger was to run the partnership for only 10 years, returning to Germany when he "had it made" in 1871. That year he and Hackfeld admitted J. C. Glade and one Ed Fursteneu to the partnership. Glade, a Hackfeld neighbor in Bremen, was made manager. Fursteneu did not last long, but Glade served until his retirement in 1883 and the name was to endure among the shareholders of the firm until liquidation of the German interests in 1918. In its early days the partners were busy selling everything from Harzer Saurbrenner, a mineral water, to Steinway pianos.

They were also involved in a major brannigan with the government over the failure of a company they represented, the United States, New Zealand and Australian Mail Steamship Line, to fulfill its contract to deliver the mails to and from the West Coast. The partnership also represented the California, Oregon and Mexico Steamship Co., which was anxious to step into the breach, as was another client, the Pacific Mail Line. The partners danced a tightrope as they corresponded, in fine Spencerian hand, with "His Excellency, E. O. Hall, H's M'y's Minister of Interior." Their phrases were elegant as well. They wrote, "The other contents of Your Excellency's letter are noted by us and will be enunciated to our principals." In another communication they said, "Inasmuch as this eminent Company is now undertaking to run the route and its previous reputation for over twenty years in this ocean gives earnest of its acceptability to travellers and shippers, we trust that we may be excused if we suggest to His Majesty's Government whether or not it would appear ungracious to withdraw from them this favor hitherto enjoyed by their predecessors."

In this period in Hawaii there was little to suggest the Islands of today. Glade organized a German Club, Der Deutsche Verein, long since disappeared. Even the spelling of place names was still confused. Maui was often written as Mowee and Molokai as Morokai. Groves of trees like kukui and acacia surrounded the scattered buildings of downtown Honolulu. There were still taro patches in Nuuanu Valley, and the approach to Waikiki wound through acres of duck ponds. You could rent a horse for $1.25 a day or readily buy opium smuggled in by clipper ship. Smuggling, in fact, was common. Even the King was detected sneaking in sherry and brandy, not only to avoid the duties but to escape the ire of the missionary element. A special breed of "poi" dogs was still being raised, in size like small sheep, and they were delicious when cooked over hot stones for a luau. The "upper store" was doing a big business in Manila hats covered with black lace. The partners did their work standing up at high bookkeepers' desks. Glade's most lasting contribution as manager in these days was the purchase of the bulk of the site of the present Amfac Center from the Hawaiian government. This included the old courthouse where the lower store was moved in 1874.

The courthouse, which was to stand until 1969, had quite a role in Hawaiian history—such a role, in fact, that there was some protest on its demolition. Erected in 1852, it served, before Iolani Palace was built, as a symbol of the authority of the monarchy, particularly the Kamehamehas.

When that line died out in 1872 and a successor, Lunalilo, passed on a year later, a contest for the throne developed. The widow of the next to last of the Kamehamehas and a prominent chief, David Kalakaua, carried their fight to an assembly of representatives elected from all the Islands. Queen Emma favored the British; Kalakaua favored the Americans. The gathering convened on February 12, 1874, to choose between them. Isenberg was one of the Kauai representatives and, though long a staunch supporter of the Kamehamehas and named a noble of the Kingdom by Lunalilo, he voted for Kalakaua, who won 39 to 6. The dignity of the proceedings was marred by the fact that one of Isenberg's fellow representatives from Kauai was too drunk to walk over and put his ballot in the box. While he made no recorded comment on it, this must have greatly distressed Paulo. As a vehement teetotaler, he was to refuse to share in any profits from liquor when he became a Hackfeld partner.

Emma's disappointed supporters rioted. The police threw their badges away and joined them or Kalakaua's faction as their personal conviction dictated. The courthouse, with its Kamehameha associations, became the center of the disturbance. When sailors from American warships, then in port, finally restored order, the building was completely gutted. In the temper of the time, its future became a political issue, and after prolonged debates in the legislature the forces favoring sale, rather than repair, prevailed. So it was that it became Amfac property, serving first as the Hackfeld office and from 1903 until 1968 variously as warehouse or office space.

By this time Isenberg had been widowed for many years and had remarried. His second wife was a young pianist named Beta Glade, whom he had met on a visit to Bremen at the home of Captain and Mrs. Hackfeld. Beta was 23 and the sister of J. C. Glade; she was also the sister of Mrs. B. F. Ehlers, wife of the manager of Hackfeld's "upper store." Isenberg's two children by his first wife, Maria, and "Mother" Rice, Maria's mother, were also in Bremen at the time. Isenberg married Beta in a matter of weeks with Mother Rice's encouragement. It was very much a family affair, with Isenberg's pastor father conducting the ceremony. On the honeymoon they stopped off to show Maria's children to their Rice great-grandparents in Tennessee. Returning to Lihue at the end of 1869, Paul and Beta established themselves with Mother Rice in Koamalu, the old Rice home, where they lived whenever they were in the Islands.

The devotion between Isenberg and Mother Rice was so great that it has become a legend among the Islands' *kamaainas*. Mother Rice remained a member of his household during his lifetime and survived him by 8 years.

Continuing the tradition of family ties, two of Isenberg's brothers, Carl and Otto, also sought their fortune in the Pacific. Carl arrived in the Islands in the 1860s. In the early days of Hawaiian plantations, boiling sugar was regarded as a form of alchemy, so Paul arranged for a French sugar boiler on the plantation, one Victor Prévost, to teach his younger brother the art. Prévost usually charged $500 for this instruction, but in this case he only extracted a pledge to keep the craft secret until he retired. Carl saved enough money to return to Germany in 1871, but only after teaching the more newly arrived Otto the wizardry of boiling sugar.

Changing Times

Reciprocity, a treaty with the United States giving dutyfree status to sugar produced in Hawaii, was the goal of those who supported Kalakaua, and its negotiation preoccupied both Isenberg and Glade throughout 1873 and 1874. By that time U.S. tariffs had become so onerous that the bulk of the Islands' 1873 sugar crop had been sent to Australia and New Zealand, where a more favorable net return was gained. There was much talk of seeking reciprocity arrangements with the British colonies should efforts with the United States fail. The Hackfeld "line" favored a treaty with the United States, as they were often at odds with British interests who, in sponsoring Queen Emma's cause, resisted closer American ties. Isenberg and Glade were also opposed to the minority in the Hawaiian community who favored annexation with the United States. They felt that reciprocity, with the implied American protection of Hawaiian sovereignty, presented the best of all possible worlds.

In this period whaling was in a decline. Discovery of kerosene in Pennsylvania and the tragic loss of ships to early ice in the Bering Sea were major factors. Civil War blockades, shipowners' displeasure with Hawaiian prices, and the local discipline meted out to their rowdy crews contributed to the whalers' desertion of Hawaii as a base. In an effort to save the trade, there was a time when 19 Hawaiian-owned vessels joined the fleet in a "we'll beat 'em at their own game" attitude. Though Hoffschlaeger and Stapenhorst owned three such vessels, the Hackfeld partners avoided the waning business and were content to act as chandlers to such of the fleet as remained. Their interest in shipping lay in other directions. One of the reasons J. C. Pflueger had moved to Bremen in 1871 was to build a fleet to ply the trade routes to the Islands. These craft, with names like *Wood* and *Glade*, were a great pride to the partnership and flew a nostalgic flag, the white cross of the Hanseatic League on a field of German red.

Sugar, though it had its ups and downs, was growing in importance. When Isenberg took over at Lihue there were only five plantations in the Islands and Hackfeld was agent for three of them. In Isenberg's first full year there, the Hackfeld plantations produced 781 tons. When Wood sold out Koloa 10 years later and Isenberg took over as manager there as well, Hackfeld shipped 3,359 tons, a fourfold increase in a decade. This was to quadruple again in the next 10 years with the addition of 12 new, small plantations to the Hackfeld string. In 1875, when the Hawaiian planters finally won a reciprocity treaty with the United States, there were 35 plantations in the Islands. Under the stimulus of dutyfree entry into the mainland market, the number grew to 63 five years later.

Herr Boss

A strong foe of reciprocity was a California sugar refiner and fellow German from Landstadt in lower Saxony, Claus Spreckels. He and the Hackfeld partners were to clash for years. It all began when Pflueger urged Spreckels to get the mainland refineries to reverse their opposition to reciprocity. Finally, by threatening to send Hackfeld sugars elsewhere for refining, he forced a reluctant Spreckels to agree. When reciprocity was granted in September 1876, the West Coast magnate was on the first boat for Hawaii to establish himself in sugar production in the Islands. His career there was a hectic and colorful one. Building a palace on Honolulu's Punahou Street, he proceeded, through loans, to get the high-living Kalakaua under control and install a business associate as Prime Minister.

Isenberg warned in writing, "We are likely to have serious trouble in regard to a market for our sugar. A . . . millionaire, Spreckels, has the San Francisco market under his thumb and will do all he can to crush other planters, as he neither fears God nor regards man." This was after Spreckels had sought an accommodation with the Hackfeld partners, telling Isenberg, "Both of us must work together, and then we will put all the Islands in our pocket."

The time was to come when, in a row over waterfront rights

in Kahului harbor, Pflueger told Spreckels to "get out or be thrown out" and Spreckels replied that he would "rue the day and see the day when grass grew where he now stood." When you imagine that all this went on in German, as they all spoke limited and accented English, it must have made for some pretty gutteral debate.

During Spreckels' reign there was scandal after scandal. One involved a land deal for Crown property on Maui which became the basis for the Hawaiian Commercial and Sugar Co. Another related to a special coinage arranged for Kalakaua on the mainland on which the sugar baron took a discount of 16 percent.

Spreckels' expenditures on irrigation and mill machinery were lavish, and he built a plantation that was nothing short of magnificent in its day. But his man, Prime Minister Walter M. Gibson, was a menace. He once wrote Hackfeld & Co. that Spreckels would refuse to refine their sugar unless the mail contract with their clients, the Pacific Mail Line, was transferred to the Oceanic Steamship Co., which Spreckels controlled.

The community regard for Gibson is probably best reflected in some popular doggeral of the day called the Gynberg Ballads. In these Spreckels was thinly disguised as "Herr Boss" and Gibson was "Nosbig." Of the latter one stanza said,

> You rascal of the deepest dye—unmitigated fraud! You panderer to silly waste, while 'bums' and beats applaud.

The story of Spreckels' invasion of Hawaii is, and has been, a book in itself. It ended in 1894 when his sons, C. A. and Rudolph, forced his withdrawal. This followed the collapse of Hawaiian Commercial and Sugar Co. stock, which sold at a high of $60 a share in 1882 and fell to 25 cents in 1884. Ironically, the sons named H. Hackfeld & Co. as their agents and the partners continued in that role until 1898, when the plantation was sold to Alexander & Baldwin.

This was not to be the end of the Isenberg-Spreckels confrontation, however. That was to resume when some Island plantations, Hackfeld's among them, undertook to refine their own sugar on San Francisco Bay (see Chapter 4).

Changing of the Guard

In the 20 years that Isenberg managed Lihue, the growing of sugar became an industry rather than a more or less hit-or-miss affair of gardening and cooking. In this period one vexing problem after another was solved. There was an increase in the labor supply, the clarification of juices was improved, and "Lahaina" cane was introduced from Tahiti and superseded the native varieties. All this was only a prelude to a century of innovation and invention, which led to the preeminence of the Islands among sugar producers throughout the world; and, of all the Hawaiian planters in his day, Isenberg was himself preeminent.

In 1878, at his wife's insistence, Isenberg had moved to Bremen. There Hackfeld and Pflueger prospered from the Big Man's genius for problem solving. Aging, they determined to reorganize the partnership and put Isenberg in it with H. W. Schmidt and Ed Muller. This was in 1881. Captain Hackfeld and the Pfluegers set themselves up as "special" partners, a position that was to be exchanged for preferred stock on incorporation. The senior Pflueger died in 1883 and Hackfeld sold out in 1886. When Hackfeld left, on September 1, 1886, the structure of his firm was as shown in Table 1.

One asks, who were Schmidt and Muller to be admitted to the club? Schmidt, brought to Hawaii by Hackfeld, was an accountant with a background in merchandising in Bremen.

TABLE 1

General partners		
H. W. Schmidt	4/15	$100,000
P. Isenberg	3/15	75,000
H. F. Glade	3/15	75,000
J. F. Hackfeld	3/15	75,000
E. Muller	2/15	50,000
		$375,000
Special partners		
J. C. Glade		$100,000
J. W. Pflueger		50,000
Dr. H. H. Pflueger		50,000
J. C. Pflueger, Jr.		50,000
		$250,000
Total capital		$625,000

He ultimately became the manager of all wholesaling and was also the consul for Sweden, a trustee of Queen's Hospital, and a senator from Oahu. In 1890 he left the partnership, taking the agency for Waimea with him, and formed his own company, H. W. Schmidt & Sons. Then he became bankrupt while his former partners flourished. The incident left no damp eyes in the old courthouse.

Less is known of Muller. He, too, was an accountant and a consul (Austria-Hungary). He disappeared from the scene when Isenberg and J. F. Hackfeld took over as the sole general partners in 1894.

In these years H. Hackfeld & Co. was serving the Kilauea, Lihue, Hanamaulu, Grove Farm, and Koloa plantations on Kauai; Heeia, Waimanalo, and Waianae on Oahu; Pioneer, Olowalu, Grove Ranch, Hana, Kipahulu, and Lilikoe on Maui; and Ookala on Hawaii. The total production of this group was 13,636 tons in the first year of Isenberg's partnership. The two identifiable survivors among this group, still a part of Amfac, produced nearly 130,000 tons in 1973. Remember that Amfac's Kekaha on Kauai, Oahu Sugar Co. outside Honolulu, and Puna on the Big Island, which produced 220,000 tons in 1973, were no more than a gleam in Isenberg's eye in the 1880s. He founded all of them in the 1890s. Contrarily, whole districts that could support small plantations under the cheap labor conditions of his day have been forced out of sugar production. Kilauea on Kauai, two of the three listed on Oahu, the last four named on Maui, and Hawaii's Ookala are all gone now. Hanamaulu sugar lands have been merged into Lihue and those of Olowalu into Pioneer, and they continue in production under those names.

An 1883 valuation of some of the plantations represented by Hackfeld looked like this:

Kilauea	$300,000
Lihue	$920,000
Koloa	$340,000
Kekaha	$400,000
Pioneer	$500,000
East Maui	$100,000
Hana	$250,000

The Quiet Accumulation

Emphasis has been given here to the evolution of the sugar plantations because in that period, quietly, the basic resources of Amfac were assembled. That the control of land in Hawaii, which is the substance behind the six operating groups today, was put together noiselessly is not to suggest it was surreptitious, as Table 1 in Chapter 7 will show. Hackfeld's earnings from sugar itself were small. As in Isenberg's purchase of Koloa from Wood, it was the custom for the individuals, rather than the agency, to take ownership in the land. It was only at the turn of the century, with incorporation of the older plantations and the formation of the three newer ones, that H. Hackfeld & Co. became the principal owner of the sugar companies and, indirectly, their land.

There was, of course, the collateral growth of the merchandising, shipping, and insurance businesses that were fed by sugar that built profits and reserves. In the year that Isenberg became a partner, his $75,000 investment earned him $9,638.73. By the time of incorporation, 15 years later, it seems to have brought him a total of over $500,000, primarily from collateral activities. This figure is an estimate, however, as the interests of the general partners changed frequently until 1894, when, as noted, Isenberg and J. F. Hackfeld became the sole general partners, each with a 50-percent interest.

While the building of the inventory of land and the accumulation of reserves from the collaterals were going on, certain major events were happening that would influence the present posture of Amfac. For example, in 1880 Isenberg, with employment for his brother Otto as one consideration, joined the Wilcox family in buying a sugar mill from Scottish manufacturers and establishing it on westernmost Kauai. Cane already was being grown there on land leased from the Crown, but it had to be shipped to distant factories for milling. The new company developed artesian water, took in new land, and then dug a network of ditches and drained 1,800 acres of rice paddies, planting them to cane. Thus began Kekaha, for years a highly profitable enterprise with Hackfeld as its agent.

There were other ventures with the Wilcox family, notably the formation of a company to import guano from Laysan Island, 700 miles west of Kauai in the Hawaiian chain. This speculation became the antecedent of the Pacific Chemical and Fertilizer Co., a major processor of modern chemical nutrients on all the cane-bearing islands. The holding in this very successful company became a minority interest with the passage of time, and it was one of the few Isenberg developments to be sold off in 1960.

In 1885 there was a foreclosure of a mortgage on Pioneer Mill Co. for $250,730.30, giving the partnership a half interest in that venture. Ten years later the balance was acquired. Thus Isenberg assembled the lands of Pioneer, molded the present-day plantation, and unwittingly provided Amfac with the thriving resort site of Kaanapali.

August Ehlers, who succeeded to his father's interests in the "upper store," returned to Germany in 1893 and sold a one-half interest back to the partnership for $11,000. In 1896 H. Hackfeld & Co. bought back the remainder for $9,000 and in the following year increased its capital to $30,000. From this seed Amfac's $276 million a year in retail sales germinated.

In 1893, while Isenberg was in Bremen, his partner, H. F. Glade (son of J. C., by then retired), became concerned over the growing advances to Pepeekeo Plantation, for which Hackfeld was then agent. He offered to sell the partnership interest in it, along with the agency, to T. H. Davies. On his return Isenberg was, to say the least, annoyed. Glade had not reckoned with the advent of some new cane varieties. Nevertheless, Isenberg honored the commitment while easing Glade out of the firm. It was then that he and J. F. Hackfeld became its sole proprietors.

There was not much doubt that Paulo dominated the company's affairs. Minutes of an 1890 Lihue meeting read:

> Mr. Cooke also presented Mr. A. M. Sproul's report on constructing a wharf at Hanamaulu. . . . Mr. Hackfeld said he had not received any instructions from Mr. Isenberg in regard to this matter; therefore, motion was made and carried that action on the report be deferred.

Isenberg continued through the years to oppose annexation of Hawaii by the United States. Writing to W. R. Castle, then in Washington as its advocate, he said:

> I hope that the Islands will remain independent. My reasons are that the conditions and circumstances of the Islands are entirely different than those of the States. The Islands need cheap labor, if the present sugar plantations, the backbone of the country, shall successfully be carried on. Also, if necessary, improvements such as good roads and railways shall be built to develop the country. The United States are not in favor of Asiatics, that is, its people. The contract law might be done away with under an independent Hawaiian government. And if from 8,000 or 10,000 Chinese were allowed to come into the country, not at one time, but say within a year or eighteen months, so that the Chinese and Japanese had to work or be hungry. . . . As regards a protectorate, this would probably be worse than annexation. . . . Have a Regent for a time until Princess Kaiulani is at least 24 years old, and if a gentleman like Judge Dole was Regent, with a number of able advisors, the country would soon be prosperous again.

He was not to prevail. In the business boom that followed annexation in 1898, Hackfeld profits were to rise from $164,516.96 in 1897 to $352,251.97 in 1898 and to $829,315.01 in 1899. Isenberg couldn't have minded too much about Kaiulani.

Preparation for a Successor

With time passing, Isenberg and Hackfeld sensed the need to provide a means to pass their interests on to heirs. Since their holdings in the firm had become too big for new partners to buy, they agreed on September 1, 1897, to incorporate. This was effected on Christmas Eve of that year. In the exchange of stock for partnership interests, there were 7,000 shares of common and 3,000 of preferred authorized, each at a value of $100. Isenberg and Hackfeld took 2,750 apiece of the common and divided the remainder among their executives, W. Wolters and Ed Suhr receiving 750 each with H. A. Isenberg, Paul's son, being given 500 of the shares allocated to his father. Preferred shares were exchanged for the special partnership interests of the Glades and the Pfluegers. The first slate of officers read:

Paul Isenberg, President
J. F. Hackfeld, Vice President
William Wolters, Director
Ed Suhr, Director
H. A. Isenberg, Secretary
C. Bosse, Treasurer
W. Pfotenhauer, Auditor

Initially capitalized at $1 million, the sum was increased to $2 million with the earnings of 1899. That year the Isenbergs, father and son, collected a total of $226,510 in dividends. Also in that year the company celebrated its fiftieth anniversary with a reception in the courthouse office and music by the Royal Hawaiian Band.

Hackfeld & Co. was, of course, the focal point for the German community, and the band-loving Germans had as their favorite the leader of the Royal Hawaiian Band, Captain Heinrich Berger. Born in Berlin in 1844, he came to Hawaii when Kamehameha V asked the German government for the loan of a master to reorganize the Hawaiian military band. Berger arrived in 1872 and presented more than 30,000 concerts in a 43-year career, many of them in the Hackfeld offices and on the docks for arrivals and departures of vessels owned or represented by Hackfeld. A gifted composer, Berger wrote "Hawaii Ponoi," the Hawaiian national anthem, and made a new arrangement of the "Hilo March." Both are among the most moving pieces of Hawaiian music, despite their beer-hall beat.

At the fiftieth anniversary celebration of Hackfeld & Co., Paul Isenberg and J. F. Hackfeld took the occasion to give bonuses to employees based on length of service and to make a number of personal charitable contributions, the most conspicuous of these being $25,000 apiece toward the construction of a Lutheran church in Honolulu.

The big news of the day, however, was that Hackfeld & Co. would erect a new office building adjoining the courthouse. It would extend a full city block from Queen Street toward the water and be three stories high. It was to be decorated at each corner with the imperial eagle of the German coat of arms and was to cost $250,045.50. To prove that times haven't changed in all respects, it finally cost, when completed in 1902, $432,911, the $200,000 excess being advanced by Paul Isenberg.

It was in this period, 1900 to be exact, that the company hired a chemist by mail to come to the Islands to work with the plantations. When Marshall Klein arrived, generations before the women's liberation movement struck the company's Board room, "he" proved to be a "she."

On January 16, 1903, word reached Honolulu by the new cable that Paulo had died the same day in Bremen. It was a shock of immense proportions to a community that regarded him as almost Herculean. Business houses closed, flags flew at half-mast, and the evening paper wrote, "Paul Isenberg was of the type of pioneer which does honor to his country." He had, it said, "amassed great wealth and done no man wrong." Another writer said that he led "a life without secrecy."

One of the most remarkable things about this remarkable man was that for 25 years he had guided the destiny and growth of Hackfeld from Bremen by correspondence and an occasional inspection trip. The files show him writing to prod Lihue "to get along with the railroad"; authorizing a charity fund "for all laborers, including Chinese and Japanese, who have grown old in the service of the plantation"; observing of striking Japanese that their desire to have Japanese doctors was natural; and defining a 10-hour day as follows: "I count the 10 hours from the time they leave home and go back again"— all the minutiae of management from 10,000 miles away.

Succession

With the momentum generated by Isenberg (capital had been increased to $3 million by the issuance of 10,000 new shares the year before his death) the firm continued with J. F. Hackfeld as President and H. Alexander Isenberg as Manager. In 1906 the company suffered another severe shock when the latter died of pneumonia, at the age of 34, while on a business trip to New York. Pfotenhauer then took over as Vice President and Manager.

It was not until 1908 that the senior Isenberg's estate was settled; his wife was the prime beneficiary. The following year 10,000 new shares were issued as a stock dividend and there was a further increase of capital to $4 million. The company's ownership at that time is shown in Table 2.

Other than making money (annual profits ranged from a low of $99,664.51 in 1904 to $766,741.71 in 1909 and averaged over $550,000 in the period), the Pfotenhauer administration did little to distinguish itself. The lot behind the new office and the old courthouse was bought for $38,977.75 (about $1.75 per square foot) for grinding and roasting coffee. A San Francisco office, under J. F. Humberg, was opened in 1905. In 1911 Humberg was transferred to New York, being succeeded in San Francisco by his son.

Perhaps presaging the guns of August that were soon to

TABLE 2

Stockholder	No. of shares	
J. F. Hackfeld	15,260	
Mrs. Paul Isenberg	4,985	
Assorted Isenberg children	13,015	
Assorted Pfluegers	2,740	
Pfotenhauer, Humberg, Rodiek, and Klamp (the management group), 250 each	1,000	
Common	37,000	
Preferred	3,000	(as previously stated)
	40,000	

sound in Europe (or the passage of income-tax legislation), J. F. Hackfeld incorporated his Hawaiian holdings in 1912 under the name J. F. Hackfeld Co., Ltd., and, with Pfotenhauer's death, named George Rodiek the General Manager of Hackfeld & Co. So the stage was set for the corporate drama of the next 5 years.

Early in World War I, while the sympathies of most of Hawaii inclined toward the Allies and against the Boche, Hackfeld did business more or less as usual. There was a certain hostility between the German and British clubs and, at Hawaiian Sugar Planters' Association meetings, a certain tenseness between the T. H. Davies and Hackfeld spokesmen. Still, 1916 was a banner year, the after-tax profit was $1,458,-018.33, and income taxes were less than $30,000. Those were the days.

Problems in the early war years centered on communications. J. F. Hackfeld had moved to Germany for his wife's health and all the Isenberg shareholders were there. The British denied the company the use of the transatlantic cable and the management had difficulty in disclaiming support of the German cause. As agent for German vessels interned in

Honolulu harbor, it was suspected of secret support of German raiders preying on Allied shipping in the Pacific. All these doubts gained some confirmation when Manager Rodiek was convicted in a federal court in San Francisco for his participation in the plot to smuggle arms into India and stimulate a revolution against the British there. Things must have been really tense in the Hawaiian Sugar Planters' Association meetings after that.

American entry into the war presented the management with all manner of problems. Of the top echelon only Rodiek, now under a cloud, and J. F. C. Hagens had become naturalized citizens. A relative of Hackfeld, Hagens had come to the Islands as a youngster, moved up to become Manager of the fertilizer venture, and joined Hackfeld in 1913. An illustration of the problems of the time is found in his requests for legal opinions and the responses. Should the German emblems be removed from the walls of the office building? Yes. Are the proxies of aliens resident in Germany valid? No.

Abdication

Under a Trading with the Enemy Act, resignation of Hackfeld as President and J. C. Isenberg as a Director was demanded. The Pacific Mail and American Hawaiian Steamship agencies were soon canceled by their Yankee owners and the privilege of cabling, even to the mainland, was suspended. Notwithstanding the difficulties (the assets were to shrink by 10 percent during the course of the war) soaring sugar prices pushed profits to a record $1,631,265.14 in 1917.

The British had long since blacklisted Hackfeld and were insisting that Washington do something about it. By late 1917 it appeared that a take-over by American interests was inevitable. The first attempt, however, was a private one: the purchase of 11,000 common shares (out of 12,647 held) from J. F. Hackfeld Co., Ltd., by F. J. Lowrey, Walter Dillingham, A. J. Campbell, and G. P. Wilcox, who planned to take 2,000 shares each. Further, Dillingham was to act as a trustee for a four-person *hui* buying another 2,000 shares. The final thousand was to be taken by H. L. Scott, the American-born manager of the New York office. The group set up a voting trust to endure throughout the war and removed Rodiek and some German nationals from office, electing J. F. C. Hagens as President.

Within 3 weeks (January 28, 1918) Honolulu's Trent Trust Co., as agent for the Alien Property Custodian, took over 27,361 of the shares held in Germany and rescinded the sale of the 11,000 shares by J. F. Hackfeld Co., Ltd. Finally, with the British government still badgering him, the Custodian ordered the sale of all H. Hackfeld & Co. assets to American interests. With that action and the dismissal of three plantation managers, the head of the fertilizer company, and the Hackfeld treasurer, all German, the company and its plantations were removed from the British blacklist.

There were 22 holders of common stock and 7 of the preferred at the time. All but the Wilcox brothers (who had bought 1,400 shares in 1913) were of German extraction if not still German citizens.

The price of $7.5 million (calculated by averaging 10 years' earnings and capitalizing them at 12 percent) for the company stock seems low in the perspective of 55 years, but at the time the company desperately needed cash and its management was a shambles. While the Germans asked $30,000,000 in their suit, Rodiek offered to settle for $8,180,000 plus interest. There were 37,000 shares outstanding, which had been traded (although rarely) at $180 to $200. Taking $190 as the market value, you arrive at something like $7 million for the common stock, leaving a balance of $500,000 for application to the preferred on which the dividend was only $30,000 a year—a rather low return.

Following a contest among employees for a $10 prize for a new company name to replace the old Hackfeld one, the winner proved to be American Factors. The company was organized on October 10, 1918, with 50,000 shares sold to the "public" for $7.5 million. Actually, the buyers were not the "public"; they were in a sense "insiders," as they knew the assets and the potential of the company very well.

After the Armistice, litigation was bound to come. The contention of the Germans that the price given them in settlement for their holdings in H. Hackfeld & Co. was too low was supported in the Hawaiian courts. John Francis Nylen, then noted as the greatest trial lawyer in the West (and William Randolph Hearst's principal advisor), represented them. His confidence was such that he bet $10,000 in the course of a golf game at the Burlingame Club, down San Francisco's peninsula, that he would win on appeal. He drew the case out so that it became one of the longest civil trials in the history of the U.S. Ninth Circuit, but he lost both the golf and the legal encounters and, in the absence of a constitutional issue, the U.S. Supreme Court refused to hear a further appeal. Individual shareholders continued to litigate the question for 20 more years, the final decision being rendered in 1943. There are still men around who participated in the first of these cases. Among them was C. Hutton Smith, retired President and Board Chairman of Amfac, of whom more will be heard later.

In its final days Hackfeld, under J. F. C. Hagens, tried to be a good corporate citizen. In 1918 there was a first half-year contribution to the Red Cross of $1,214.30 along with $250 for the Salvation Army War Fund and a $100 purchase of War Savings Stamps. However, the take-over process was under way and finalized on July 19, 1918, when a unanimous vote of the shares represented joined with the Alien Property Custodian to vote "aye" on the proposed sale of the assets. Such names as Isenberg, Hagens, Humberg, and Rodiek were all spoken for as favoring the sale of the properties so carefully assembled over 70 years. The purchaser, self-styled American Factors, Ltd., was, in fact, a consortium including Alexander & Baldwin, H. P. Baldwin, Ltd., C. Brewer, Castle & Cooke, Matson Navigation Co., and Welch & Co., each with 2,300 shares. They knew what they were getting, and in 1919 they used Amfac credit to buy out the German interest in the Koloa, Kekaha, and Lihue plantations.

So ended the German phase of the dynasty Hackfeld founded, but the corporate creature they forged and the "factoring" pattern Isenberg had refined were to endure for another half century. Then there followed a major redeployment of assets plus a redesign in the manner of doing business. Yet the German burghers were flexible too, and had they retained control they might have taken much the same course as the present management.

4

Sugar, the Source of It All

Sugar, the cheapest form of carbohydrate in the world, is also the most abundant. Save for man-made restraints, tariffs, wars, and such, there has usually been an oversupply of sugar. How the relatively minute Hawaiian Islands, which produce less than 2 percent of the sugar consumed by the world, became rich from this common commodity is a story combining business acumen, scientific pursuit, and political strategy. Amfac, as Hawaii's largest sugar producer and long associated with the Island's oldest plantations, is a conspicuous figure in that tale.

Think about sugar for a moment. It is the best illustration of the function of photosynthesis in the conversion of radiant energy into a form man can use. Meat, coal, and the other storehouses of energy are far less efficient than sugar. Expressed in terms of food calories per acre per year, Hawaiian-grown sugar leads all states in its contribution. For example, sugarcane in Hawaii produces 17,470,000 calories per acre per year; sugar beets in California, 9,311,000.

Pacific explorers found sugarcane planted around Hawaiian huts and taro patches to define boundaries. Its stringy, juicy stalks were munched for their flavor and nothing more. Whether washed ashore or imported, along with pigs and poi by the Islanders in their eighth-century migrations from the South Pacific, is not known. Captain Cook, the Islands' discoverer, found it a useful base for sugar beer, writing, "It has the taste of new malt beer. I believe no one will doubt it being very wholesome." Less wholesome was his fate at the hands of the natives, though sugar figured in that as well. He was stabbed to death in a skirmish with some natives. When they returned his body to his crew, the contrite Hawaiians formed a great procession, bearing gifts of tropical foods, and each man carried over his shoulder a bunch of sugarcane.

In the 75 years following Cook's death in 1779, the ranks of deserting seamen, scheming traders, and Calvinist missionaries, all categorized as foreigners, grew in Hawaii, and in the first census of the kingdom they numbered about 2,000 persons. In those years the foreigners, about half of them Caucasian, had experimented with a score of crops—cotton, tea, rice, pineapple, tobacco, and coffee—along with sugarcane. In fact, the first sugar planting had been begun by some Chinese on the Island of Lanai in 1802. There were those who tried to make sugar by crushing the juice from cane stalks with stone poi pounders. Two years later a man named Wilkinson was growing cane in Manoa Valley (where the University of Hawaii now stands) to make rum. The missionaries' convert, Queen Kaahumanu, the widow of Kamehameha I, put a stop to that.

How the "Fac" Got in Amfac

As observed in Chapter 1, one of the reasons that influenced Hackfeld to settle in Hawaii was the promise of sugar. Shortly after his arrival he sensed a place in the business for an agent, or "factor." While the concept of producers operating through agents was not new (traders had used them from the time of the Phoenicians) their development in Hawaii was to become a bit different. Hackfeld paved the way, with Dr. Wood's Koloa in the early 1850s, to be followed shortly by Castle & Cooke, C. Brewer, and others. The end of the gold rush and the cost of money—12 percent interest was regarded as favorable and 18 percent not unheard of—made this decade a trying one for the infant industry. Plantation bankruptcies were prevalent; demands on the agent were unremitting; but by consolidating faltering plantations and making advances at the constant risk of bankruptcy to themselves, the factors pulled the sugar industry through.

The growth of population in the West and the Civil War, which cut off Caribbean sugar from the North, created new markets in the 1860s. More importantly, Hackfeld had reversed the roles of principal and agent in fact if not in name. Where Dr. Wood had employed the captain to serve Koloa, within a decade the Captain ended up running it. When Wood sold out to Isenberg's group, Big Paul became the farmer but even he looked to the factor for what is regarded today as corporate management. This was to become generally true throughout the industry except where there was family ownership, as with Grove Farm, which the Wilcoxes ran, calling on Hackfeld for services only.

The Hackfeld dynasty was to share the destiny of the Hawaiian sugar industry and, in fact, lead in shaping it throughout the last half of the nineteenth century. Displeasure with the indolence of Hawaiian labor led to the formation of the Royal Hawaiian Agricultural Society in 1852. Hackfeld was a founder. While he was silent on one motion that the missionaries sponsored, to oppose the manufacture of rum, he found it hard not to favor a second of their resolutions. It read, "Has the state no right to remove women who repair to the large seaports with the evident and avowed intention to make their living by prostitution, nay, 'horrible dictu,' are even sent there for this purpose by parents and husbands—has it no right to send them back from whence they came?" His real interest, however, was in the Society's intention to foster the importation of labor. Hackfeld was in the forefront in this undertaking and soon dispatched the first of the recruiters to Whampoa. The first year they induced 200 to go to Hawaii. Working through his old friends among the Co Hong, the recruiters were ultimately to send over 20,000 Chinese to the Islands from Kwangtung Province.

This was to be but one of the labor sources for the Hawaiian planters. Subsequently, Hackfeld's worldwide network of sailing vessels and shipping agents led the Island industry to look to his partnership to probe the possibilities of labor procurement in Europe. In 1877 Manager Glade sent 2,000 marks from Bremen to Dr. W. F. Hillenbrand in Madeira to initiate the emigration of Portuguese. In 1881 Glade arranged with Captain L'Orange, father of a man who was later to run Amfac's Oahu Sugar Co., to bring in 243 men, 84 women, and 65 children from Norway. In the span of 20 years Isenberg recruited over 1,000 of his countrymen. At Lihue, as late as 1893, 38 of the 41 supervisors there were German. Nevertheless, Europe, except for the Portuguese, was not to be a major font of plantation manpower. Japan was the next source, and Hackfeld represented the Pacific Mail Line, which brought most of the recruits to Hawaii. After the Japanese, Filipinos came, many of them on Pacific Mail ships. The final labor importation of 4,000 from the Philippines soon after World War II was engineered by the Hawaiian Sugar Planters' Association (HSPA), whose president at the time was also Amfac's president, the senior Walker.

Pauper Plantations

Not all the early problems shared by the Island industry concerned labor. Power to grind the cane and pull the plows came from men and mules. Oxen were eventually imported to haul the big plows originally drawn by as many as 30 Hawaiians, who worked for $0.125 an hour plus a ration of poi. There was no Hawaiian currency in those times so labor was paid in script redeemable at the company store. Mules, plodding in circles, turned the wooden presses that ground the stalks of cane, which were fed by hand. In 1838 there were 20 fledgling mills in the Islands. Two of them were regarded as technologically advanced when millraces were built to replace the beasts with water power, though the pipes were still fashioned from wood.

The process of milling sugar was well known. The Indians and Chinese had practiced it for several thousand years and there were factories in the Caribbean to copy; but money was scarce. Further, the companies that supplied the mill machinery were in Scotland and Germany, 180 sailing days away and not disposed to extend credit.

Then there was the business of interisland transportation, no simple matter in sailing ships that had to stand off landings rather than berth in snug harbors. The little barks that launched longboats through the surf to debark passengers and freight and to pick up mail and sugar called at the primitive ports irregularly. Often weather delayed them for days, making a mockery of schedules. A plowshare would break and it could be weeks before a letter reached the agents in Honolulu and the needed replacement arrived.

Since cane is very susceptible to drought, irrigation was the subject of early experimentation. W. H. Rice built the first ditch at Lihue the same year he appointed Hackfeld his factor; but the ditch silted up and in places the grade proved inadequate for water to flow and formed a pond. This lack of flow obtained also in the roughly graded fields, where some patches would flood while others remained dry. Later successful efforts were to set a standard for the industry.

A drought in 1856 forced all but five of the tiny plantations to close. So it was that irrigation at Lihue demonstrated its value, and Koloa and Grove Farm were quick to follow suit. Thus began a system of ditches that eventually laced Kauai, tapping 50 miles of the slopes of Mount Waialeale, whose 5,080-foot peak, with an annual rainfall of 460 inches, is said to be the wettest spot on earth.

With the background gained on Kauai, the Hackfeld partnership spread irrigation to plantations on Oahu and Maui, where the land, without water, grew only cactus. This pioneering was also to pave the way for the Alexander & Baldwin partnership to build the biggest ditch in the Islands on Maui and for Claus Spreckels subsequently to build an even bigger one.

It was in order to bring more water to the Ewa plain than could be pumped that Amfac built the Waiahole Ditch. This 7-mile tunnel through the Koolau range, the mountain backdrop for Honolulu, delivers up to 100 million gallons a day from the rainy windward side of Oahu to cane fields 18 miles away. The six ditchmen who tend the tunnel patrol it by floating through on wooden rafts with packing cases as seats and kerosene lamps for lights. A hard hat is necessary for protection against rocky outcroppings from the tunnel ceiling. There is an almost graveyard-like serenity to the tunnel. (Riding through, powered only by the current, I found my thoughts turning to what would happen if an earthquake should rock the mountain or how this bore could be commercialized as the longest "tunnel of love" in the world.)

Thirsty Fields

Fancy apart, one can reflect also on this tunnel as a symbol of the rugged independence asserted by the Hawaiian planters in building their industry. They are unique among American farmers in providing a complex of tunnels, main supply ditches, and pumps on all sugar islands that was built, every foot of it, with private funds. HSPA engineers say it would cost roughly $500 million to replace it today.

While there is constant maintenance and expansion of the basic system of delivering water to the plantations, the major changes in more recent years have concerned ways of applying water to the fields. There was first the familiar flooding technique, but the industry converted to the furrow system early in the game. This provided economies in the use of water and, by running it through a pattern of trenches dug between the standing stalks of cane, delivered it closer to the roots. For generations irrigators were the most skilled of field hands, opening and closing the little earthen dams that diverted water from the supply ditches to the furrows.

Labor scarcity, disinterest in field work, high wages following unionization, and technical advances have contributed to reducing the reliance on irrigators. First, there was the development of the portable concrete flume, a series of yard-long, U-shaped blocks that could be laid end to end to serve as a supply ditch. Metal gates in their walls could be raised to release water into the furrows more readily than through earthen dams. This improved the productivity of the irrigators.

At Oahu the best of them could cover 10 acres in a day. That meant walking 5 miles, opening and closing gates as they went. Equally important, the concrete flume saved water previously lost to absorption in the ground and, being portable, could be removed to facilitate mechanization of field operations.

Next was the bouyoucos block, a sort of clinical thermometer to tell the moisture content of the soil and to signal its need for water. Previously, the managers' judgment was guided by rain-fall records and a seasoned eye, alert to any browning of the leaves.

Now a semiautomatic system is being installed on Amfac plantations, where a clock timer ingeniously controls a mechanical device that drops the gate in the concrete flume when a furrow is filled.

Amfac plantations, along with others in the Hawaiian industry, have long experimented with overhead irrigation as a means of further mechanizing the application of water and eliminating the need to trench the fields. This would also simplify mechanical operations and conserve water lost to evaporation. Giant sprinklers capable of spraying water over 100 acres have yet to prove feasible, primarily because shifting trade winds cause them to spread the water in erratic patterns. Kekaha has even experimented with smaller "risers" only 60 to 90 feet apart.

The present betting among Amfac managers is that a "drip" system, now becoming operational, will be the method of the future. This entails laying plastic pipe in the furrows with little holes, at appropriate intervals, through which water drips at rates regulated by pressure. The pipe itself is cheap enough to be abandoned when the field is plowed, thus eliminating an age-old conflict with mechanical operations. As with most innovations, one wonders, "Why didn't they think of this before?"

The standard for evaluating performance on Amfac plantations is expressed in terms of the tons of sugar per acre per month (TSAM) produced. Development of this measurement requires maintenance of records of each field as its cane is harvested and processed through the factory. The general practice in Hawaii is to nourish the growth of the plant over some 22 months, then burn it to remove leaves and trash. It is then harvested with bulldozers equipped with massive rakes that snap the stalks and windrow them for loading to trucks by mobile cranes with clawlike grabs. Amfac plantations, in general, follow this practice.

Still, there are subtle variations from one to another plantation, as it is in the harmonization of growing time, fertilization, and irrigation that the maximum TSAM is gained and that harmony changes from one locale to another. Thus Puna, in the high rainfall belt, is unirrigated and has some fields in cool uplands on the slopes of volcanic Mauna Loa that take a full 2½ years to produce their maximum TSAM. Yields can be as little as a quarter of a ton of sugar per acre per month in that low-cost environment. Kekaha, on the other hand, being irrigated, and under a blazing sun, has fields that nearly triple that figure; yet both plantations survive. While attainment of the maximum TSAM is the test of the plantation manager as a farmer and it is notable that most managers advance through the field rather than the factory, there are many other elements of expense to be controlled.

The Only Constant Is Change

Transportation of harvested cane from field to factory can be a quarter of all the costs of a crop from planting to the time the cane enters the mill. Though the problem has manifested itself in different ways at different times and, more recently, in various locations, it has always been, and will remain, a major cost item.

In the early days of Koloa, for example, the hand-cut cane was loaded into carts pulled by oxen. When Isenberg took over at Lihue, one of his first plans was to build a narrow-gauge railroad to serve the mill. It took until 1886 to get all the money to build it, and then the cane was packed by mule to the main line. In time portable track was laid in spurs, permitting the switching of cars by manpower or mule power into the harvest field. In other areas where rainfall was abundant, wooden flumes were built; water flowed through them and bundled cane floated down them, with the speed of surf, from field to factory. It was a rare plantation boy who didn't learn to swim in an irrigation ditch or ride a bundle of cane as a raft on the surging waters of a flume.

Spurred by soaring labor costs and the availability of new mechanical devices, transportation practices changed. Just as mechanical harvesting replaced hand cutting, so the hauling of cane by truck replaced the "in field" movement by rail. These trucks are no ordinary vehicles. Amfac plantations rely on various makes of truck-trailer combinations with capacities of up to 50 tons per load. Operation of these behemoths generates new problems from strengthening bridges to community relations.

Because they carry mud from the fields and make the highways slick and hazardous, they have been an environmental headache since Ralph Nader was in rompers. The solution has been to build private "haulcane" roads. Amfac plantations have over 200 miles of them. These roads in turn introduce new community problems, proving quite enticing to everyone from drag racers to philanderers.

At Puna, cane historically was bought from outside planters in the Pahoa district 18 miles from the mill. When the railroad was abandoned, it became impractical to haul the growers' cane on anything but the public highway. After 25 tenacious years, this proved just too costly and too provocative a public relations problem with touring motorists. So Puna abandoned the practice and has turned to opening up dank jungle land much closer to the mill. This rocky property, which defied clearing by manpower through generations, has become available for cultivation with the development of monster bulldozers. It is this technical interplay, the rendering of one method obsolete by the introduction of another, that is the principal characteristic of industrialized agriculture as practiced in Hawaii.

It extends on into the factory. In the early days, cane was relatively clean when it arrived at the mill. The major problem was to dispose of the stalks after they were crushed. The milling process was so inefficient and left so much juice in the cane that the bagasse, as the crushed stalks are called, would not burn. Isenberg built great drying sheds with slanted walls at Lihue. Laborers spread the matted cane out to evaporate its remaining juices before returning it to the mill as fuel. Through the years, the problems in receiving the cane changed. Conveyors superseded hand feeding. Devices for tilting the cane cars as they were shunted past the conveyors were introduced. Everything seemed solved until the introduction of mechanical harvesting. Then the cane arrived muddy; rocks picked up by the rakes and grabs came in with it, often enmeshed in it. Tramp iron, never before a problem, broken off equipment in the fields, would, like the rocks, jam the mill rolls, stopping the whole operation, sometimes for hours. Dirt adhering to the cane was carried in with the juices, further prolonging and complicating the clarification process.

To solve this problem a unit was built to clean the cane before it entered the mill, called, not suprisingly, a "cane washer." Essentially, it consists of a conveyor under an indus-trial-sized shower bath, which washes the dirt from the cane. The conveyor floats the cane across a tub of mud the size of a small wading pool, the theory being that rocks and tramp iron will plummet to the bottom as the cane floats back onto another conveyor and so to the mills. These washers, though expensive (the one at Oahu cost $1.2 million), have resulted in added land at some plantations. Faced with the problem of disposing of all the muddy water—18 million gallons a day at Lihue—many plantations with waste, rocky, or coral land near the mill have fashioned fields with dikes and pumped the muddy water into them. When the water evaporates, the remaining soil, rich with the fertilization of its prior habitat, makes fine cane land. Amfac has added nearly 2,000 acres that way and so increased annual production by nearly 12,000 tons.

There have been improvements, of course, in the milling process: ever-increasing extraction with the development of better mill trains, some turbine-powered (here Kekaha is the Islands' leader), and better centrifugals and instrumentation of the boiling process. This process is a far cry from that of Victor Prévost, Isenberg's French sugar boiler. However, it is still fascinating to peer into the glass porthole of one of the towering vats where cane juice is boiling and watch the brown crystals form.

Probably the greatest departure from conventional milling practice has been Amfac's espousal of the diffusion process. It was tried early in the history of sugar in Hawaii. Ewa, recently purchased by Amfac and merged with neighboring Oahu, nearly went bankrupt with it in the 1890s. Its manager then complained, "This mill couldn't crush an egg," and he changed over at great expense to the conventional mill train principle; but after pilot plant experimentation at Kekaha, Amfac, faced with a major factory renewal problem at Pioneer, opted for diffusion. It was a daring move, which was greeted skeptically throughout the Hawaiian industry, but it worked. Extraction was increased by 6 percent. So pleased with the results was Amfac that it spent $8 million replacing the mill at once-foundering Puna with a diffuser. Agriculture Group Chairman Karl H. Berg says, "If we ever replace a present mill or build a new one, it will be with a diffuser. At Puna, we have increased extraction 5 percent."

Ships as Sugar Bowls

A final revolution in production has occurred in the means of getting the raw sugar to the refinery. In Captain Hackfeld's time it was a matter of standing off a landing and swinging aboard, by block and tackle, cask after cask of sugar and molasses from a longboat powered by Hawaiians gleeful in their element, the surf. At one time a score of such landings were scattered throughout the Islands. When steam replaced sail, the Hackfeld partners were among the first to recognize that most of the landings were obsolete. Ben F. Dillingham, founder of the Dillingham clan, with his railroad running from Honolulu to the north shore of Oahu, paved the way in bringing sugar to the larger harbors. Later he joined the Hackfeld partners in developing a similar road on Hawaii. Thus the natural harbors, Nawiliwili and Port Allen on Kauai, Honolulu on Oahu, Kahului on Maui, and Hilo on Hawaii, came into their own. While each of them required improvement, they contributed to economies in shipping. Some of the landings, notwithstanding, continued to be served by small coasters until World War II, but with the advent of highways and high-capacity trucks they were abandoned along with the very railroads that had developed the major ports.

Amfac's Oahu Sugar Co. was a founder of the Oahu Trans-

port Co., which replaced the Dillingham railroad in the carrying of sugar. On the other islands, the plantations American
Factors represented turned to trucking for themselves or hired
others to haul for them as the first step in the evolution of new
means of movement of sugar from factory to market. Jute bags
from India replaced barrels and kegs in the shipment of
Hawaiian sugar as early as 1890. By World War II over 200
million bags of raw sugar moved out of Island ports each year
to be deftly stowed in the holds of Matson freighters. The
warehousemen were small-boned Filipinos weighing little
more than the 100-pound bags they flipped about.

Mechanization, prompted by the 410 percent increase in
waterfront wages that followed World War II, required extensive and integrated changes in shipping methods. This affected
warehousing at the plantations, storage in the ports, and the
design of the holds of ships as well as the receiving facilities
at the Island-owned California and Hawaiian Sugar Refinery
(C and H). Amfac, as the operator of seven sugar mills, trucker
and stevedore on Kauai, shareholder in the Oahu Transport
Co. that built the sugar storage facility in Honolulu harbor,
owner of Matson stock, and spokesman for its plantations'
holdings in C and H, was deeply involved in the change-over.

The system was to set aside the scales, sewing machines, and
clacking cleat conveyors that attended the bagging of sugar.
It was to replace the labor of stacking it in railroad cars and
dockside piles and the loading of slings to carry it into ship-
board holds. It was to eliminate the rehandling of bags there
and the laying of dunnage to prevent the stacked sacks from
shifting in heavy seas. It was to supplant the whole laborious
process—which was then performed in reverse at the refinery.

Machines were substituted for muscle throughout the
scenario. At the mill now, conveyors move raw sugar in bulk
to overhead silos, where it is stored and then dumped into

trucks, designed much like those that carry sand, which take it to the ports. There, specially built warehouses accept the sugar from conveyors that move it overhead and spew it out to warehouse floors by trimmers that scatter it in a fashion that suggests a snowstorm. Again, when ships are to be loaded, conveyors move the sugar up and over their holds, where other trimmers direct it to every nook and cranny and, finally, to the brim of the deck. Once arrived at C and H the ships' holds are emptied and the raw crystals are placed in storage to await the refining operation. Thus it is that sugar moves unpackaged, as much as 30,000 tons of it in a single shipload.

Something of the scale of all this is evidenced by the Honolulu bulk terminal built in 1954, which, when full, holds a pile of sugar 50 feet high on a floor as large as eight basketball courts. The 37,000 tons of sugar it can accommodate would frost 500 million cakes or meet the needs of 725,000 Americans for a year.

Even when under common ownership, C and H long felt that Matson was compromising the competitive advantage gained from the control of the up-bound haul of sugar with the down-bound movement of general cargoes. In the past this posed some soul-searching problems for Matson directors, who met in the morning on the second floor of the Matson building in San Francisco only to adjourn for a domino lunch at the Pacific Union Club and reconvene at 2 o'clock on the twentieth floor of the same building as C and H Board members. Now that the interests of C and H are clearly distinguishable from those of the shipping company, the realities have emerged. If there is an advantage to the plantations in vessels structured purely for the movement of sugar, let the plantations invest the capital. Matson can employ its funds better elsewhere. Launched in 1973 was a C and H owned bulker, the *Sugar*

Islander, with a capacity of 31,489 tons, 200 times that of Hackfeld's *Wilhelmine.*

The Uncooperative Cooperative

C and H has not always been entirely responsive to the will of all the Hawaiian plantations. It was fashioned by some of them in response to Claus Spreckels' monopoly of the refining and sale of sugar in the West. Initially, only a fragment of the group was convinced that the Islands' interests were best served by setting up their own organization in California. Isenberg was among those who, in 1897, concluded that this was the case, while the plantations represented by T. H. Davies and the Brewer-Irwin-Spreckels group continued to deal with Spreckels' refinery in San Fransciso.

The differences with Spreckels centered no less on his personality than on his insistence that the margin between what he would pay for raw sugar and the price he got for it would be $7.50 per ton, whereas the dissident Islanders held out for $5. But there was more to it than that. Spreckels' invasion of Hawaii still rankled the Islanders and they just really didn't want to do business with him.

An opportunity for the Islanders to run a Hawaiian-owned refinery presented itself in 1897, when an ambitious attempt to establish a giant flour mill at Crockett, on San Pablo Bay across from San Francisco, failed. Left behind was a massive rectangular structure 200 feet by 250 feet six stories high with a 6,000-foot frontage on deep water. Under Isenberg's leadership, the California Beet Sugar and Refining Co. was established there, programmed to process both beet and cane sugar in a 5-to-3 ratio. It was destined to fail because the area around Crockett proved incapable of producing beets economically and the wells on which the refinery relied for fresh water developed heavy salinity. By 1899 the word "beet" had been removed from the name, and although the problem of supplying fresh water was on the way to being solved (by barging it from the Sacramento River), the undertaking was never profitable. If this was not enough, the Spreckels monopoly prevailed in the marketplace, leading to the demise of the Hawaiian enterprise in 1903. A further humiliation occurred when the operation was closed, for 17,361 tons of Hawaiian sugar were pledged annually to Spreckels at his demanded margin. His sole concession was to pay $200,000 per year rent for 3 years for the closed refinery as an "emergency" facility.

In 1904, restless with the arrangement, all but the eight plantations controlled by Spreckels and Davies formed Sugar Factors Co., Ltd., and acquired all the stock of the old C and H outfit, the only remaining individual shareholder being Colonel Z. K. Spaulding, part owner, with Lihue, of the neighboring Makee Plantation on Kauai. H. Hackfeld & Co., representing the Island interests, provided a consulting engineer and fellow German, Max Loranz, to convert the old flour mill and abandoned sugar refinery into an efficient factory, which he did. With the expiration of the 3-year agreement with Spreckels, it reopened with Germanic efficiency, with Loranz being known throughout the plant as Herr Ober Ingenieur.

Thus began a competition with the Spreckels interests for the sugar market in the western United States that was to endure for over 40 years. While Spreckels' refinery continued to receive the product of those Hawaiian plantations in which his associates had an interest, its primary reliance was on Philippine production. In times of war or sugar shortages this was sometimes an erratic source. Increasingly, Spreckels turned to processing sugar beets in other mainland factories. Finally, in 1948 the Western refinery was closed and sold to C and H and the Spreckels-Irwin interests in Hawaii were sold to C. Brewer. This development put all Hawaiian production in the hands of a single mainland refiner and marketing organization for the first time.

This was not, however, to lessen the competition. The fact that more sugar, both cane and beet, was being produced in the West than its population could consume remains unchanged today. So does the battle for the major share of the market in the 11 Western states. Historically, excess production from the area has been forced to go to consumers in "high freight absorption" territories. This has cost as much as $12 per ton in a business where the refiner's margin, the difference between the cost of raw and the selling price of refined, averages $40 per ton.

All Is Not Sweetness

While the basic C and H problem in marketing Hawaiian sugar in the Western states is overproduction, it has other headaches. The first is operation under the Sugar Act. Sugar has always proved an issue in Congress. It was the tariff on sugar that provided the federal government with 90 percent of its revenue until the income-tax amendment was adopted in 1913. The impact of the current legislation on Hawaiian sugar plantations has been discussed earlier. But C and H, because of its ownership, is alone among the major refiners in sharing the growers' interest. That means seeking a low estimate of consumption by the Secretary of Agriculture each year so that foreign imports will be low. It means opposing the addition of new domestic beet acreage so that U.S. production will not soar. Both positions favor a higher price. Eastern refineries and the beet processors, having no stake in production, prosper with volume and so work the other side of the street. Refineries, reliant on foreign-grown raw sugar, are understandably sympathetic to the cause of Latin American, Philippine, and other alien cane areas. Beet processors almost universally buy their raw material under contracts which share returns with the growers on a percentage basis. The after-tax effect of the formula is to penalize the processors only about 1 cent in the event of a 50-cent reduction in the price of 100 pounds of refined sugar while passing on 38 cents of the cut to the grower. As a consequence, the politically potent beet processors, with the support of 18 congressional delegations, also have a greater interest in volume than in price. In fact, there are circumstances where added volume at a lower price will give them a higher return on their investment than otherwise.

While these and other differences continue, there has been an accommodation between C and H and the other refiners since the early days when the senior Walker fought to insure Hawaii's place as a domestic producer. In fact, James Marshall, the president of C and H and a one-time director of the sugar branch of the Department of Agriculture, headed a committee that presented a solid front on behalf of all elements of the domestic industry in the course of congressional and departmental deliberation on extension of the Sugar Act in 1971. At this writing, with the world price of sugar soaring and the shortage of commodities for domestic consumption provoking a consumer-minded Congress, the future of sugar legislation is clouded.

The second headache for the C and H management has been labor problems since World War II. Historically, the refining of sugar has demanded the assembly of a number of highly skilled craftsmen and, as a consequence, the involvement of the AFL-CIO; but Crockett, on deep water adjoining San Francisco Bay, which is Harry Bridges' territory, has 145 warehousemen to handle the incoming raws from Hawaii and the 3,250 tons per day of refined which it can produce. Warehousemen are in Bridges' fiefdom. In the past 25 years differences between the two unions, strikes by one or the other over contract negotiations, waterfront strikes on the West Coast or in Hawaii, along with sugar strikes on the plantations, have closed down the refinery for 6.8 percent of its normal number of operating days.

The refinery was converted from a stock company to an agricultural cooperative in 1921. One reason was to permit its refinancing after it was caught in a bind in the World War I inflation of sugar prices. This plagued all refiners who were committed to pay suppliers soaring New York quotations while bound by contract to sell industrial users at fixed prices. There was also an income-tax advantage to be gained in being a co-op. A modest factor then, it had come to have real advantages under the tax brackets prevailing later. At that time seven Amfac plantations became members of the cooperative. They were Kekaha, Koloa, Lihue, Makee, Oahu, Pioneer, and Olaa (now Puna). Today the number has declined to five, but they produce over three times as much sugar as the 1921 assembly.

The Agriculture Group

Among the six groups into which the operation of Amfac is divided, sugar is assigned to Agriculture. Ironically, for years it made the smallest "contribution" to income of the lot. Yet if the balance sheet were adjusted to reflect the land holdings at their market value and improvements at replacement costs a clear majority of Amfac's assets would be concentrated there. Times have changed. The recent boom in commodity prices has tripled the plantation's earnings. However, after 35 years' experience under the Sugar Act, and almost as many with Mr. Bridges' ILWU, few in Hawaii expect the bonanza to continue.

For the time being, though, Senior Vice President and

Group Chairman Karl H. Berg is greeted with smiles when he meets with the Operations and Financial Review Committee. As a major "contributor" to Amfac profit and custodian of the basic values that made the expansion and acquisition of the other activities possible, he no longer has to talk poor mouth.

There couldn't be a better man to run the Group. German-born, Island-bred, 61-year-old Berg is the epitome of the modern Hawaiian plantation manager. It would be hard to picture him in a pair of puttees or the whipcord riding britches that characterized planters of a generation past. In fact his shirts, like Jacob's coat, are of many Joseph Magnin inspired colors and no one on the executive floor can match his cuff-links in size or range.

Berg is a product of the University of Hawaii School of Tropical Agriculture and the Harvard Business School's Advanced Management Program. He can talk in terms of gram calories or balance sheet ratios. He is also a talker in Walker's regular noontime cribbage game. His running comment includes such phrases as "inexplicable performance," in criticizing his partner's play, or alluding to the doctrine "avarice spawns error," when referring to an opponent's mistake. In the Hackfelds' day his five-syllable words would have made him a good correspondent with "H's M'y's Government."

While an Australian adventure and expanded production of fresh papaya for mainland markets fall under Berg, the plantations are his preoccupation. Of these the oldest is Lihue and, as with all of them, its history is so intertwined with that of Amfac as to be inseparable.

Lush Lihue

Founded in 1849 by a three-man partnership, headed by Charles Reed Bishop, whose wife, heir to the Kamehamehas, was to endow the Bishop Estate with 10 percent of the land in Hawaii, The Lihue Plantation Co., Ltd., had an initial capital of $16,000. Reflecting the difficulty of the times, 4 years later (the year Hackfeld became agent for neighboring Koloa) it had produced 350 tons of sugar as its first crop. In the time it took to clear and plant the land, William Harrison Rice, an early manager, had built a dam in the Nawiliwili Valley adjoining the factory, giving him water rather than mule power to grind it. Since one of the basic problems encountered was drought, Rice embarked on the first irrigation project in the brief history of Hawaii's sugar industry. He reported that "a trench 10 miles long, about 2½ feet wide, and the same depth has been dug." It cost $7,000.

Isenberg, who succeeded Rice, came to an understanding with George N. Wilcox that cane from Grove Farm would be ground by Lihue. The two men were jointly to develop mountain water for their lands in the Hanamaulu district and set up the first telephone net on Kauai, a three-instrument affair, one step advanced over tin cans and a string, joining Lihue, Grove Farm, and the Island's only doctor. When the men had differences, as with the tolling rate charged by Lihue for grinding Wilcox cane, they found ways to reconcile them, though at one point Wilcox had to go to Scotland to do it. This was in the 1870s and no mean undertaking. He bought a complete sugar mill there, but by the time it arrived on Kauai they had settled the problem. Isenberg bought the mill, set it up in Hanamaulu to enlarge Lihue's capacity, and put Albert Wilcox, G. N.'s brother, in charge of running it.

At the turn of the century Lihue was producing over 10,000 tons of sugar per year and had been incorporated. Isenberg and the former Hackfeld partners owned 43 percent of it personally and others in his family had enough more to give him outright control.

In an industry marked with a high degree of cooperation in research as well as marketing, a claim to being "first" may mean only that a plantation is the first to try out an idea developed cooperatively, a "next step" in a constantly shifting technology Island-wide. From Rice's "first" ditch, however, Lihue has had a history of innovation. Recall that Isenberg built sheds adjoining the mill to speed the drying of the bagasse. Nearly a century later, mill engineer R. G. Watt tackled the problem created by mechanical harvesting, which brought in so much soil that it again became difficult to burn the bagasse. Watt's answer was to introduce a vortex of air to the factory furnace so that most of the combustion occurs before the dirt-laden bagasse falls to the floor.

Lihue was to go from the 1903 production of 10,000 tons to today's 60,000 to 70,000 tons primarily through internal improvement. The only significant addition of substantial cane land came with the acquisition of the remaining Spaulding interest (49 percent) in Makee Sugar Co. and its production of 25,000 tons in 1933.

As with all Amfac companies, Lihue has had many names long associated with its operation. One is C. E. S. Burns, who managed Lihue during the period of its greatest growth and the 1933 acquisition of the balance of Makee as well as its greatest tribulations with World War II and unionization. His son, after his own stint on the plantations, is now Senior Vice President for Administration of Amfac in Honolulu and a director of the sugar companies, among them Kekaha.

Torrid Kekaha

Also on Kauai, but on the burning hot dry side, is the Kekaha Sugar Co., Ltd., a relative newcomer, which was incorporated in 1898 when many of the sugar ventures were encouraged by annexation to incorporate. Originally it was the Kekaha Milling Co., founded by H. P. Baldwin in 1870, and it ground cane for Augustus Knudsen, who had a lease on some 1,500 acres of lands owned by the monarchy. German growers who took leases and settled in the area also contributed to the mill's output. By the end of 1898 its name had become the Kekaha Sugar Mill Co., Ltd. Its first crop in 1899 yielded 7,593 tons of sugar. Irrigation was limited to artesian wells. Some of the agricultural practices of the time would make a modern agronomist shudder. Dried blood from Australia and bone meal from Norway were its fertilizers. Furrows were 6 feet apart (they are 5 today), and cane once planted was allowed to ratoon 20 times. Now only two or three crops are harvested from the same planting.

Kekaha continues to operate on leased land, much of it in areas descending to the state from the Crown lands of the past and some holdings still leased from the Knudsen family. The 50,000 to 55,000 tons of sugar it now produces make it profitable year in and year out.

Several factors contribute to this success. First was the diking and filling of an 1,800-acre swamp that was growing rice when the company was founded. Even now, this swampy area, 1 or 2 feet below sea level, must be pumped 24 hours per day and in heavy rains will stand 3 feet in water until the pumps can pull it down again. Second was the construction of a network of ditches to import water from Mount Waialeale. More recent was the 1968 acquisition of adjoining Waimea Plantation, owned by the Faye family, which added 4,000 tons to Kekaha's output.

Here, again, the Amfac custom of close family ties appears. Lindsay Faye, father, son, and grandson, have managed Kekaha and family-owned Waimea through the generations. Still another Faye sought a career in Amfac and was briefly its President.

Captain L'Orange, already mentioned in connection with the importation of Scandinavians for the Hackfelds, had a son, Hans, who was long-time manager of Oahu Sugar Co. While Knudsen, Faye, and L'Orange were Scandinavians, many Germans worked for them. Hackfeld's Glade was first employed at the Kekaha Milling Co., and a big German mill superintendent named Schultze is still remembered for his police dog. While many managers affected sidearms as a means of intimidating idlers, Schultze's dog was menacing enough to make any malingerer hustle. Lindsay Faye, Jr., recalls Schultze as well as many a noisy beer bust and *hoch der Kaiser* in the days before World War I.

Kekaha is proud of the number of ditches built between 1910 and 1927 to supplement the pumped water. It is even more proud of its turbine-driven mill that gives it the highest extraction (the percentage of available juice removed from the cane stalk) of any sugar mill not employing the diffusion process. Remember that it was at Kekaha that a pilot plant proved, to Amfac's satisfaction, the merits of diffusion. The tests also proved that the system was not enough better than Kekaha's excellent factory to justify replacement.

Pearl Harbor's Oahu

Oahu Sugar Co., Ltd., headquartered on the central plain of the Island of Oahu, is a complex of 55 square miles, scarred with housing developments, freeways, military establishments, and shopping centers that make management as much a traffic problem as an agricultural one. None of this bizarre accompaniment to agriculture was visualized by the three men who sponsored the plantation in 1894 and incorporated it in 1897. The first was James Campbell, a canny Irishman who had bought the arid Ewa-Waipahu plain in the 1880s for $90,000, convinced that, with water, it would grow sugar in abundance. Having first demonstrated the practicability of drilling artesian wells there, he set about attracting tenants. The second in the group was the founder of the vast Dillingham enterprises, who, having built the railroad of his dreams as far as the Ewa mill, sought developers for the land in between and with them more freight across his tracks. Finally, as often was the case in those days, there were the Hackfeld partners led by Isenberg. Wise about sugar and well endowed with funds, they provided the tenant for Campbell and the freight for Dillingham. Most importantly, as events 75 years later were to demonstrate, they were to avoid the mistake of Ewa's founders by insisting on owning the mill site in fee. So it was that Oahu Sugar Co., dominated by Isenberg, acquired 70 acres adjoining Dillingham's main line, overlooking Pearl Harbor. They and another 1,415 acres, acquired between 1897 and 1951, were to prove a real estate bonanza in the late 1960s as well as insure Oahu's survival at the expense of Ewa.

By contrast with the faltering beginnings of Koloa and Lihue, Oahu's start evidenced Isenberg's professionalism. From the time of its founding in 1895 to its first crop 2 years later, wells were dug, fields planted, a mill built, a labor force recruited, housing erected, and over 7,000 tons of sugar produced. Berg says, "It would be hard to do better today."

With ample land available, Oahu's limitation was water. From the day the first manager, August Ahrens, set foot on the place, he and Isenberg were eyeing the distant Koolau range as its source. While the underlying water table was adequate for pumping artesian wells to irrigate low-lying fields, upper unirrigated areas were subject to drought and needed moisture. Gravity feed was one answer. The first survey of the Koolaus as a source was made in 1905. It took 7 years of negotiation to acquire the water rights and easements

(1) Amfac headquarters, despite a half-dozen moves during the years, has always been on Honolulu's Queen Street. This scene, photographed in the 1860s, shows at the extreme left the single-story building built for Hackfeld's "expansion" in 1853.

(2) In 1874 the partners bought the old courthouse. It served variously as an office and a warehouse until 1969, when it was demolished to make way for Amfac Center. The crowd, shown gathered at the corner of Fort and Queen streets, was celebrating the fiftieth anniversary of the partnership.

(3) Left: A popular figure in the German community was Henry Berger, the bearded leader of the Royal Hawaiian Band. He played for many occasions, including the arrivals and departures of Hackfeld's vessels. They plied the seven seas, carrying sugar outbound and returning with a wide assortment of merchandise, such as mill machinery from Scotland, gin from Holland, dried blood for fertilizer from Australia, and tobacco from the Philippines.

(4) Right: The end of an era is shown as a workman removes the Hackfeld name from the building Isenberg built. This occurred in 1919, when the new name, American Factors, Ltd., was adopted.

(5) This view of Honolulu harbor shows the dome of the new Hackfeld & Co. office building, completed in 1902, in the left third of photo. To its right is a Hackfeld warehouse sign; another sign appears behind the stern mast of the ship at the far right.

(6) Left: This is Honolulu harbor today, 125 years after Hackfeld sailed in with his merchandise and set up shop. The twin Amfac Center towers stand on land the company started acquiring in 1874.

(7) Craft like the Paul Isenberg, right, made up the Hackfeld fleet in the late 19th century. There were a dozen of them, bearing the names of the partners and their associates. One was the R. W. Wood, named for the druggist who appointed Hackfeld "factor" or agent for Koloa plantation and so introduced him to the sugar business. Another vessel was the J. C. Glade, named for the managing partner from 1871 to 1883.

(8) This park, at the same intersection of Fort and Queen streets shown in Figure 2, marks one entrance leading to Amfac Center. Behind the fountain, a gift of the Walker family, stands the gate that identified the premises in partnership days.

(9) Left: In this illustration, used as an annual report cover, the artist has suggested not only the increasing scale of the headquarters offices since 1849 but the magnitude of the enterprise that has emerged from once dusty, dirty Queen Street.

(10) Below: This corner, at Stockton and O'Farrell streets in the heart of downtown San Francisco's shopping district, will house a Liberty House store. The building will also provide offices for Amfac operating groups based in the continental United States. The property, once part of the City of Paris department store founded by a French family in 1850, was acquired when Amfac bought up the faltering enterprise and determined to revitalize it.

to move it across to Oahu's fields. Another 4 years was needed to dig the tunnels and the ditches to serve them; but the effort brought 3,000 new acres into cultivation and doubled the yield from hitherto unirrigated areas. The first water that gushed from the new Waiahole Ditch was greeted with much the same celebration that attended driving the golden spike that joined the initial transcontinental railroad.

While the Germans did their job well, the Oahu plantation had its problems. Though there was water under the plain, as Campbell had demonstrated, pumping it was another question. Ahrens was to write, "It is a fact (not to be made public) that the wretched work of this pump so slighted something over 200 acres that the yield was not quite 4 tons per acre, plant cane!—and taken in all its various phases it is my honest opinion that this miserable pump has lost us 2½ million dollars." Later, Oahu survived destruction by a pest, the leafhopper, which finally was brought under control by a parasite discovered by HSPA scientists. The experience, involving the loss of hundreds of thousands of dollars, stimulated research for new varieties of sugarcane by an industry still reliant on "Lahaina" introduced from Tahiti over 50 years before. Problems with the old variety persisted and in 1918, rootrot, know as Lahaina disease, spread over half the plantation. This demanded the substitution of new breeds, a feat accomplished within 3 years. As a result of this, a precautionary HSPA now plants 2.5 million seedlings each year, from which 70,000 to 80,000 are selected for field trials and about 2,000 are crossed for new varieties.

Oahu had planted all its available land by the end of World War I. In the following 35 years, production increased from 40,000 tons in 1922 to 70,000 in 1947, the growth due entirely to improved practices. In the latter year 3,000 added acres were acquired from the adjoining Aiea Plantation. This gave

Oahu 15,000 tons of increased production. In 1970 purchase of its remaining neighbor, Ewa Plantation Co., brought it still another 60,000 tons, making Oahu the second largest producer in Hawaii and the third largest in the United States.

The plantation's ability to make these acquisitions rather than itself be acquired is rooted in its strategic location as it relates to the growth of Honolulu. Aiea found so much of its land being withdrawn for military purposes that it no longer could sustain a volume that would permit an economic operation. Ewa, facing renewal of a lease with Mr. Campbell's trustees, found them adamant in demanding rights to withdraw areas for urbanization that would, in time, reduce its sugar production to unprofitable levels. The trustees' demands were strengthened no end by the fact that the estate owned the factory site. Oahu, with a bigger base to begin with and owning nearly 1,000 acres including its mill site, was in a better position to bargain and so bought out Ewa's position for $5 million. A tip of the hat to Mr. Isenberg!

Oahu can claim some industry firsts. It had the first 14-roller mill in the Islands. This was back in 1917. Following that, innovations occurred in every decade, the last being the installation of the largest bagasse-operated boiler in the world. At one time there was even thought of opening its own port in Pearl Harbor. To that end, it contributed $643.62 to the Republican party in 1902.

In the history of the company, undoubtedly the most dramatic event was the Japanese attack on Pearl Harbor. The plantation's population were shocked witnesses to the pandemonium of that Sunday morning. By noon its hospital was filled with Navy casualties and its heavy equipment had been commandeered by the military to help restore order to bombed-out areas. The jute bags, inventoried to ship sugar, were filled with sand by nightfall to guard improvised air-raid shelters. The very fact of being in the midst of the military activity for the ensuing 4 war years was to bring spectacular change to the plantation. It had to abandon burning cane and harvesting at nighttime because of the blackout. Some 3,000 acres of productive land were diverted to military uses. There were more than 100 installations, from warehouses to antiaircraft batteries, from barrage balloon platforms and searchlight installations to prisoner-of-war camps spotted among its fields. Production was to drop by a third. Shortages of labor shrunk the work force to a similar extent. As a consequence of the war and unionization, the basic wage rose from $0.25 per hour to $0.705 in 5 years.

Among the names associated with Oahu Sugar, in addition to L'Orange and to C. E. S. Burns, Jr., who managed it from 1957 to 1965, is that of bluff Ernest W. Greene. The contributions of this man, who ran the plantation until 1934, were of vast importance to the Island sugar industry and ultimately to Washington, D.C., as a community rather than as the nation's capital. Greene was first dispatched as technical adviser to the senior Walker in the drawn-out fight before New Dealers and Congress to obtain recognition of the Territory of Hawaii as "an integral part of the United States." His solid integrity, his complete knowledge of the Hawaiian industry, and his persuasive abilities made him the unanimous choice of the HSPA to remain in Washington as the Islands' representative for 20 years. It didn't hurt the cause of the industry (or Hawaiian statehood) that in time Greene became so respected by his fellow Washingtonians that he became a principal fund raiser for St. Alban's Cathedral and chairman of the house committee of the prestigious Chevy Chase Club. Among other roles, he served as president of the Rotary Club and a director of the National Savings and Trust Co. Greene was of such character that, when called on to register as a lobbyist, he refused. He thought it was a tainted word. He was so respected in Congress he got away with it.

Populous Pioneer

Moving eastward across the Island chain, the next of Amfac's plantations is Pioneer Mill. It was, like Kekaha, first a milling company adjoining the port of Lahaina, processing cane grown by others on West Maui. In fact, five plantations once functioned where now only Pioneer remains. The first formal undertaking to grow and process sugar in the district was led by a Hawaiian, David Malo, in 1845. His work as a reporter of Hawaiian legends and history has survived his reputation as a planter. This venture was to change hands twice before a missionary offspring, O. H. Gulick, put a 1,000-acre parcel together around it in 1849. Five years later he planted the first of the fabled cane from Tahiti that was to become known as the "Lahaina" variety.

With the end of the whaling economy on which Lahaina had thrived, businessmen at the tiny port turned to planting sugarcane all along the coast. In 1859 a storekeeper, the customs collector, and the sheriff jointly founded the Lahaina Sugar Co., and the following year Pioneer Mill was formed by Henry Turton, a mason as well as the proprietor of the town's billiard hall and bowling alley. His partner for a time was a carpenter, freshly arrived from Tahiti, named James Campbell, who later bought much of the land on which Oahu Sugar operates. The mill was rated as "two-mule power," with the animals driving wooden rollers as was done elsewhere. It did boast a small centrifugal to spin the molasses into crystals after the cane juice had been boiled in try-pots salvaged from the whaling ships. Originally, the partners ground cane grown by planters bearing such familiar sugar names as Makee and Baldwin; but in 1861 they mortgaged all their assets for $3,000—some indication of the scale of sugar plantations of the day—and began to plant cane.

Ten years later, King Kamehameha V set up a plantation to the west of Lahaina and relied on Pioneer to mill its product. At that time Campbell sold out to his partner. Lacking Campbell's sage counsel, Turton soon went bankrupt, and in 1885 the plantation was bid in by Campbell and Isenberg. Apparently Campbell's participation was an accommodation to Turton and Isenberg, as he sold out shortly to one Walter Horner, who, in turn, sold his interest to Isenberg soon after the incorporation of the present company in 1895. Such is the checkered career of many of the plantations in Hawaii. Pioneer was to have only one substantial expansion thereafter. That was the purchase of adjoining Olowalu in 1931.

The fluctuating fortunes of these early ventures are well illustrated by a quote from Mark Twain, who, though never noted for his financial acumen, fancied himself a businessman. Visiting Hawaii in 1866, he wrote of a Maui sugar venture:

> One of the best plantations in the Islands, though not one of the largest by any means, cost, with its appurtenances, $100,000. All bills were promptly paid and no debts allowed to accrue and bear interest. The consequence was that three years after the first plow disturbed its virgin soil, it had paid for itself and added a dividend of $200,000.

This particular plantation failed and has been a cattle ranch for the past 80 years.

Even after annexation, Pioneer had its difficulties. Pumps, operated by a secondhand engine once used to power San Francisco cable cars, began to lift water with a heavy saline content, forcing Pioneer to make a deal with the Baldwins to tunnel the West Maui mountains as an irrigation source. At various times, to supplement the income from sugar and molasses, the company ran a store and a dairy, grew vegetables, manufactured ice and ice cream, bottled soda water, and operated the Lahaina Light and Power Co. In the years after World War II, these activities were phased out, but it was not until 1973 that it got rid of the last of them: the 1,700 head of cattle it ranched.

The manager during and after World War II, John ("Jack") T. Moir, was one of the last Scotch autocrats to run a plantation. Dressed in the riding britches of an era that was fast disappearing, he was also a practitioner of labor relations in a fashion that was fast disappearing.

Despite his neolithic social views, Moir knew sugar and recognized that, with enforced mechanization, the only way to continue sugar production in his area was to clear it of rocks. He set about the mammoth job of digging up the boulders imbedded every few feet in the fields. In hundreds of instances, they weighed a ton or more and totaled 5,000 tons of rocks per acre. His stubbornness is reflected in mounds that dot the plantation and rise from the natural skyline 50 to 100 feet. They are some 200 feet long and nearly as wide. These man-made patterns, which resemble Diamond Head, probably will puzzle archaeologists eons hence.

Sugar production is still no cinch at Pioneer. The fields that were cleared of rocks seem to grow new ones and more are constantly unearthed in the course of mechanical planting and harvesting. Yet this plantation, also, has had its "firsts." It was the first to install and demonstrate the high recoveries available from the diffusion process. It was also the first to analyze the relative economics of land used for sugar in comparison with its use for resort purposes. This is an undertaking more complex than appears on the surface, for in the economies of scale it is the final acres harvested and tons of sugar produced that generate a plantation's profit, and Pioneer is too small as it is. The analysis, however, dictated the diversion of land adjoining the beautiful beach at Kaanapali for recreation; so Pioneer became the first plantation to learn to operate around people. It lives now in an atmosphere of *mai tais* and bikinis while providing such support functions as the irrigation of golf courses and the suppression of tourist-annoying dust and noise.

Periled Puna

Where Oahu and Kekaha have been the sugar man's dream, profiting in every year since their incorporation, until recently Puna, on the Island of Hawaii, has been a sugar man's night-mare. Every problem cited for other plantations—transporta-tion, rocks, Lahaina disease, labor costs—in fact, everything but drought (it averages 165 inches of rain per year), has hit Puna. To complicate matters, it lies on a slope below two active volcanoes which, on occasion, send lava flows burning their way through its fields. Organized by Isenberg's friend Dillingham in 1898, around land originally bought for coffee production, it paid only two dividends in 60 years. Its financial position deteriorated to a point where it relied on centrifugals 50 years old, and a quarter of them broke down each day.

No plantation felt the costs imposed by unionization as much as Puna. When struck in 1946 it had 1,200 employees. This had to be reduced to 400 if the plantation was to survive. The 400 figure was not to be approached until the appointment of the junior Burns as manager in 1951.

In fact, the plantation, which owed the agent $2.5 million in 1946, was to increase its indebtedness to over $4 million when Burns took over. By 1968, when it merged with Amfac, the overdraft had disappeared. The reversal of Puna's fortunes can be credited primarily to management, not the least to William Henry Bomke, who nursed the aged factory from 1958 to 1969.

The plantation's major landlord, an authority on Hawaiiana, Herbert Shipman, also claims a share in its success. Called Olaa for its first 60 perilous years, the plantation, Shipman insisted, had to change its name. In Hawaiian the word "Olaa" has an association with death. Since the name change all has gone well. The 1969 investment of $10 million in the new boiler-diffuser complex and the clearing and planting of 5,000 added acres are, however, a reflection of Amfac's confidence in more than the new name.

From the point of view of the Operations and Financial Review Committee, the plantation's profits, in terms of return on investment, were inadequate until 1973. Put another way, the hierarchy would never agree to invest the capital required to start a sugar plantation with its attendant irrigation system and mill in Hawaii today, given the best of soils and growing conditions. The capital outlays they authorize involve essential replacements or improvements that offer a quick "payback" in terms of savings in operating expense. Sugar, "the source of it all," while currently profitable, is probably a long-term holding operation for Amfac—a means of continuing employment and keeping the lands policed and property taxes paid while earning only a slight return on the massive capital commitments of past generations.

Sugar Futures

Despite their reputation for reproduction, not many more rabbits are going to be left for Berg to pull from his hat. The point of diminishing returns from mechanization, consolidation, and centralization has been reached. It was far easier for Amfac to cut Puna's work force from 1,200 to 400 than it would be to cut it proportionately from today's 390 to even 300.

While Lihue has recently arranged to lease 40 percent of Grove Farm, the opportunities for expansion are limited. Kekaha might outbid neighboring Olokele for its ground leases when they expire. Oahu lands threatened by urbanization might be expanded to include pineapple fields if that industry continues to phase out. That could also happen at Pioneer. There is more jungle around Puna to be cleared if the present project proves successful, but that is the only place where land is available without negotiation or acquisition of existing enterprises.

While some of these limitations may be overcome, the future of Amfac's sugar lands will ultimately be determined in the halls of Congress, at the Department of Agriculture, and in labor negotiations. Even if present prices are maintained, the research laboratories of HSPA and the talented resources of Berg's group will be hard-pressed to keep up with production controls imposed by the government, on the one hand, and increased labor costs imposed by the union, on the other.

5

The Collaterals

M issionary descendants in Hawaii call those they marry
who are not so descended "collaterals." The services
Hackfeld and his partners devised to serve the plantations
might well be called "collaterals."

As sugarcane nourished the enterprise from shortly after the
opium wars until the American take-over following World War
I, they plucked many profitable leaves from its stalks. The
company, employing sugar profits, was to abandon its worldwide trade and concentrate on Hawaii and, while exploring the
opportunities in diversification there, acquire land and contrive
added, profitable services to the plantations themselves.

Vertical Integration—Bremen Style

Part of the basic agency or factoring function established by
Hackfeld and molded by Isenberg provided for stevedoring,

storage, and shipping, all commissionable or profitable to the agent. There has been substantial change in these collaterals since Hackfeld first conceived them. The plantations now merged with Amfac no longer pay for those that remain and many—insurance, stevedoring, and shipping—are gone. Yet in their day they built Amfac.

Consider first the sale of management services to the plantations. The historic relationship was a charge of 2.5 percent on the selling price of the sugar marketed and an additional 2.5 percent as a commission on all purchases for them. This compensation was earned by providing corporate management as well as purchasing services and shipping and marketing arrangements. There were, at times, some requests for unexpected assistance. An example is reflected in this 1897 paragraph from correspondence between the agent and Lihue:

> That Chinaman we wrote about yesterday as having escaped, we beg to say, has returned again this morning to the hospital, but tried then to go out again when he was stopped by hospital authorities. We notified the police about this deserter and arranged with them to send a policeman to the hospital and keep him there until the *Mikihana* should sail. You will kindly send someone down right away to obtain this man. For hack hire we have paid 75 cents for him which we have debited to your account.

As further compensation for such annoyances, there were the commissions earned from others for casualty, fire, and marine insurance and the sale of supplies. By the time of the Spanish-American War the agent also owned 11 of the ships that carried plantation provisions and products, at a profit, naturally. Just what went on in Bremen is not clear, but evidently there was a further "skim" there, first by the company set up by Hackfeld and later by the one set up by Pflueger.

As early as 1851 Hackfeld was in the business of importing lumber and, except for a short period, his successors have done so ever since. By the turn of the century, cement, paint, and plumbing and lighting fixtures—in fact, well-established lines of all industrial materials—were being represented. Food, liquor, and tobacco had long been items in the Amfac line. The industrial needs of the plantations and the consumer goods sold through their stores were the backbone of its distribution business. If a plantation needed a pump, Amfac happened to represent Worthington and so, as purchasing agent for the plantation, bought it a Worthington pump. This was the Hackfeld approach to getting as many commissions from a transaction as possible. If the plantation's needs were for paint or hardware, plows or plumbing, the story was much the same.

Paulo Pioneers

"Sweet potatoes, potatoes, taro, tomatoes, and bananas could be raised and sold very cheaply; we need cheaper labor and must supply them with food cheap," Isenberg wrote from Bremen. The possibilities in diversification intrigued him throughout his lifetime. On his arrival in Hawaii, he found rice growing at Hanalei and pineapple near Lihue. He learned that tea and silkworms had been tried along with less exotic wheat, corn, and castor and lima beans. As an agriculturalist, he had an interest in plants, unlike Hackfeld. While the captain was glad to ship Island-grown potatoes to California during the gold rush, he never thought of planting or digging them.

In contrast, the young farmer from Dransfeld in Odenstat was to introduce the dynasty to the concept of orderly research with the establishment of an experimental farm at Kona on the Big Island. This interest in botany has characterized Amfac for a century.

In his early days on Kauai, Big Paul's diversification efforts were, like taro, pretty well confined to the immediate needs of the sugar operation. Cattle, hogs, and fowl were raised to be sold through the Hackfeld store. He set out a forest of redolent eucalyptus above Lihue as a source of firewood for the cook and bath houses in the plantation camps. He also experimented with hardwoods, hoping to fashion staves for the casks he used to ship Lihue's sugar. It is not clear whether he knew that the stands he planted would serve today as a watershed and a forest reserve that is an integral part of the plantation's irrigation system.

In Isenberg's time the ideas that had produced the Royal Hawaiian Agricultural Society led to the formation of the Planters' Labor and Supply Co. This in turn became the forerunner of the present-day Hawaiian Sugar Planters' Association. It is some reflection of the way Isenberg operated that Glade, the partner who nominally represented the firm on the Board of that company, subscribed for 10 shares, whereas Isenberg, remaining in the background, personally subscribed for 3,000, as much as any of the plantation members had.

The nascent Planters' Labor and Supply Co. had plenty to occupy it in problems of labor importation, sugar production, and government regulation. Experimentation with other crops was left to the individual members. Thus Isenberg's restless mind focused the resources of the partnership on diversification.

Trial and Error

This is where the Kona venture came in. Isenberg's original efforts to grow sugar there had failed because of spotty rainfall patterns and the lack of a source of water for irrigation. Nevertheless, the soils were good, the climate was favorable, and a labor supply was available for crops less demanding of water. Early in the project sisal was set out. Cordage and binder twine were important in those days and there was much speculation in the crop throughout the Islands. For a brief time the fiber was commercially produced.

Isenberg encouraged tobacco to be planted. Some of the drying sheds are still to be seen on the slopes above the carefree Kona coast. George Vancouver, the English explorer and naturalist, had been the first to plant oranges there and small groves were subsequently started from his stock. No longer cultivated on a significant scale, they still bear a tangy flavored fruit that finds its way to rural Island produce markets. Canna and hemp were tried. While everything would grow, yields in some cases, as with sisal, did not approach those available in more tropic climes.

The Hackfeld partners were to find that they could get their cigars cheaper by buying them in Manila, as they always had, than by rolling Kona leaves closer to home. In other instances, failures were due to disease and, most frequently with temperate-zone crops like peanuts, pestilence.

The one product on which Isenberg was persistently bullish, however, was coffee. Amfac was to continue to participate in its production and distribution for 75 years. Unquestionably, the coffee bean grown in Kona has a flavor that distinguishes it from that grown elsewhere. Early in Isenberg's plantings it found favor with blenders not only along the West Coast but in Europe. Even today, one nationwide restaurant chain will serve nothing but "Kona" coffee. The Amfac practice was to encourage growers by clearing land and making cash advances to them, then buying their crop, packing it, and marketing it, primarily through Hawaiian retail outlets but, in part, on the mainland. For years after the "new" building was completed in 1902, coffee was roasted in a small plant immediately behind it. In those days before air-conditioning, the Hackfeld office was known for its aromatic halls as well as its imperial eagles.

Languid Land

Turn, now, to the quiet collateral—the land in Hawaii. The myth that the Calvinist missionaries "stole" the lands from the Hawaiians clearly doesn't apply in the case of the Lutheran Hackfeld partnership and its successors; but, as a matter of fact, the pattern in its acquisition is much the same as occurred with the plantations developed by missionary-associated names like Castle & Cooke and Alexander & Baldwin.

Remember that with minor exceptions related to the warehousing and distribution of merchandise all the land was acquired for agricultural purposes, primarily for sugar. Whereas the profits from services for and sales to the plantations ended up as dividends to Amfac shareholders or as assets in the ever more substantial balance sheet, the land accumulated value quietly, its growing worth nowhere stated. Once acquired, it slept languidly alongside beaches fringed with the green of sugarcane or removed from passing view by lava flows or algarroba thickets. It came into Amfac's portfolio only with the recent plantation mergers but it came under Amfac management back in the days of the partnership. Much of that which is owned in fee was acquired by the partners individually and passed into the hands of the plantations in exchange for stock on their incorporation. In turn, when Amfac bought out the German interests in the plantations, it was the plantations' stock that was bought, not direct title to their lands.

"High Class in Our Dealings"

As these holdings were being accumulated, politics, as it related to monarchy and reciprocity, was a Hawaiian preoccupation. While seeking to avoid encumbrances, the partners were compelled to take some role in such matters.

Isenberg was certainly a royalist, as his advocacy of a regency for Princess Kaiulani, rather than a republic or annexation by the United States, manifests. He would return from Bremen periodically to attend meetings of the House of Nobles. But as J. F. Humberg, an early employee of the partnership and ultimately the first manager of the San Francisco office recalled, "The firm, during all my service with it, never mixed in politics. We were solely concerned to carry on business on the highest plane and in the most dignified manner, high class in our dealings with the public, never monopolistic; 'live and let live' was our principle."

Collaterals in the Caretaker Years

The astronomical sugar profits attending World War I contributed greatly to the substance of Amfac. Through dividends derived from the plantations and the 2.5 percent "marketing" commission on the sale of their sugar to C and H, the balance sheet flourished. From the time that C and H reorganized as a farmers' cooperative until it merged with its plantations, Amfac had no investment in the C and H refinery but it did hold two seats on the C and H board, representing the plantations' ownership. This, and the fact that it held one of the five trusteeships in the HSPA and, until recently, a seat on the Matson Board, gave Amfac officers status in both Honolulu and San Francisco. It gave, as well, valuable access to the business and political communities on the mainland that has proved, in itself, to be a collateral.

Related to the refining activity has been the ownership of a small part of Bay and River Navigation, a freighting operation in San Francisco Bay. This company moves sugar from the C and H refinery to railroad piers on the city's *embarcadero*. While rail lines serve the factory, the existence of Bay and

River is due to more favorable rates available at terminals across the bay.

Before the Germans' departure the growth of the Islands had so expanded the list of their suppliers and customers that distribution had become far more than a sugar collateral. There was a time when an Amfac employee could buy everything but an automobile from the company. When the Americans took over they moved to correct that and, in the 1920s, had won the agency for several General Motors cars representing, among others, such makes as Chevrolet and Oldsmobile. They exhibited poor judgment—rare for them—in giving G.M. up in 1927 in favor of names now long forgotten, like Auburn and Star.

At about the same time May & Co., a major retail grocer in downtown Honolulu, was acquired. The establishment of a six-unit chain of supermarkets built around it was authorized by the Board. The minutes are not clear, but somebody dropped the ball. When the possibility of a chain of supermarkets was again referred to, it was to the effect that the competition was too intense to permit it. Eventually, May's itself was forced to close. In fact, the expansion of supermarkets in Hawaii, as elsewhere, resulted in the elimination of food wholesalers, Amfac among them.

Following the transfer of the Hackfeld assets to American hands, there seemed no further interest in getting mixed up in politics. This may be because the new owners had their own political apparatus and saw no reason for another management to become involved. Brewer associate George P. Cooke was President of the Senate, Castle & Cooke's T. H. Petrie was on the Honolulu Board of Supervisors, and so on. Under the territorial structure Amfac was never to become deeply involved in that government.

Among the other collaterals under the Hackfeld dynasty there was always shipping; but a majority of the American interests who took over the assets were owners of Matson as well and saw no reason to reestablish Amfac as a competitor. In 1925 Walter Dillingham, a long-time antagonist of Matson and the part owner of a competitive firm, made an all-out effort to disrupt the arrangement. The matter was finally submitted to Oscar Sutro, the San Francisco attorney retained to defend Amfac in the Hackfeld litigation. As arbitrator, he approved the Matson contract. Thus the shipping collateral remained only an agency one and a stevedoring business on tiny Kauai, where even those operations were confined to one port, Nawiliwili. A second port was served by an Alexander & Baldwin subsidiary. Amfac was never to enjoy returns comparable to those of Alexander & Baldwin on Maui and C. Brewer on Hawaii. By far the largest importer in the Islands, it stood placidly by while Castle & Cooke, with its Oahu orientation and control of Dole's pineapple, enjoyed the advantage of being agent and stevedore in the Islands' only major port, Honolulu.

For many years the principal U.S. life insurance companies resisted covering Orientals because of the fear of a high mortality rate. Later, when a major new source of premiums developed in the 1930s with the emergence of group life insurance and formalized pension and health plans, they relented. With its thousands of employees in Hawaii and its leadership in the practice of modern industrial relations, Amfac attracted a heavy volume of business of this character. It installed one of the first formal, private pension plans in the Islands in 1941 and has been a leader in expanding employee benefits ever since.

Amfac and the Wars

Armed conflict figures prominently in Amfac's history. More than most venerable companies, its destiny has been influenced by war. The opening of China stimulated Hackfeld's trade in the Far East. It was then that he engaged his Hong Kong representative, W. M. Pustau & Co., to insure the cargo he loaded aboard the *Swallow* on his fateful return to Honolulu in 1846. The relationship was to endure. Years later, his accounts show him still trading through Pustau for such items as "rope at $8 a hundred weight, 268 cases of tea and $535.50 worth of crystal glassware."

Amfac has survived as many governments as wars. There was first the monarchy of Hackfeld's day. The Hawaiian kingdom may appear to have had its comic-opera aspects, but it was no joke to those who lived in Hawaii during that epoch. Pflueger took pride in his role as a fiscal adviser to Kamehameha IV. Royalty was also the social arbiter of the time. In 1860 the King, his Queen, Emma, and their two-year-old son, Prince Albert Edward Kauikeaouli, paid a state visit to Kauai. At a costume party the monarch played the role of a fearsome ghost to the fascination of the children. This became the greatest social occasion in the Island's history. It also provided the name for a ranch, long owned and operated by Amfac, Princeville.

It was the American Civil War that shut off Caribbean sugar from the Union and gave the Hawaiian industry access to the markets of the North and so an opportunity to recover from a depression that followed the brief gold rush boom.

When the revolution of 1893 led to the formation of the Republic of Hawaii, with Judge Sanford Dole as President, Isenberg, in Bremen, still hoped for a restoration of the monarchy. But he admired Dole, and when Isenberg visited the Islands in the following year he expressed confidence in the economic stability achieved under the Republic. While opposing annexation, which Dole favored, he felt that becoming only a protectorate of the United States "would be even worse."

When his friends, Judge Dole, W. R. Castle, and L. A. Thurston among them, succeeded in securing annexation in 1898, Isenberg had no choice but to go along with it. As it developed, he prospered under it and in Humberg's words "never mixed in politics." This may well have been a matter of policy but it was probably also due in part to the fact that Hackfeld & Co. was so blatantly German that the American, British, and Hawaiian elements which constituted the electorate didn't welcome any company interest in the conduct of public affairs.

Still Another War

The Spanish-American War ensured the annexation of Hawaii to the United States and thus the future of the sugar business. In 1897, the year preceding that event, Hackfeld plantations shipped 46,259 tons of sugar. Five years later this had grown to 70,223, and in 10 years more that figure doubled.

It remained for still another war, one that encompassed the whole world, substantially to change Amfac's destiny. Before then H. A. Isenberg, Paul's son, and then William Pfotenhauer guided the company along the course Paulo set.

World War I was accompanied by an inflation in sugar prices that induced Hackfeld & Co. to expand production from 108,636 tons in 1913 to 144,075 tons in 1918. Meanwhile, the price per ton increased from $66.26 to $284.52. On the plantations compensation was related to the price of sugar and bonuses of 40 percent were not uncommon as late as 1919 and 1920. Even field hands, accustomed to $8 a day, were getting $44. Hawaii's soaring prosperity, then largely reliant on sugar, generated a second wave of profit for Hackfeld in its collateral activities. Merchandise earnings, $246,470.59 in 1913, reached $570,123.62 in 1917.

Nonetheless, on the American entry into the war the alien character of the firm got it in all sorts of trouble. Provisioning the German ships interned conspicuously in Honolulu harbor (which someone had to do) fueled the antagonism directed against the concern. There were threats of boycotts and civil demonstrations. Despite J. F. C. Hagens' obtaining loyalty oaths from all employees, the firm remained closely tied to Germany. J. F. Hackfeld, its President, rode out the war in Bremen. Given the benefit of hindsight, there was no tolerable solution but the one evolved by the Alien Property Custodian (see Chapter 3).

Day of Infamy

In the early wars, though cause and effect is now evident, the martial events were far removed from Hawaii. In fact, the word of Hawaii's annexation to the United States came by the same ship that brought the news of the battle of Santiago Bay.

World War II was a different matter. Oahu Sugar Co. fields flow down from the uplands to Pearl Harbor's rim. Its factory, sited on a hill, looks down on the hull of the sunken battleship *Arizona*, marked now by a memorial. On the day of the Japanese attack, Oahu Sugar found itself very close to the scene of action. Its buildings, in fact, still show scars from machine-gun bullets. Incendiary matter set cane fields afire throughout the property. In the ensuing 4 years Hawaiian plantations were to face every conceivable demand on their resources. Oahu, because of its proximity to the military, suffered more than any of them. By war's end it had provided 3,000 acres of cane land for over 100 military installations, ranging from warehouses to ammunition dumps.

Once the naval victory at Midway rendered the Hawaiian chain secure, the impact of World War II on Hawaii was largely social and economic. Blackouts, travel restrictions, and material scarcities complicated private life as well as business. During the war some 8,000 firms closed their doors for lack of supplies, yet 12,000 new ones sprang up in the service trades. Kapaa on Kauai, for example, where Amfac's Hawaiian Canneries had its plant, had 3 restaurants before Pearl Harbor, 22 by war's end.

Amfac, of course, was in the heart of the economic maelstrom. The senior Walker, always on cordial terms with the military, was called upon to regulate distribution of food and materials under martial law. There was no one better positioned to take on the thankless chore. His company, as the Island's major importer in peacetime, knew the buying patterns and volume of business done by the various suppliers of the civilian community. This helped Walker maintain historic competitive relationships in the face of swollen demands and persistent shortages. Walter Dillingham, Walker's confidant and a senior Board member, was called on by the military to stimulate the local production of food, a program which required Oahu to divert 500 acres for the production of potatoes. Their roles were more than advisory; they operated from desks in the military governor's office at Iolani Palace and had staffs of employees, some of them in uniform, to carry out their directives.

Notwithstanding the senior Walker's intimacy with it, the military government became an ever-increasing burden to Hawaiian business. It imposed wage and price controls, rationing, and material allocations and finally mired itself down in regulations by the carload. One executive put it well when he said that it seemed "as though the winning of the war had become a secondary matter in the welter of questionnaires, regulations, rulings, and interpretations hurled at us. It is utterly impossible to keep pace with all of them; there is a confusing mass of instructions and directions, which often admit of no intelligent application."

In the long run the war had little effect on Amfac earnings. Despite excess profit levies that quadrupled its federal income taxes, its net improved slightly between 1941 and 1945. Its increased sale of merchandise, reflecting the demands of the military, more than offset the decline in sugar production. On renegotiation of its government contracts, a postwar precaution against profiteering, Amfac was required to return less than $5,000 to the federal agencies it had served.

Diverse Engagements

Freed, with the sale of Castle & Cooke and C. Brewer interests, to operate independently, Amfac turned to new horizons after World War II. Meanwhile, it had anticipated a return to a peacetime economy by opening up an entirely new line of endeavor in 1944 with the purchase of W. A. Ramsay & Co., the distributor of all General Electric products in Hawaii. This introduced Amfac to the highly competitive business of retailing and servicing appliances and the problems and profits of wholesaling electrical products for industrial purposes.

Acquainted with the Philippines through ownership of stock in several sugar plantations there and the HSPA recruitment of Filipinos, the senior Walker was acutely aware of the demand for goods that wartime destruction had generated. Piers, factories, sugar mills, and warehouses had to be restored; food, appliances, plumbing fixtures, and roofing had to be supplied. As merchants with established sources for all these materials and experience in marketing them, Amfac's expansion into the void was inviting. Too, because of the kinship of Hawaii and the Philippines, it seemed almost a charitable thing to do. Amphil was the name of the corporation estab-

lished in Manila to do the job with an initial capitalization of
$500,000. In 1950 it was decided to abandon it.

Industrial Bargaining Battles

The 5 years of labor strife in Hawaii that followed World
War II were a management's nightmare. There were all-night
negotiating sessions, week-long fact-finding hearings, strikes
running for months, as well as years of employer-union propa-
ganda campaigns.

Despite this long and costly experience, Amfac is not anti-
union. Vice President for Industrial Relations Don Nicholson,
square-jawed, superfit if graying, says:

> We recognize the unions that represent our employees, strive
> to have good day-to-day relations with them, and do our best to
> establish good communications. We are tough bargainers at the
> negotiating table and don't give the store away, but at the same
> time, we will not bypass NLRB or state election procedures in
> a union-organizing situation to be party to a sweetheart contract.
> We attempt to keep our nonunion operations nonunion and use
> the legal weapons available to achieve this aim. Finally, as a
> company, we recognize good labor relations, including the
> prompt settlement of grievances, as an important part of our
> operations, for poor relations can severely affect our profits.

Of the 22,000 Amfac employees, 10,000 are represented by
a score of different bargaining units. While there is an attempt
in Hawaii to keep plantation and headquarters compensation
structures in similar patterns, the diversity among the newly
acquired companies defies any short-term attempt to gain
consistency. Even if there were no union contracts, the
practices in the various lines of business would defy it. Retail
managers, for example, are highly paid by comparison with
hotel managers. Except for the Agriculture Group and headquarters staff, Nicholson provides philosophy and, if asked,

advice, but he does not intervene in the conduct of the labor relations of the subsidiaries.

Throughout the travails of the postwar period Amfac, in common with other Hawaiian companies, avoided long-term debt and, with an almost pious attitude, prided itself on paying cash for everything. But the strikes of the 1940s, the problems at Puna, and the demands of such capital-devouring ventures as land development forced a change in position. The fact that modern management believes in substantial debt as a contributor to corporate capital had no influence on Amfac's original resort to debt in financing its affairs. Borrowing was forced on it by collateral activities.

6

Troubled Times

With the retirement of the senior Walker as President in 1950, Amfac management suffered one resounding shock after another. His successor, long groomed for the Presidency, had spent his career in the company and made some notable contributions to it. Yet he committed a serious sin of omission in neglecting to pay his income taxes, a circumstance, when it surfaced, that forced his retirement after 2 years as President.

Next in turn was a brilliant, financially trained executive who had come to Hawaii as an Army officer and draft administrator during World War II. Emmett Solomon became a protégé of the senior Walker, who brought him into the company at war's end to manage labor relations. Solomon proved an excellent choice, performing in the difficult, strike-torn, transitional postwar years in a fashion that commanded community respect. His wife's health, however, was a problem,

111

and he sought and got the assignment as Amfac's San Francisco office manager. When the Presidency was abruptly vacated, Solomon was induced to return to the Islands and fill the chair, but the same health problems required him to resign within a year and return to San Francisco. Some indication of what he might have done at Amfac is found in his ascendancy to the Presidency and Chairmanship of the Crocker-Anglo Bank and the engineering of its subsequent merger with the Citizen's National of Los Angeles. Now known simply as Crocker, it is California's fourth largest bank.

George Sumner, a naval officer who had married Eva Focke and so had ties with the German community, succeeded Solomon in 1953 and was President until 1959. Sumner, after becoming a civilian, had served as an officer at the Bishop Trust Co., where he had earned the confidence of Walter Dillingham and Gaylord Wilcox. Long an executive of Amfac, Sumner was essentially a sugar man and above all a gentleman. He had the rigidity of purpose that is often associated with the military and his administration proved somewhat abrasive, if successful.

The decade following the senior Walker's retirement was troubled, not only by executive changes but by predators loose among the stockholders and politicians. Through no fault of Sumner's, but of the passing years, the dominant voices on the Amfac Board, Dillingham and Wilcox, were growing feeble. The vacuum in stockholder influence was evident and there was no lack of candidates to buy enough stock to assume a significant voice on the company's Board of Directors.

One of the first was a Philadelphia broker, Howard Butcher III of Butcher and Sherrerd. He is a Philadelphian with many of the traditions of Ben Franklin, such as the University of Pennsylvania and thrift, behind him. His interests range from tennis to a personal pleasure and a pun, a ti-house restaurant in Waipio Valley on the Island of Hawaii. He also likes to make money and use peppery financial phrases like "Don't try to disguise profits; disclose them." Speaking of his losses in the Pennsylvania Railroad bankruptcy, he said: "12 million clams is a lot of clams, but the same year we made over 30 million clams out of our ships cruising the Caribbean."

Actually Butcher knew Hawaii well. He had honeymooned there in the 1930s and determined to buy Island stocks when they were low in price and mainland securities were high. His oldest son was nicknamed "Olaa" (the original name for Puna) because, while vacationing at the neighboring Volcano House, Butcher had bought some Olaa stock and made a profit, with which he paid the cost of the boy's delivery.

Butcher is not a quiet man. He made no secret of his feeling that the plantations' profit and loss statements should be consolidated with those of Amfac and that its share of C and H earnings should be reflected in Amfac's financial reports. He wanted all the profits accruing to the parent to appear and so benefit the price of Amfac stock. He also wanted the company to rely more on borrowings for the leverage so provided and to become listed on the New York Stock Exchange. To reduce overhead, he urged Amfac to merge with C. Brewer, where he had acquired large holdings as well. While he sat on the Board from 1957 until 1962 he was not heeded by the conservative management. Rather than start a battle he sold out and found a more responsive haven in C. Brewer; he and his investor clients finally took over its control.

Butcher was only the first clap of thunder to warn of the gathering storm. He was followed by a pride of lions smelling raw meat in Amfac's exposed carcass. J. C. Earle, a Los Angeles insurance millionaire who was later to figure in the Royal Lahaina Hotel at Kaanapali, was also on the prowl.

There were overtures for a take-over by Georgia-Pacific in 1965. For a time the Chase Manhattan Bank held $7 million worth of stock, by far the most influential holding.

Changing the Palace Guard

Traditionally Republican Hawaii was to face a string of Democratic governors beginning with appointees of Franklin Roosevelt. The first were ineffectual and they showed no great desire to disturb the status quo by building the Democratic party within the state.

Beyond the walls of Iolani Palace, however, where the Territorial Governor made his office, a former policeman, John A. Burns, was providing the leadership the dormant party needed. Sensing the possibilities in a coalition of recently organized labor, the numerically dominant Japanese, and those with a general anti-Establishment attitude in the community, Burns built a shadow cabinet of sorts. It met on Fridays for lunch to exchange ideas, identify likely candidates, and strategize. With Burns as chairman of the Democratic Central Committee, the party won a majority in the Territorial legislature for the first time in 1954 and then put Burns in as a delegate to Congress in 1956. When statehood came in 1959, three of the state's four members elected to Congress were Democrats. Ironically, Burns, who piloted statehood through the Capitol, was defeated in the state's first election for governor, but he prevailed in his next try and now is serving his third term.

Amfac had been reluctant to support statehood. Dillingham was strongly opposed to the idea, and Sumner, as an old Naval Academy man, personally shared the strong Navy opposition to the admission of Hawaii as a state. Finally, however, community sentiment and support for admission by most of the remaining business community led to a change in the company's position, though "Old Warrior" Dillingham was never convinced.

Statehood itself brought no change in the company's participation in political matters. It was not statehood that led it to support occasional Democrats; it was the political reality· that the Democrats had taken over the electorate.

Transfer of control of the legislature to the Democrats presented Amfac with new problems. These took various forms. Under new antitrust laws, Harold C Eichelberger had to resign as a Director of the Bank of Hawaii because it and Amfac both engaged in the mortgage business. Amfac executive C. E. S. Burns, Jr., appointed to chair the Land Use Commission (the agency that classifies and zones land as urban or agricultural), found he had to resign the post. In this case, it was not forced upon him. It was merely that with Amfac trying to urbanize and develop its Oahu lands, he felt obliged to abstain from voting whenever company property was involved. Under the wording of the law an abstention is, in fact, a vote against a rezoning, so he found himself voting against Amfac's interests no matter what their merit.

In this period of Democratic control Amfac spokesmen have joined other businessmen in opposing a stream of legislation directed at the Establishment and designed to liberalize and socialize everything from land use to workmen's compensation. They have helped stem some extreme ideas or channel them into more conservative patterns. Nevertheless, Hawaii now has the sixth highest per capita taxes of any state. Its land zoning and condemnation laws are far more extreme than any on the mainland. Its welfare payments have multiplied five times in as many years, and its labor legislation extends to all agricultural employees, ensuring union solidarity in all walks of life. The high costs resulting from this type of legislation and militant unionization have made the business climate in Hawaii less attractive than in many states.

Cannon to the Right and Left

The Sumner administration had further problems. Following the war some shareholders, as well as the unions, began to attack the conservative Hawaiian establishment. Minority stockholders, most of them seeking to embarrass the management in order to arrive at a favorable out-of-court settlement, initiated a number of actions. One such was by a *kamaaina* rancher and legislator, W. H. Rice, who alleged that Pioneer was being milked and mismanaged by Amfac. Nothing ever came of it but a day-long shareholders' meeting and a proxy fight won by management.

At that time Puna was foundering and a former Governor and Roosevelt appointee, Ingram Stainback, sought to force Puna to abandon the use of Amfac as its agent. This was settled out of court to avoid prolonged litigation. Still another suit was directed against Pioneer by Harriet Bouslog, an attorney and counsel for the ILWU with a sharp eye for real estate. She contended that the values assigned to Pioneer's land in its merger with Amfac were too low. Her case was dismissed.

In this period the retail business called for examination. There had been quite an issue at the Board level when the Ala Moana Shopping Center was built midway between downtown Honolulu and Waikiki. The differences concerned the question of whether Liberty House should undertake a major expansion and become a key tenant in a facility which was to become one of the largest such centers in the world. It was

(11) To commemorate its one hundredth anniversary, Amfac commissioned famed artist Peter Hurd to depict the history of the company. This is Koloa Plantation at the time Hackfeld became agent.

(12) As late as the 1930s many women still worked in the cane fields, weeding or applying fertilizer. This scene dates from the turn of the century, when female field labor was common. At that time Lihue was producing only a fifth of the sugar it does today.

(13) Little thought was given to the environment in the early days. In this photograph of the Lihue mill in 1890 the piles of trash are bagasse, set out to dry so it could be used as fuel.

(14) The passage of time and a growing concern with ecology have led to the parklike development that has emerged around the Lihue mill today.

(15) The opening of the Waiahole tunnel, which serves Amfac's Oahu Sugar Co. with irrigation water, on May 27, 1916, was the occasion for much celebration. This photograph shows the arrival of the first party to traverse the tunnel, which runs through 7 miles of lava mountain.

(16) On October 8, 1930, the first train ran from westernmost Kauai, where Amfac's Kekaha Plantation lies, to Lihue and adjoining Nawiliwili harbor. G. N. Wilcox, in the business suit and panama hat, was associated with Amfac in the early days of the partnership. The Wilcox-owned Grove Farm Plantation adjoined Lihue, which ground its cane for generations. Recently the Wilcox family also turned part of the farming over to Lihue.

(17) The Oahu Sugar Co. had this view of the Japanese attack on Pearl Harbor on December 7, 1941. Because of its proximity to the naval base, Oahu suffered the most physical damage and the greatest demands on its resources of any of the Island plantations.

(18) Mechanization and industrialization of the sugar plantations accelerated after the close of World War II. This was intensified by the aggressive unionization of the labor force. Today Hawaiian sugar companies are the most efficient in the world.

(19) In the Esperance district, along the Great Bight in southwest Australia, Amfac's Agriculture Group, which runs sugar production in Hawaii, is participating in the development of 1.3 million acres of government-owned land.

(20) Papaya production on the Big Island of Hawaii is a new venture for the Agriculture Group. At present over 750 acres of otherwise unproductive lava land are devoted to the crop. The main market is the continental United States, to which the fruit is shipped by air.

(21) In 1849 Heinrich Hackfeld founded Hackfeld & Co.; he remained a partner until 1886. He had structured a rapidly growing, vertically integrated business deriving profits at all levels of sugar production from merchandising and shipping to insurance.

(22) Paul Isenberg was made a partner in 1881 and a managing partner in 1889. When H. Hackfeld & Co. was incorporated in 1897, he became its first President. As a leader in building its sugar, mercantile, and shipping industries, he set a pattern for Amfac that endured until the 1960s.

(23) A. W. T. Bottomley, a banker, was recruited by the consortium of new owners that took over the interests of the Germans after World War I. He became the first President of the newly named American Factors, Ltd. His tenure was marked by litigation with the Hackfeld and Isenberg heirs over the sums paid for their holdings in the predecessor company.

(24) H. Alexander Walker, Sr., was President from 1933 to 1950. During the depression years he fought congressional action that was discriminatory to Hawaiian interests. In World War II he served with the military government. He was preoccupied in his last years with the organization of Hawaiian labor by Harry Bridges and his IWLU.

(25) In the next 17 years Amfac had five Presidents. In 1967 Henry A. Walker, Jr., was appointed President and now serves as Chairman and Chief Executive Officer. He presides over a management that completely altered the character of Amfac as established by Isenberg. Walker sold blocks of Hawaiian land and developed resorts on other parcels. He made major mainland acquisitions in the areas of food processing, retailing, mortgage servicing, electrical supplies, and pharmaceuticals.

being built by Dillingham interests on land owned by them. Walter Dillingham, then a major power on the Amfac Board, urged it. George Sumner, as President, opposed it and carried the day, but, as will be seen, his long-time friend and sponsor was persistent.

Then there was the problem of pineapple. Pineapple, grown as a fresh table fruit, was to be found on all the Islands in Isenberg's time. The smooth cayenne variety, the basis of the industry today, was introduced in 1886 and flourished. Before Isenberg died there were some canning ventures operating, primarily in the Pearl Harbor area near his Oahu Sugar Co., yet he never became enthusiastic about the fruit. Thus Amfac was slow to become involved in its production. Jim Dole, the long-limbed founder of the industry as big business, came to the Islands after Isenberg was gone. In 1909 Dole leased some 3,000 acres on Oahu's upland plain to begin the first major canning venture in the history of Island agriculture.

Amfac's entry into pineapple came in the 1920s and even then the approach was just to stick a toe in the water. Hawaiian Canneries had been operating as a neighbor of Lihue's at Kapaa since 1915. Its moving spirit was a Cleveland food merchant named Henry Haserot. Haserot needed a larger source of private-label canned pineapple for his customers. Dole was in its ascendancy and Del Monte and Libby had entered the business in a big way. Haserot approached Lihue to take stock in his company in exchange for some land. Amfac agreed on the condition that it be named agent for Hawaiian Canneries, and so it came to be. The arrangement provided it be paid 1 percent on sales, 1 percent on purchases, and 6 percent on cash advances. In the nature of things in those days it paid only 3 percent on credit balances. Primarily as a result of the depression of the 1930s, which followed tremendous packs by the major producers (Dole lost control of his company to his landlords in the course of the debacle), Amfac found itself owning 90 percent of Hawaiian Canneries. In 1938, the packer's overdraft with its agent had mounted to $343,022.17, and the prospects were bleak. While the surplus of canned fruit had been absorbed by the market, its by-product, pineapple juice, could not be sold under any label. It was World War II and the great demands of the military that reversed the trend for a time. In 1945 Hawaiian Canneries even had a credit balance of $589,000 and paid out $67,250 in dividends. Ten years later it was back in the red. High labor costs imposed by unionization and the difficulties of competing with the big brand names presented problems enough. When the market was flooded with low-cost foreign imports from Taiwan and the Philippines, Hawaiian Canneries was forced to close.

Pineapple was not the only Amfac venture with Island products other than sugar. In 1921 it found itself the major creditor of Hawaiian Tuna Packers, but rather than take over its ownership it negotiated its sale and so recovered the sums owed. In 1937 there were modest investments in Hawaiian Taro Products and the Hawaiian Macadamia Nut Co., both now long defunct.

What hurt most, however, was the abandonment of coffee, which Isenberg had started growing (see Chapter 5). Battered by extreme price changes occasioned by a world surplus on the one hand and wars and civil disturbances on the other, Amfac hung on tenaciously to Paulo's project. The rising cost of labor and a developing shortage of it made roasting and marketing unprofitable. Further, because of its low volume, the Amfac "Mayflower" brand of Kona coffee had difficulty winning shelf space in mainland outlets. The coming of chain supermarkets, with their emphasis on competitive pricing, and TV promotion of national brands added to Amfac's problems. In 1963 it abandoned all participation in the business. Lands that were once bought for coffee were subdivided to house workers in the coastal resort hotels below the groves.

Day Dawns

Sumner's successor, C. Hutton Smith, brought in an able retail merchandiser and manager from Portland, Oregon, Edmund A. Attebury, with a view to revitalizing the Liberty House operation. Under Attebury, branches were expanded at Waikiki and in a small center in Kahala, a suburban area beyond Diamond Head. When the Ala Moana Shopping Center embarked on a planned second-phase expansion, there was no question about it—Liberty House was to be its anchor with a 233,000-square-foot, three-story structure. A crisp, airy, masterfully designed showcase, it reflects Attebury's long-nourished dream of what a department store should be. It has since provided the pattern for successors in the chain. It also proved so profitable that it gave Attebury the springboard from which to launch the massive Retail Group that came into existence in the last decade.

Thus, for 20 years following World War II Amfac was trying to find its role in a Hawaii where pineapple was on the decline, sugar was no longer king, and the collaterals of the Big Five days were going fast. With a tradition in agriculture and distribution, Amfac's stubborn devotion to coffee and its investment in the Amphil venture in Manila were logical.

But people pressure, the growth of Honolulu, and tourism were to make resort and housing development the truly profitable field for expansion by a company rich in land and the related services, financing, building materials, and knowledge of the territory. They were to provide the basis for the great "thrust forward" under the administration of the junior Walker.

7

New Horizons

Quite a contrast to Sumner was his cigar-smoking successor, C. Hutton Smith. An insurance underwriter and salesman since he was 17, "Conch" Smith proved to have the cordial personality to reconcile the many problems that were to arise in the ensuing decade. Appointed President at the age of 62, his obvious role was to select and develop a successor management. That proved to be more difficult than it sounds.

Under Smith the search for diversification was begun as well. This search was occurring as statehood and the introduction of jet aircraft generated the biggest boom (in percentage terms) in the Island economy since the reciprocity treaty was signed. The rate of growth in the 1960s ranged from 8 to 10 percent a year. Tourist travel to the Islands was growing even faster. There was a tremendous demand for housing on Oahu, and tourists so crowded Waikiki that resort development on the outlying Islands became inevitable.

Getting into Land Development

Amfac had long encouraged builders to buy its construction materials by bonding them (thus gaining business for the insurance department) as well as helping finance them on an interim basis (and servicing the mortgages so generated). Accordingly, it was only a short step for Amfac to join with a builder, Joe Pao, in developing housing on Amfac-leased land that adjoined Honolulu's expansion; so a three-way agreement between Pao, Amfac, and the Bishop Estate, which owned the land and participated in consideration of Amfac surrendering its agricultural leases in the area, was a logical step. Over the years, some 3,000 single-family homes were built under this agreement. The profits to Amfac, however, were modest.

At this time the magnificent beach lands at Kaanapali, owned by Pioneer, were being eyed from many quarters for resort development. Matson, then very much in the hotel business, was the leading contender. In the discussion Amfac refused to give a lease of more than 50 years. Matson, bruised by its experience in building the Royal Hawaiian Hotel and, in fact, the whole Waikiki district around land leased for that short term, demurred. Adamant, Amfac in effect left itself no alternative but to become the developer.

It was a massive undertaking, involving $10 million, and the negotiations entailed moving a public highway inland to attain, in effect, a private enclave around the beach. Involved also was the construction of a golf course and a network of roads, which brought a multitude of problems that only a developer knows, ranging from drainage to labor supply. As the months went on and the dollars went out, the management became nervous. There is evidence of "buck fever" in the lease signed for the key hotel site, now rented by Sheraton, and another lease to a condominium structure, now operated by Island

Holidays for an association of apartment owners. The physical planning was good and the glamour of the place was in no sense marred by the early financial woes. It took some time, however, for management to recognize that everyone in the act—innkeepers, restaurateurs, cab drivers, travel agencies, entertainers, as well as employees and tax collectors—was getting his share ahead of Amfac, which was really the only one taking the risks. The tale of that recognition and what was done to correct it is detailed in discussing the Asset Management Group in Chapter 12.

In the evolution of Kaanapali and the Halawa Heights tracts outside Honolulu the management began to sense the profit potentials in land and resort development. An organization to further such projects came into being. The next project was a golf-oriented second-home venture in the oak-strewn, rolling hills of the Napa Valley, north of San Francisco. Built around a magnificent golf course, Silverado, as it is known, was bought up jointly with a West Coast builder. A second golf course was added, which became the site of the annual Kaiser $150,000 International Tournament. While Silverado appealed to a golf-playing management, it proved to be slow in developing. Present, also, were the operating problems of running a public facility merged with a private club. Many of the original concepts had to be abandoned. The partner had to be bought out. Notwithstanding its vicissitudes, the experience of offering food and lodging to the public further heightened the interest of the management in the possibilities in the hospitality field.

Amfac Associates

Amfac was not yet disillusioned about using its know-how in developing countries. In an effort that was ultimately incorporated and given the name Amfac Associates, it sought to sell its expertise in agriculture throughout the world. The younger Walker and Burns ranged the globe, became familiar with Lima and the Antilles, Libya and the Congo. Their labors produced two operating situations, as well as a corporate conclusion, on the future of this kind of business.

The first of the operations, styled Hawaiian Antilles, spawned a sugar production and milling venture with Uruguayan nationals in that country. Here again, all expectations were met: cane yields exceeded forecasts; extraction at the factory was good. But unstable government led to financial problems, notably rampant inflation, that doomed the project. Amfac was not without good advice at the outset. The knowledgeable New York banks, the State Department, and those with investments in Uruguay were queried. All gave assurance that here was the one solid economy in South America, the one currency and government that could be relied upon. It wasn't.

The second enterprise was in western Australia. The state government in Perth sought a partner to turn 1.3 million acres of wasteland in the Esperance district along the Great Bight into productive acreage. Involved was clearing, tilling, and fertilizing the soil. This was followed by the planting of grain and grass for feed, along with building up flocks of sheep and herds of cattle. Eventually 50 percent of the land is to be sold off to Australian settlers, with Amfac sharing in the profits from the sale through an undivided ownership in 18.75 percent of the developed acres. Under the leadership of Karl Berg, this undertaking has gone well and all agricultural objectives have been met. At one point two special trains were organized to carry 2,000 head of cattle across the continent to found an Amfac herd that now numbers 15,000. It has been slow, but after 10 years profits that Controller d'Arcambal can post to his financial statements are beginning to be reported.

The conclusion drawn from these experiences has been quoted in another context but bears repetition. Walker says, "We learned that underdeveloped nations are more interested in capital than guidance." So he looks to Australia, rather than the Congo, for future application of agricultural expertise.

Amfac Associates has been turned over to one of the consultants it employed, and management has turned to the search for other opportunities elsewhere.

Disappointment Nearer Home

Meanwhile, Harold C Eichelberger was active in an HSPA study group examining the possibility of using the fibers in bagasse for something with a higher value than fuel. In 1930 the company had taken a minor interest in a factory in Hilo manufacturing a wallboard called Canec. Much of Puna's bagasse was sold there at a price somewhat above that obtained for fuel; yet Canec, like Mayflower coffee, was plagued with the familiar problem of marketing a modest volume on the mainland in competition with the "bigs." The founding Island interests, Amfac among them, sold out to Pioneer Flintkote in 1948.

The conviction remained, however, that somehow bagasse could be used in the manufacture of products of even higher value. It was known that its short fiber is employed in making corrugated packing cartons in various cane-growing areas throughout the world, and in some locations fine writing papers are produced from it. Again the problem was rooted in volume, freight costs, and marketing overseas. What might be made from it that could be consumed for the most part in Hawaii?

Three possibilities presented themselves. There was the mulch paper used in planting pineapple fields to contain weeds and soil temperature. There were the packing cases, 29 million a year, used in shipping pineapple. Finally, there were the

41,000 tons a year of newsprint imported from overseas. In cooperation with the research department of the paper giant, Crown Zellerbach, Eichelberger's group found the means to manufacture each of these products; but, again, not one of them was consumed in sufficient volume in Hawaii to support a paper mill. A multipurpose factory was found to be uneconomical. Only the volume in newsprint came close to meeting the test of supporting a profitable plant, and Oahu Sugar Co. still eyes that possibility. Certainly, if anything ever materializes from this work, the facility will have to be near Honolulu, where the market for newsprint grows with the increase in population, tourism, and newspaper advertising resulting from prosperity. Amfac's Oahu, as the second largest producer of bagasse in Hawaii and the plantation closest to Honolulu, would be the logical site for such an enterprise.

Succession

During his tenure Smith was setting the stage internally for the sale of the insurance business and the dramatic expansion into retailing and land development; but he was more or less powerless to influence the ebb and flow of Amfac shares. Having passed retirement age, he named Eichelberger his successor. That was a logical choice. An intellectual, diligent careerist who had spent his whole business life with Amfac, Eichelberger was in his fifties when appointed in 1964. A temperate family man, he lived in the modest beachfront neighborhood where Smith made his home on Oahu's windward side. Eichelberger was an executive in the Isenberg tradition: "Avoid debt, work hard, abide by friends, and above all don't get mixed up in politics."

At the time Eichelberger was promoted to the Presidency, control of the Board was being contended for by two most unlikely men, either of whom would have made Butcher look like Billy Graham. One was Austrian-born Harry Weinberg, who had accumulated a fortune buying up transit companies, depleting their assets, and then selling them off to weary municipalities. Scalps from Scranton, Dallas, and New York's Fifth Avenue Coach Lines dangled from his belt. Up to the same game with Honolulu's Rapid Transit Co., he saw an opportunity in Amfac and bought up enough shares to get elected to the Board.

In dignified contrast to Weinberg was Leslie Hoffman, who, having bought the Chase shares, joined the Board at the same time. Where Weinberg was a blunderbuss, Hoffman was a rapier. Both men wanted the same thing: to put the company's slumbering assets to work, as well as run Amfac and thus run up its stock; this was in 1966.

They bedeviled Eichelberger. He tried patience, corporate decorum, and chain-of-command explanations with them but to no avail. They went around him to his subordinates, railed at day-long Board meetings, pressed so hard that Smith had to intervene repeatedly. There was even one occasion when Conch introduced a motion governing the conduct of directors. It was passed, but Weinberg and Hoffman ignored it. Perhaps the most telling attack of the two was against several of Eichelberger's subordinate executives. They didn't have the confidence of Weinberg and Hoffman to begin with. Later, when the Directors learned that they also didn't have the confidence of some of the other executives, like Attebury, the two men played all the harder on the theme. Eichelberger, a brooding, thoughtful man, stuck loyally by his friends.

While it is probable that Eichelberger had not settled on Walker as his successor at the time, the two men were good friends and respected one another. It was Walker who finally relieved Eichelberger of his problems with Weinberg. When

Weinberg demanded three seats on the Board under Hawaii's cumulative voting law, he was repulsed by Eichelberger, who reduced the number of Directors to a point where Weinberg couldn't elect even one. Walker then talked him into selling out. "Hendry," as Weinberg calls him, thus restored some quiet to the Amfac Board room. The two remain friends, and Weinberg has performed many constructive services for the company since disposing of his holdings in it.

Relieved of one of his bêtes noires, Eichelberger proceeded, with Walker, to employ E. Laurence Gay as Chief Finance Officer. This was to prove a substantial contribution to the direction of the affairs of Amfac today.

During Eichelberger's administration the development of Kaanapali was completed, retail activity was expanded in Hawaii, the stock of the company was listed on the "Big Board," and the company's name was abbreviated to its present form, Amfac. There also was a determined effort to make the company better known in financial circles, with frequent appearances by Amfac executives before groups of financial analysts and others of the investment fraternity, but it didn't work to the satisfaction of Hoffman. He wanted a more zestful approach to company affairs.

It was Eichelberger's persistent loyalty to others, however, that gradually convinced the Board, under Hoffman's prodding, that Eichelberger should be elevated to Chairman. Henry Walker, Jr., having been named Executive Vice President, then became President and Chief Executive Officer. So the way was paved in 1967 for the great thrust forward.

The New Broom

Walker, supported by his new Executive Vice President, Gilbert E. Cox, and the financially seasoned Gay, introduced many changes in the management of men and money. Perhaps the greatest departure from the Isenberg tradition was the abandonment of reliance on collaterals as major contributors to Amfac profit. The three men were prompt to consolidate the remaining plantations with the parent organization and to centralize their agricultural management. Recognizing that sugar profits had been minimal through three generations, they carefully scrutinized the whole enterprise with the intention of getting rid of the marginally profitable collaterals and employing their latent resources aggressively.

Flinty eyes quickly turned to the century-old construction material supply business (once, with food, the biggest element in distribution by Amfac) which had encountered problems in the 1960s. Intense competition had forced margins down to the thinness of a piece of cigarette paper. Strikes in Hawaiian industries, particularly in the shipping and construction fields, complicated the already costly problem of maintaining $3.5 million in inventories. There also was some embarrassment because the development of tract housing in Hawaii put Amfac in the position of competing with other builders who, in turn, were customers of its material supply division.

Walker, Cox, and Gay came to feel there were other more advantageous ways to employ the funds tied up in this end of the business. They therefore sold it for $15,700,000, mostly in paper, to an apparently successful and obviously ambitious young group who had done well in the Islands with a check-verification business they had expanded into a computer service center. In time the buyers ran into the same troubles that Amfac had encountered in the ailing business. Shortly after they bought the business there was a series of shipping strikes and a slowdown in the construction boom of the 60s. In the ensuing reorganization proceedings, Amfac found itself with no loss but again a distributor of construction materials.

By that time, however, the tract house business had been pretty well phased out, thereby reducing the problem of selling to competitors. As Walker puts it:

> We have learned a lot about wholesaling in the course of our expansion on the mainland. By applying those lessons here we have reduced the work force, cut inventories by relying on drop shipments, and greatly simplified control procedures. We think we can apply our proven wholesale 'template' to the distribution of construction materials in Hawaii and have it make a real contribution!

At this writing, it is doing so.

Get It for You Wholesale

So while Distribution continues, it is no longer as a collateral. The principal resemblance to the past is that it breaks down today much as it did when Hackfeld established his "upper store" to concentrate on retailing while using the Queen Street establishment as a base for his ship chandlery and plantation businesses. The latter phase of distribution was to grow far faster in the first century of the dynasty.

The acquisition of W. A. Ramsay & Co. introduced Amfac to the highly competitive business of retailing and servicing appliances and acquainted it with the problems and profits of wholesaling electrical products for industrial purposes. This in turn led to the decision to acquire similar businesses throughout the West. And it was the experience gained in retailing electrical appliances that caused it to sell out that part of the business in Hawaii and stay out of it elsewhere. As Walker puts it, "That's a low-margin, high-pressure operation where the only money to be made is from the financing. We can do better lending money in other fashions."

A long and successful experience in selling prescription drugs to pharmacies in Hawaii encouraged the expansion of this type of distribution on the mainland.

While the Korean war, the cold war, and the war in Vietnam were physically removed from Hawaii, Amfac Distribution, as purveyor to the military, has felt a substantial impact from them. The more than 100,000 servicemen and civilian employees and their dependents residing in the Islands, along with Defense Department procurement officers, spend $750 million a year in the Islands. Military transients moving to and from the Far East add to the market.

New Horizons Bring New Problems

The emergence of new forms of business regulation has presented new problems, as has consolidation with the plantations. The latter provoked several class-action suits, where individuals sought to obtain for minority stockholders a higher value than that offered by Amfac. None was successful. In one case the court went so far as to appoint new appraisers—an independent investment banking firm and the respected former head of the Trust Department of the First Hawaiian Bank. They arrived at values lower than Amfac had paid.

The junior Walker, who like his predecessors, hasn't elected to mix in politics, recently talked about the business climate in Hawaii quite bluntly and quite publicly. In a widely quoted speech he said:

> Somehow, those with the power to tax and to impose unfair and unwise government controls must be made to know that they are playing a dangerous game with the future of Hawaii. Any continuation of the current trend must be considered a deterrent to the attraction of new business and the expansion of our present industries. Moreover, it raises a serious question about the continued presence of many businesses here in Hawaii, including our own.

Such consequences are best evidenced by the removal of much pineapple, once a Hawaiian monopoly, to lower cost areas. While past quotas under the Sugar Act have given assurance of some continued production in Hawaii, the recent closing of three of the smaller, more marginal plantations is a further reflection of the fact that the imposition of cost upon cost can force management and money to turn elsewhere for employment. By good fortune and, particularly in the case of Puna, good management, Amfac's sugar operations, with the possible exception of Pioneer, are among the lowest cost producers in the Islands. They can endure as long as any sugar can be produced profitably there.

Other difficulties arose under the price controls initiated by President Nixon in 1971. Price increases at the wholesale level were not supposed to exceed a stated percentage over a base period. In pricing the 12,000 items of electrical equipment offered by the Distribution Group, Amfac practice was to follow a historic markup over the manufacturers' quotations. The manufacturers' prices, however, were not directly controlled. It was their profits that were regulated. Amfac was perfectly prepared to accept a limitation of the earnings of its Distribution Group but literally could not comply with the regulations as written. This took the Group's Chairman, John P. Richardson, and Senior Vice President C. E. S. Burns, Jr., to Washington, where an adjustment was made.

The Hospitality Group also had its difficulties with the Price Commission. In the June preceding the imposition of controls, it had announced through travel agents an increase in room rates to become effective January 1, 1972. It proceeded to sell tour groups and conventions for the following year on the basis of the new rates. When the fact came to the Commission's attention in the spring of 1972, it brought suit against Amfac. Without prior notice, it sought restoration of over $100,000 to specific customers and a rollback of the rates. After litigation, the issue was resolved by letting the increase stand and paying a token $22,500 penalty.

While the various groups have almost complete autonomy in operations, when contention of a regulatory or legal character surfaces the firemen at headquarters slide down their brass poles and go to work. Any event or policy that threatens the reputation of the parent starts the alarm bells ringing.

Luxuriant Land

The bureaucratic battles have only drawn attention to Amfac's basic asset. The Islands found themselves propelled by World War II, jet aircraft, and statehood into a period where land became too expensive to be used for agricultural purposes. Part of this was due to population pressure, part to the fact that overseas investors "discovered" Hawaii in the 1960s, and part to the demand for resort development generated by the tourist boom. While there is ample land to satisfy these pressures, many don't think so. On an island the amount of available land is visible to all and may seem frighteningly scarce.

Table 1 presents the most valuable rural land holdings of Amfac in Hawaii.

Lacking minerals, in fact, any natural resources save abundant water and sunlight, there is no more productive use for the cane land than it now has. This is particularly true since pineapple production is on the decline. Thus, but for the normal appreciation in value owing to inflation, higher and better use must relate to people-oriented needs. These are essentially housing, resort development, and government. In the last category schools, parks, recreational facilities, and the military demand large areas. Housing near Honolulu will require 25,000 acres by 1985, it is said. Amfac is in a good position to provide 1,400 acres of it but faces competition. The Campbell Estate has the right to withdraw up to 4,000 acres from the Oahu Sugar lease for housing development. Castle & Cooke has announced that it will cut pineapple

TABLE 1 Major Amfac Land Holdings in Hawaii

Operator	Fee acquired			Lease acquired			Present use
	Acreage	From	When	Acreage	From	When	
Lihue Plantation, Kauai	2,374	M. Kekuanaoa, W. Lee, H. A. Pierce & Co.	1849–1867	2,660	Territory of Hawaii	1919	Agriculture, conservation, urban
	19,928	V. Kamamalu, J. O. Dominis, P. Isenberg	1861–1870	7,055	Territory of Hawaii	1923	Agriculture, conservation
	1,024	W. H. Rice, P. Isenberg	1880	2,430	Territory of Hawaii	1930–1974	Agriculture, conservation
	837	W. H. Rice and Lihue Plantation Co.	1921	−831	Withdrawals and expirations		Agriculture, conservation
	7,433	Various sellers	1900–1955	Net 11,314			
	Net 31,596						
Kekaha Sugar Co., Kauai	37	Territory of Hawaii	1922	38,938	Territory of Hawaii (some by assignment from Knudsen Estate)	1922	Urban, agriculture, conservation
	30	Territory of Hawaii	1932	−10,434	Withdrawals and expirations	1926–1974	
	67	Various sellers	1906–1950	Net 28,504			
	Net 134						
Oahu Sugar Co., Oahu	397	M. P. Robinson	1897	3,100	Campbell Estate, B. F. Dillingham	1897	Agriculture, conservation, and urban throughout. Amfac's ability to capitalize fully on urbanization of leased lands is circumscribed by lessors' rights of withdrawal.
	705	Hawaiian Pineapple Co.	1951	2,800	M. P. Robinson	1897	
	135	Capital Investment Co.	1957–1962	3,400	C. A. Brown	1897	
	248	C. J. Robinson	1951–1971	1,318	Ii Estate	1925	
	77	Various sellers	1951–1971	3,408	Campbell Estate	1929	
	−761	Various sales	1951–1971	31,557	Various lessors	1925–1974	
	Net 801			−11,100	Withdrawals and exemptions	1925–1974	
				Net 34,483			
Pioneer Mill, Maui	1,280	Campbell and Turton	1863	1,972	Territory of Hawaii	1919	Fee: resort, urban, agriculture, conservation
	2,282	H. Turton	1877	1,378	Territory of Hawaii	1912	
	4,619	Campbell and Isenberg	1886	2,397	Bishop Estate	1918	Lease: agriculture, conservation
	1,021	Isenberg and Horner	1889	12,890	Territorial Public Lands Commissioner	1906	
	2,217	Predecessor Mill Co.	1895	1,521	Territory of Hawaii	1928	
	1,285	Lahaina C & F Co.	1900	−10,945	Withdrawals	1920–1974	
	1,039	Lahaina Ag. Co.	1924	Net 9,213			
	1,178	Olowalu Co.	1931				
	−280	Various sales	1906–1974				
	Net 14,641						
Puna Sugar Co., Hawaii	400	Kilauea Coffee Co.	1899	3,812	W. H. Shipman	1899	Agriculture, conservation
	439	E. D. Baldwin	1899	219	W. H. Shipman	1907	
	300	A. W. Carter	1899	583	Bishop Estate	1910	
	935	Capital Coffee Co.	1899	715	Roman Catholic Church	1929	
	500	Aloha Coffee Co.	1899	4,877	W. H. Shipman	1936	
	304	Wolters and Rodiek	1899	Net 10,206			
	1,804	Hawaiian land	1899				
	1,906	B. F. Dillingham	1899				
	299	N. McStocker	1902				
	10,449	Various purchases and sales	1899–1974				
	Net 17,336						

production on its Wahiawa plantation, leaving 2,000 acres fallow. This will provide a larger area for its development of adjoining Mililani Town. Nevertheless, given the growth rate in Hawaii, even at substantially less than the 8–10 percent rate of the 1960s, and a continuation of present zoning policies, Amfac's Oahu land will undoubtedly be further urbanized. It should provide a significant share of the housing needs of Honolulu for the foreseeable future.

Barring a major mainland depression or another war, there is no end in sight to the growth in travel to Hawaii. In 1973 there were over 2.6 million visitors. The consensus among the squad of analysts that constantly tests the economic pulse of the Islands is that the figure will be 4.5 million by 1985. While a visitor doesn't take up much land per se (Kaanapali's 325 developed acres accommodated 384,823 guests last year), the support functions are demanding. Employee housing gobbles up land and, in turn, requires its own supporting areas such as schools and parks, shops and parking. While there is ample acreage suitable, and planned, for the development of high-rise hotels and golf courses, the peripheral needs of resort development will have to be met from lands now in agriculture or lesser uses. Amfac, with Kaanapali established as a leading neighbor island destination and owning 15,000 adjoining agricultural acres, should be the beneficiary of much of this kind of growth as the resort expands. If and when it is able to start a similar undertaking on its ocean-front cliffs on Kauai, it could enjoy another such multiplier effect.

Amfac's Hawaiian properties are situated on small islands where the bordering sea is a constant reminder that land is finite. All the land there is you can see. Even the population boom is more manifest on an island than on a continent because everyone knows how much space is left to accommodate it. The resulting feeling of scarcity in Hawaii stimulates a demand for land that may have little current, but some long-term, justification.

In considering the worth of real estate in Hawaii it is important to consider where it lies. An acre of pasture is worth more on Oahu than on a neighboring island just because it is nearer Honolulu. An acre of cane land under the hot sun of Kehaha is worth more than an acre of cane land at rainy, rocky Puna.

Amfac in recent years has acquired substantial lands outside of Hawaii. There are the 20,000 fabulously fertile acres along the Columbia River that the Food Group is now opening up to plant potatoes. There are the two feed lots of Wilhelm Foods in Colorado. As has been noted, Amfac is the managing partner of a joint venture in Australia which has the concession to clear and develop 1.3 million acres of lands for agricultural and ranching use. These once sterile fields are being brought into production by the addition of minute quantities of trace elements.

At any one time the Asset Management Group may be dealing in land in the West, most of it large blocks for planned community development. In a similar "in and out" fashion, it can, briefly, be a part owner of a condominium structure or a shopping center; but to it real estate of this character is just so much merchandise. On the other hand, the long-term holdings on the mainland and in Australia are not unlike other areas just as vast. It is the land in Hawaii that is, to repeat, obviously finite. Though Amfac may sell parcels of it from time to time, the management is Hawaii-oriented and, in Hawaii, you don't often sell land. You use it or lease it to others.

8

Management of Men

Of his 10-hour workday, Henry Walker spends two-thirds of it with people. Of his social engagements during a week (excluding a beloved noontime cribbage game), on the average half are with people having business with Amfac. His schedule is not unusual among the executives of this people-oriented company. Cox calculates that in a normal working week he will talk business to over 100 men he knows by name. He may also talk to a gathering of security analysts or speak at a convention of company controllers. While this confrontation with people is part of the management process that has evolved in all American business, it is Amfac's policy to make the company and its executives better known in all circles. This springs in part from its relative anonymity in the past. It is also attributable to the recent increase in new customers, new investors, new bankers, and new environments. This emphasis on executive exposure to people is achieved more by persuasion than dictation. Occasionally there has to be a "bench call," but in general the management emphasis on people is a pattern set at the top and emulated down the line.

The Owners

As might be expected, the presentation of management views and desires takes different forms with its widely different audiences. In common with other large corporations whose stock is traded on the "Big Board," Amfac expends a major effort on communicating with its shareholders. There are over 13,000 of them in every state in the union and 10 foreign countries. This and the fact that the owners range from mutual funds to the traditional widows and orphans require the company to be quite simplistic in its presentation of complicated matters. Thus, Amfac in its reports emphasizes the common denominator that everyone can understand: profit and profit potential.

In addition to handsome annual statements, costing 85 cents a copy to produce, quarterly reports are published to show progress as the fiscal year advances. There are some 80 press releases annually, detailing everything from the promotion of subordinate executives to Walker's speeches on such matters of importance to the company as the growth of travel to the Islands and land tenure in Hawaii.

Occasions to present the more complicated facts concerning the company's affairs are sought with those who are conduits to investors. These are the brokers and bankers, security analysts and business-page editors whose interpretations guide the financial public. These opportunities are sought as a means of conveying more than the story of earnings—to give some feel of the substance of the company, the fiber of its people, the nature of its problems, and the plans for their solution. All this effort is supported by the belief that a fully informed share-holder will be a contented one and that fully informed investors will provide a wholesome market for Amfac stock. If it can also give stockholders a feeling of pride in their Amfac hold-ings, such as they have in more intimate assets like their homes and their country clubs, so much the better.

The Amfac effort to appeal to the diverse interests of share-holders is nowhere better evidenced than at the annual meet-ings. Some open with fashion shows to draw out the ladies, though hard-nosed trust officers voting thousands of shares seem to respond as well. These affairs are staged after office hours, and tea is served to induce greater attendance. From one meeting to another different Amfac interests are empha-sized: property development on one occasion, hospitality on another. At the 1974 meeting fresh papayas, one of the com-pany products, were distributed.

Three reasons, by no means unique to Amfac, motivate costly, time-consuming management efforts of this character. The first is that responsible men managing $500 million of other people's money feel impelled to account for their stewardship. It is not enough to have their books closed and their financial statements audited; they also want to expose their conduct of affairs, social attitudes, and business philoso-phy to the full light of day. Thus, management hopes to gain credibility not only with the owners but with the vast public with which it must deal.

The second factor prompting these activities is that the financial community favors corporations that are open about disclosing information. It was this very flow of facts about Amfac that made its 1971 public offering of 1.2 million shares and its 1972–1973 refinancing of over $70 million of debt eagerly greeted by buyers and lenders. There is a certain contagious enthusiasm in the financial community. This bolsters the price at which Amfac stock is traded and in turn encourages further investment—in a sense, a whole recycling of a favorable attitude toward the company.

The final consideration fostering this outpouring of information is the reasonable desire of the members of management to remain in office. The company that shelters the facts and camouflages its earnings invites proxy fights and take-over attempts by corporate raiders. As has been detailed, Amfac learned this from brutal experience in the 1960s.

Of course the company has competitive secrets. Just as Macy's won't tell Gimbels, Joseph Magnin's design of next year's Christmas shopping bag is a secret that is not shared even with Liberty House. The manner in which an upcoming convention is to be wooed into one of Fred Harvey's hotels is very much a private matter. Such competitive concealment is transitory, and consequently it really is not important so far as the long-term investor in Amfac is concerned. In the year of inquiry that went into this book, I encountered no significant fact relative to the problems or the prospects of the company that had not been printed or would not be made available to any responsible party on request.

The Directors

It is the practice in American industry for the Directors who act as surrogates for the shareholders to face reelection every year. Actually, in companies the size of Amfac, with its large number of stockholders, this is something of a myth. So long as management performance is such that proxies keep coming in, permitting balloting on behalf of the owners, it is the management that is reelected and its nominees for Directors are really appointees following that election.

In the case of Amfac, this generalization must be tempered

somewhat by two considerations. The first is a Hawaiian law, not uncommon among the states, that calls for "cumulative" voting. Thus a candidate for a directorship on a board of 10 can elect himself to a seat, notwithstanding management objection, if he owns or can obtain representation of 10 percent of the stock; but there is a management alternative. So long as it represents over half the outstanding shares, it can cut the number of seats on the Board. This is what Amfac did in the face of Weinberg's demands.

The second limitation on management's freedom in naming the slate is rooted in the fact that a seat on the Board is often a consideration in the acquisition of a particular company. This is the case in 2 of the 17 Amfac Directors. These people have, however, brought a welcome storehouse of knowledge of their respective businesses with them.

Other "outside" Directors have been named for qualifications the management thought would contribute to the conduct of company affairs. These range from successful careers in a line of endeavor important to Amfac, such as travel, retail trade, and investment banking, to exposure to a broad segment of the public, for example, knowledge of the military and of the California financial fraternity. In every instance the major factor influencing selection is management's desire to benefit from experienced judgment.

Cox and Walker use this experience as a sounding board and modify their positions to adapt to the collective advice of the group. Their employment of the Board doesn't stop there. Once a course of action has been adopted, they rely on the members to go their separate ways and interpret Amfac's actions to the "universe" each represents. Back together on the Board, they report the reactions they have encountered.

Before considering a typical Amfac Board meeting, let us review the principals. The discussion of these individuals, however appealing and distinguished they may be, is presented here only as an illustration of how Amfac is governed. Before this ink is dry, names and personalities will have changed, for "the Captains and the Kings depart"; but these types of people, with the same kind of intellectual resources, will govern the company as long as its management continues successful and our present economic system endures.

Representing the management are Chairman and Chief Executive Officer Walker, President and Chief Operating Officer Cox, and Vice Chairman and Chief Finance and Administrative Officer Gay.

"Hanko" Walker, 52, is about as far removed from the popular image of a scion of a wealthy family as one can imagine. While retaining all the polish of *kamaaina* upbringing, St. Paul's, and Harvard, he prefers yard work to the symphony, the Dodgers to the Giants, and Sunday TV pro football to attendance at St. Andrew's Episcopal Cathedral. During World War II he was a communications officer in the Navy and was once assigned as an aide to President and Mrs. Truman when they visited his ship, the *Missouri*. He observes that his military career seemed doomed when, in escorting the First Lady up the gangway, he nearly dropped her in the drink. After the war Walker studied business administration at Columbia and then returned to Hawaii to become a trainee in Amfac. During this period he married Skidmore graduate Nancy Johnston of Port Leyden, New York.

Walker advanced to manager of the plantation department in the late 1950s when that was still one of the two prestige jobs in Amfac. With merchandising on the decline, sugar was the "be all and end all" of the company in that decade. By 1965 the problems of the distribution end of the business had become so serious and Walker's performance had become so distinguished that Eichelberger, then President, transferred him to management of that distressed area. Walker was quick to dispose of unprofitable lines, such as the retailing of appliances, and to consolidate departments to eliminate deadwood. It was, in fact, his decisive approach to the troubled affairs of this division that determined his future elevation to the Presidency. As Chief Executive Officer, Walker is very decisive. Notwithstanding his easy smile, he moves fast and speaks positively. "No, that's wrong," "It wasn't that way," and "The way to do it is" are phrases he uses. Probably the reason he heads the company is because he is usually right and, when wrong, is the first to acknowledge it.

Walker and Gil Cox, as Chief Operating Officer, are perfect foils. Cox, a long-time attorney for the company, 5 years Walker's senior, clearly has Hanko's complete confidence. Walker frequently says, "I'll talk to Gil about that," or "Gil thinks," or "Let's see Gil." The two men are complementary in every respect but physical appearance. They find humor in the same things, love cards and Tanqueray Gibsons, and, while mutually dependent, do not lack for self-confidence.

Cox, who pushed bombers around during World War II, came to Hawaii with a law degree from the University of Texas in 1947 to join the leading law firm in the sugar-coated town of Hilo on the Big Island. His work on complicated problems arising from the Sugar Act brought him to the attention of Amfac and its Honolulu attorney, J. Russell Cades, then a Director of the company. For 8 years Cades had exerted a strong influence on the Amfac Board, quitting only when its size was reduced during the Weinberg affair. Cox soon joined Cades' firm as a partner and became an Amfac Director when the Board was again enlarged. Cox has proved to be an effective communicator with the complex public addressed by

Amfac. His talks before security analysts and financial editors, shareholders, and customers have made him, in 4 years, one of the best-known Hawaiian businessmen in the country.

He is an indefatigable man. I remember lunching one day at Oahu Country Club when suddenly a golf cart with a single occupant appeared, going all out for the first tee. It was Cox. My companion exclaimed, "What the hell is he doing here? He ought to be home in bed. He just got in from a 20-hour flight from Lima." Of all of Cox's contributions to Amfac, perhaps the greatest one is his ability to make the most of scarce executive time. He can winnow out the trivial from the important.

A Harvard-trained lawyer with a Wall Street and Litton Industries background, 51-year-old, no-nonsense Gay also brought a seasoned approach to Amfac's acquisition program. His interests include Honolulu's symphony orchestra and the Iolani School in Honolulu. Gay was elected to the Amfac Board and named its Vice Chairman in 1974 following his designation as Chief Finance and Administrative Officer on January 1.

Amfac policy formerly required its Directors to retire at age 75 (it is now 70). C. H. Smith, President and Chairman of the Board before Eichelberger, reached that point in life in 1972 and so was named Chairman Emeritus. While no longer a voting member, his attendance at meetings is encouraged, and the trip from Walker's twenty-first-floor office to Smith's, three stories below, is not a long one. Self-effacing Smith arrived in Honolulu to work for the Hackfelds as a marine underwriter in 1917, and he is the only one in the Amfac management to have worked under the Germans. For years he confined his energies to the insurance end of the business, emerging as a Vice President in 1950. From then on he moved rapidly to the Board in 1954 and the Presidency in 1959.

Another golf enthusiast, who lives modestly outside Honolulu in suburban Kailua, Smith deserves much credit for the present positive posture of Amfac. He brought in Attebury and got the go-ahead for the Liberty House expansion. It is a measure of the man that he recognized that his love of 40 years—the insurance end of the business—was phasing out and he had the wisdom to initiate its sale before it became valueless.

Eichelberger, long a Director, resigned at the end of 1973 to become a trustee of the Campbell Estate, Oahu Sugar Co.'s landlord. He feared the conflict of interest that might follow.

Closely related to the management Directors are those who sit on the Board as a consequence of having sold their business or merged it with Amfac. One such is a Chicagoan, Daggett Harvey, grandson of Fred Harvey, who, as chairman of the family-controlled company, engineered its joining Amfac. His office is something of a museum of mementos of the days of the old Harvey House restaurants along the Santa Fe tracks. The walls display Staffordshire serving plates, especially made for his English-born grandfather, along with one of the gongs used to warn diners that their train was about to depart. While he is as familiar with the boulevards of Paris and the Greek Isles as he is with the Grand Canyon, Harvey has an almost fierce affection for the Southwest. Though trained as a lawyer, he lists himself in *Who's Who* as a restaurant executive.

A fellow chevalier of the French Legion of Honor joined the Board with Harvey when Amfac acquired the chain of Joseph Magnin specialty shops. Cyril Magnin is, in a sense, "Mr. San Francisco." Long-time President of San Francisco's Port Authority, he is also chief of protocol, the official greeter for the city. He, too, reveals his affection for this post by listing himself in *Who's Who* as a city official. Magnin is a great asset to Amfac not only because of his stature in San

Francisco, where he is much beloved, but also because he has vast experience in the retailing field, the area from which much of the company's revenues are derived. Shortly after World War II Magnin, sensing that everybody thinks young, directed his staff to emphasize goods and merchandising that appealed to youth.

The recent purchase by Gulf & Western Industries of approximately 19 percent of the outstanding common stock of Amfac, along with its stated intent to acquire up to 20 percent, certainly entitles it to representation on the Board. However, G & W, a $2 billion a year conglomerate with a wide range of interests, declared that its interest is investment and that it does not desire representation.

Among those individuals who are helpful in the investment community, there is one who would cause Isenberg to raise a shocked German eyebrow. He is 60-year-old Charles de Bretteville, whose credentials are impeccable—but he is Claus Spreckels' grandson! Chairman and Chief Executive Officer of the Bank of California and a string of Spreckels companies, Stanford graduate De Bretteville moves in the highest San Franciscan social circles. He has put Walker on the board of his bank, thus strengthening Amfac's California ties.

The anchor in the southern California financial community is Ralph E. Phillips, 71, retired executive of the investment banking firm of Dean Witter. Quiet-spoken Phillips has counseled Amfac through its major refinancing in recent years.

A further tie with the investment fraternity is provided by long-time Director Fred Merrill, past Chairman of the Fireman's Fund Insurance Co., who engineered its acquisition by American Express. Merrill, a Stanford graduate and now a trustee of that institution, had some years in Honolulu with the Hawaiian Trust Co., thus acquiring certain *kamaaina* credentials. This furthers the long-standing association between the Hawaiian and San Francisco business communities.

Chauncey E. Schmidt, President of First National Bank of Chicago, is a recent addition to the Amfac governing body. With Daggett Harvey, he contributes the Midwestern geographical point of view to Amfac's interests.

An outsider's experience in retailing is brought to Amfac by Richard Rich, Chairman of the Executive Committee of Atlanta's great institution, Rich's Department Store. In Atlanta, Rich's is part of every family: counselor on graduations and weddings, gentle creditor when money is tight, the place to rest and have a cola when shopping. A book about it, *Dear Store*, is more a family letter than a business account.

As a matter of policy, their capabilities and stock ownership notwithstanding, none of the Senior Vice Presidents is a member of the Board. One of them, Lyle Guslander, in the exchange of his Island Holidays hotel chain for Amfac stock, became the largest individual shareholder in the company. He continues to labor with equal willingness without Director's status.

Representation of the hospitality field is provided by his good friend, the former head of Western Airlines, Terrell C. Drinkwater. He and Harvey provide the Board with knowledge that spans the whole gamut of the travel business: transportation and recreation, resort and commercial hotel operation, restaurant and entertainment management.

Amfac's choice of Directors is dictated by other considerations than its requirements in administering its many commercial endeavors. The biggest source of revenue for the state of Hawaii, and a major customer of Amfac's Distribution Group, is the military. John Joseph Hyland, retired commander of the Pacific Fleet, reflects the military viewpoint in the conduct of company affairs. Further, his extensive knowledge of the Pacific, along with his background in government administration, fill a void in the experience of the Board.

Ralph Yamaguchi, 61 but who looks 41, was one of the first of the Nisei to break into the ranks of the major haole corporations. As a young lawyer he was fortunate enough to join Wilfred Tsukiyama's firm. That jolly gentleman, later a Republican Chief Justice of the Hawaiian Supreme Court, was probably the first Nisei to win acceptance in the haole business community.

The third of the long-time outside directors is a true *kamaaina,* 56-year-old Kenneth Brown. A Princeton Phi Bete, the wealthy Brown is a successful architect, a Democratic state senator, and a confidant of the powerful and rich, among them Governor John A. Burns and resort developer Laurance Rockefeller.

In 1972, although not unaware of the upsurge of the women's liberation movement, but prompted principally by the fact that fashion has a major influence on Amfac's sales, the Board added two women to its group. The nomination of Ellen Newman, a mother of three and daughter of Cyril Magnin, was based not on stock ownership but on her background as a fashion consultant and in consumerism. The latter interest has led her into a thorough study of Amfac's conduct of customer relations.

Patricia Saiki is an attractive mother of five who taught school while raising her family. Her father was an Amfac employee for over 40 years. She has been a member of the Hawaii State Legislature since 1968. She also serves on the President's Committee on the Status of Women.

The most recently elected member of the Board is John A. Scott, the 57-year-old publisher of the Honolulu *Star-Bulletin.* In announcing his nomination, Walker said: "Scott's background in business and education, his dedication to improvement of the communities where he has lived and worked, and his understanding of the often counteracting forces in the nation and world today will prove of great value in the further development of Amfac."

The Group Chairmen

The Board meets regularly on the third Friday of every other month, usually in the impressive Board room on the seventeenth floor of the Amfac Building in Honolulu. Walker, Cox, and Gay sit at the base of a U-shaped arrangement and are flanked by the Directors and the officers of the company involved in the matters to be decided by the Board. Customarily, the proposition is introduced by Walker or Cox. Usually, when the speaker is done, the other man fields questions. Fully familiar with all topics that are presented, they often conduct whispered conversations on upcoming subjects or occasionally, one suspects, tomorrow's cribbage game.

The identity and background of the performers, the operating men who carry the burden of these Board presentations, are described later in this book when their particular areas of responsibility are discussed. It's enough here to say that a composite description of them would read: "He is a Caucasian with an Anglo-Saxon name (though there is a D'Arcambal among them and a Hamamoto in the wings). He is just under 50, a college graduate (only 3 of 18 lack a degree), mainland born (4 are Island boys), and very fluent. He is also a golf zealot."

From their meetings with the Board, the group chairmen emerge with the authority delegated them by Walker and Cox to run their separate businesses. Except for Board and management meetings and the competition among them for funds before the Operations and Financial Review Committee, there is little that links them together. However, they all share one Amfac identification in common: each of the constituent groups labels its stationery and advertising with its own trade name and then the phrase "An Amfac Company" subordinate to it.

Below the group chairmen are a myriad of personalities and talents inevitably insulated from the management not by choice but by the limitations of time. There is "Skeeter" Harris, past retirement age now but so enthralled with his work, buying curios and novelties to sell in Harvey gift shops, that he won't quit. German-born Hella Rothwell, managing all of Island Holidays' public relations, visits places like Marrakesh to woo convening travel writers to turn their eyes to Hawaii. The Retail Group's prime researcher, Helen Lamoureux, can tell you the composition and buying power of any market area in the West. At Oahu Sugar, David Cayetano, an immigrant laborer from the Philippines 42 years ago, is a self-taught safety engineer and lives a life of ease from profits made in Hawaiian real estate. The diverse talents and backgrounds of such individuals as these are the hard core of Amfac and the root of its success.

While General Electric and some of the other socially concerned members of the "Big Board" have emphasized community relations policies nationwide, Amfac is just beginning to expand programs it has had under way in Hawaii for years. Probably this is because it has grown so fast. For example, Arizona legislation and dealings with the National Park Service, once of considerable concern to the Harvey family, are now the responsibility of the Hospitality Group. The irrigation rights to Columbia River water, essential to the success of Lamb-Weston's farming venture in that basin, are the concern of Executive Vice President John L. Baxter, Jr., Food Group Chairman.

In short, Amfac headquarters busies itself with people in the financial community (including the directors, shareholders, and financiers). It allocates funds and delegates authority to the men running the operating groups. It maintains corporate relations with citizens in the communities where it is active. It concerns itself with trouble wherever it may arise. All this involves, primarily, the management of men and women.

9

Management of Money

There would soon be no women and men to manage if the money funding their endeavors were not managed with equal skill. Hackfeld's first undertakings in this regard are reflected in financial records that are little more than notes to himself. "12/12/1849, Ship *Hansa*/Commissions—2.5 percent Commission for endorsing a draft on Bremen $2,000, $50" is one example. Another is even more terse: "12/27/1849, John Hackfeld/Merchandise—2 dozen shawls, $18."

With J. C. Pflueger's admission to partnership, the accounts became less murky but continued quite simple. From his year-end statements it is evident that he and Hackfeld were employing credit, that is, managing money, to fuel the business in the 1850s. There were no banks or insurance companies in Hawaii and the monarchy, far from being a source of funds, was borrowing from every available quarter.

The partnership obtained its local credit from the coterie of Kauai businessmen and neighbors. Representative of such transactions is Pflueger's borrowing $2,000 from E. Kopke for 8 months at 12 percent interest and Isenberg's advancing Wilcox a $6,000 mortgage to help buy Grove Farm. A second source was the private banks in Bremen, the font for Hackfeld's original outfitting.

Still, the venture built cash fast and if there was resort to borrowing after the founder departed for the fatherland it was to finance the private ventures of the partners as individuals. H. Hackfeld & Co., as such, had $2,562.00 in cash and $10,972.54 in receivables in 1855. By 1860 the comparable figures had grown to $20,431.73 and $26,086.33. In 1860 about $45,000 was due them from debtors as far removed as D. H. Watjen & Co. in Bremen and the East Maui Plantation. In turn, they owed $95,030.57, about $30,000 of it to Hackfeld and Dr. Wood.

On incorporation in 1897 the balance sheet had grown to the amounts shown in Table 1.

TABLE 1 *H. Hackfeld & Co. Balance Sheet*

Assets		Liabilities	
Cash	$ 124,690.75	Notes payable	$ 330,000.00
Receivables	1,554,211.36	Accounts payable*	2,345,922.89
Land	102,718.11	Capital	1,000,000.00
Vessels	116,834.62	Reserve	180,639.02
Investments	1,083,661.68		
Other†	874,445.39		
	$3,856,561.91		$3,856,561.91

*$1,261,765.77 payable to stockholders for partnership interests.
†Primarily inventory.

Changing Views on Debt

The Hackfeld enterprise thus entered the corporate phase of its existence relatively debt-free and so founded a tradition, an abhorrence of debt, that was to continue through the World War II years. Debt was bad, debtors were suspect, pay cash and take your discounts—in short, always be a lender, never a borrower. In the 50 years following incorporation, Amfac engaged in long-term borrowings only to buy out the German interest in certain of the plantations. In the seasonal nature of the sugar business, short-term loans were a routine affair.

But problems encountered after World War II changed the pattern. In the late 1940s mainland banking connections and credit lines were established. The 1949 waterfront strike, the cash demands of Puna, the requirements in the development of Kaanapali, and the acquisition of Silverado forced a reluctant management into long-term debt. First, there was the sale of commercial paper in 1954; then came a $7 million issuance of debentures which was taken by a long-time associate, the John Hancock Mutual Life Insurance Co., in 1955. Amfac, inexperienced in this phase of money management and inexperienced in the rate at which land development devours cash, borrowed too little in 1962. Going back to the trough in 1966 compelled the acceptance of a higher interest rate, plus tight restrictions on working capital and borrowings imposed by the lenders. Thus, the use of credit for land development was severely circumscribed. These restrictions were imposed at a time when the company's interest in expansion in that field and in the retail area was beginning to peak.

These were the circumstances that confronted Walker and Gay when they began to take over the management of money.

The first step was to trade out the restrictive covenants of the loan agreements. This Gay did in 1968. The action freed the company to proceed with the construction of single-family housing on Oahu, the further development of Kaanapali, and the initiation of several mainland projects. It broke the logjam in other quarters as well. Edmund Attebury had ideas for retail expansion. Paul Cassiday, then head of the Finance Group, who had been forced to cut back his activities (which had been confined to leasing and servicing of mortgages), found other avenues opened up. So limited had his operation become that his number 2 man, Howard Hamamoto, quit. With the reversal of the company's posture on expansion in the financial field, Cassiday lured him back. Hamamoto now heads Amfac Financial Corp. and has expanded it to Guam.

Redeploying Resources

As they straightened out money matters, Walker and Gay also set about analyzing the employment of Amfac's resources. Sugar operations, land holdings, distribution services, and development activities were studied with a view to liquidating those showing a low return on investment and meager growth prospects. The objective was to redeploy the funds so freed to more promising areas such as retailing. At various times Amfac had an interest in a mixed bag of companies that included Hawaiian Airlines, Honolulu Iron Works, San Miguel beer, Philippine Telephone, Budget Finance, and Hawaiian Philippine (sugar), but these had already been disposed of. In 1968 the new regime sold its minority interests in McCabe, Hamilton and Renny (stevedoring), Hawaiian Western Steel, and Oahu Transport Co., all in Honolulu, and the Princeville Ranch.

There was solid support on the Board for all of this. Hoffman had, in effect, been demanding it and in trying to enforce his demands voted "no" on many management propositions. He so welcomed the new program he never voted "no" again on anything. (His nature was sufficiently dogmatic that he did abstain at times.) Conch Smith, the balance wheel in those troubled days, encouraged the approach, and Gil Cox, then attorney for the company, provided a third strong voice in its support. It was in this period, in fact, that Cox, as counsel, gravitated toward the management team. His name is found on negotiating committees and in memoranda commenting on management problems well before his appointment as Executive Vice President in 1969.

A Board resolution adopted in this period sets the tone for all that has followed. It directed the management to "capitalize on the opportunities for growth and profit in the Pacific Basin with particular emphasis on Australia."

This introduces the Operations and Financial Review Committee: Cox, Gay, D'Arcambal, Baxter, Richardson, and Hagberg, with Walker ex-officio. They review the budget proposals of all the groups as well as their 5-year plans and, most importantly, their performance as related to plan. The committee does not concern itself with the need for a new drinking fountain at El Tovar Hotel in the Grand Canyon or the inventory of wines carried by Liberty House's Normandy Lane. How the dollars are employed is the group chairman's decision. The committee's interest is in performance as measured by contribution to profit and rate of return on investment. It would be appropriate for them to paint dollar signs on their eyeglasses as they convene in a small meeting room between Gay's and Walker's offices. Here they analyze the reasoning of a group chairman as he presents his financial needs. Poring over the supporting figures presented by his controller, they probe every program. There is no danger of overstating the importance of this committee: suffice it to say no proposal they have turned down has ever reached the Board for consideration.

Finding Funds

The acquisitions of recent years, all of which have survived extensive examination by this committee, have imposed vast demands for cash and credit. These needs have been satisfied in several fashions. Cumulative convertible preferred stock and convertible debentures have been employed, as has the issuance of common shares. In other cases cash has been paid. In 1969 over $11 million and in 1970 over $13 million was used in purchasing businesses. These demands required extensive bank borrowings and the use of commercial paper. To reduce these obligations, the company offered 1.2 million shares of its common stock to the public in an underwriting combined with the sale of 522,997 shares owned by the members of two families—Hoffman's heirs and the Lambs of Lamb-Weston. The fact that 147 underwriters throughout the country participated in an offering that overnight generated nearly $37 million in cash for the company was greeted with corporate pride. It demonstrated that Walker, Cox, and Gay had succeeded in putting Amfac on the map with the financial community. It was no longer regarded with skepticism as a tropical curiosity with a speculative potential in Hawaiian land. In the money markets of America, Amfac had come of age.

This offering was followed in 1972 by another bit of sophisticated money management. In a step toward further reduction of short- and intermediate-term bank loans and as a general sprucing up of the liability side of the balance sheet, a major refinancing of Amfac's long-term debt was undertaken. Accomplished in two phases, the $71,250,000 program was finished with the issuance of a final $30,000,000 of new notes in the spring of 1973. The purchasers were eight large insurance companies. Walker, in announcing the refinancing, observed: "The provisions contained in the new notes are geared to the requirements of Amfac of the seventies." At a subsequent shareholders' meeting, Gay said: "The current ratio of 1.75 to 1 and the debt to capital ratio of 41 percent evidence the soundly balanced and leveraged capital structure we have."

This matter of balancing debt, senior and subordinate, with capital has been only one of Gay's major contributions at Amfac. His tireless work in educating the financial community on the company, his restructuring the earlier long-term loan agreements, and his encouragement of the financial group have all been noted. He will be a force at Amfac for years to come.

While the external acceptance of Amfac's money management program is a flattering reward for the thousands of miles of plane travel, the scores of committee meetings, the endless lunches in the financial centers of the country, and the patient preparation of prospectuses, reports, slide shows, and interviews, it is a reflection of internal change as well. In fact, it could not have been achieved without far-reaching revision of money management practices introduced in part by Gay and forced in part by the very growth of the company with the consequent demand for intricate controls.

The 7-Pound Summary

J. C. Pflueger's first "statement of the affairs of H. Hackfeld & Co.," dated June 30, 1855, showed assets of $93,711 and a balancing of "our net capital" of $45,652. The respective figures today are $659,246,000 and $259,354,000. Where Pflueger's statements were patiently compiled by the junior partner in longhand after hours, Senior Vice President and

Controller D'Arcambal's come to him in computer printouts. These reports, of as many as 160,000 retail transactions, 11,754 hotel-room rentals, and 78,900 meal services in a day (not to mention potato inventories and feed-lot population, mortgage loan transactions, and pharmaceutical sales), are summaries only. They are reported on a monthly basis for convenience in handling and review, yet they weigh 7 pounds and cover 550 pages. Summaries they are but when D'Arcambal, who is known in the company as the "enforcer," senses trouble, details down to Howard Hughes's credit rating or the number of transformers in stock in Santa Rosa are available in minutes electronically.

When Gay arrived in mid-1967, he found a computer center that had been in operation for 5 years. Both the quality of its product and its extravagant use of manpower displeased him. One of his first undertakings was to revise the system and cut the force from 80 to 50. Now, with all the mainland growth, an additional computer center has been built in an industrial park at Brisbane, south of San Francisco. This modern one-story structure, with a staff of 80, was set up under a retired Marine colonel and former All-American, Charles Greene, Jr. Still very much a Marine in bearing and appearance, he learned the computer business in the service during the Vietnam war, where expenditures of everything from ammunition and rations to weapons carriers and field artillery pieces were tabulated electronically. As levels of supply fell below established support tables, requisitions were transmitted by satellite to computer centers and supply points in Da Nang, thence to Okinawa and on to Philadelphia. Greene is now on special assignment to set up new Amfac offices in San Francisco. Brisbane remains his pride and he sees the day when it and the Honolulu center will consolidate their data via satellite in true Marine fashion.

The employment of these centers by the several groups varies in degree. The traditional Amfac operations are all on-stream; in fact, the Amfac plantation offices, once bustling with bookkeepers and storekeepers, industrial engineers and statisticians, each with his adding machine or calculator, are empty now—an eerie, Orwellian comment on the relationship of man and machine.

Perhaps the optimum use of the computer is reflected in the "Uni-tote" operation of the Joseph Magnin and Liberty House chains. It is a system being rapidly expanded throughout the whole Retail Group. Under this scheme, every cash register (2,032 of them at this moment) in every store will be keyed into the computer. By the time a salesclerk has punched the appropriate keys, and it doesn't take as long to do it as to write it, the center has confirmed that the customer's credit is good, has noted that the items sold have been removed from inventory, has charged the customer's account with the amount of the purchases, and has credited the particular store with the sale. This done, the computer is ready for the next transaction, which may be occurring 2,000 miles from the previous one.

Lamb-Weston, with a business-school-patterned management, already had an excellent system of computerized accounting, and it was readily integrated with Brisbane. Some of the more individualistic organizations have been slower for "the enforcer" to bring into the fold. Guslander, for example, whose own system had served his purposes very well, changed his somewhat grudgingly. Other organizations acquired by Amfac, particularly some of the drug and electrical firms, have operated traditionally with smaller business machines and have yet to key into Brisbane electronically. They do, however, provide it with their data, which get punched into the system there. Some of them give the impression that they are not too anxious to rush into the world of whirling tapes and devices that type 1,400 lines a minute. These operators have made their way as green-eyeshade, know-your-neighbor operations and want to stay that way. The one thing Distribution Group Chairman Richardson wishes to avoid is the pitfall of becoming an impersonalized "big" which the computer world symbolizes, but Gay and D'Arcambal may prevail with their technology.

Centralized Banking and Risk Taking

While it is Amfac's policy in the course of its acquisitions to continue existing management and programs, headquarters must manage the money. In its management not only must the accounting be controlled but the placement of funds as well. Deposits must be made where they will best serve Amfac's interests, whether it be for treasury bills or for meeting the compensating balance needs of a lending bank.

The one thing centralized as soon as a company is acquired is its banking. The treasurer of one of the new members of the Amfac family complained to me: "Everyone around here is doing what he always did and is pleased to have this new financial muscle behind him. That is, everybody but me. I don't have anything to do any more." That is true. Every such treasurer has seen his banking connections and responsibilities removed to San Francisco, where they are centralized under Hagberg and Eugene W. Faust, Treasurer. On the other hand, the controller's function in each of the new companies has become more critical and more demanding than ever before.

Hagberg and Faust know the banking structure of Amfac inside out: who has the short-term loan capability, what the compensating balance requirements are, what the terms of the revolving credit agreements may be, and which banks have been friends in time of need in the past. While they are not insensitive to the long-time relations of Lamb-Weston with U.S. National in Portland, or Harvey with Harris Trust in Chicago, it is now Amfac's money and they have to place it where the total needs of the company dictate.

Not the least interesting part of their job is management of the $4 million of float the company enjoys in any given day. This becomes money that can be used, interest free, in the business.

As with the computerization of accounts, Gay has made greater progress in revising the insurance of Amfac assets with the companies traditionally managed by the parent than with the newcomers. Called Risk Management, the unit he has established would be the insurance department in most organizations. This section has reviewed all the exposures of the Hawaiian activities, undertaken self-insurance within certain limits, consolidated policies in other cases, and negotiated new premium rates whenever possible. The annual saving in the areas already covered runs to $1 million a year. Gay foresees an equal saving as the activity is expanded to the mainland. He has already set up a branch there. The latest step has been to set up a corporation under Colorado law, which permits a subsidiary to underwrite high-risk exposures among its affiliates.

The growth and expansion that make Captain Hackfeld's enterprise what it is today could not have been achieved without these radical changes in the management of money. They have unearthed the slumbering resources that have made possible the acquisition and expansion of recent years.

To see what money management can accomplish, turn now to Amfac's affairs as they appear after 125 years of growth. Remember that sugar, already discussed, is, along with money management, the source of it all.

10

Vendors of Vogue

"Hard goods," "soft goods," "credit cards," and "manufacturer support," terms in common use today among Amfac's 92 retail outlets and 6,000 retail employees, would have had little meaning to Captain Hackfeld. He talked in terms of "specie," "doubloons," and "agencies" when he opened that first little shared salesroom on Honolulu's dusty Queen Street. It is remarkable, however, that of all the items listed in his inventories in those early years only silver suspender buckles, gold waistcoat chains, joss sticks, and ladies' riding crops would be hard to find in an Amfac store today. True, there have been some design changes in razors, field glasses, and ladies' hats. Guernsey frocks and seidlitz powder are no longer hot items. Nevertheless, ink, tacks, coffee, cigars, muslin, Irish linen, and scores of other items he carried are still in demand.

Retailing has been a slow-blooming flower in the Amfac

garden. Since Ehlers helped open it, there has always been the "upper store," renamed Liberty House and Honolulu's only department store until the arrival of Sears Roebuck in the early 1940s. At the retail level were the plantation stores dating from Hackfeld's days. They disappeared with improved transportation, home ownership, and Amfac's desire to eliminate the company-town atmosphere of the plantation villages. May's Market, once the leading food retailer in sleepy prewar Honolulu, was acquired in 1924. Its expansion into a supermarket chain was considered, even given Board approval, but it didn't materialize. When reexamined years later, the idea was abandoned. The field had become too competitive and May's itself was closed thereafter. There was no longer a place in Honolulu for a store that offered charge accounts, order by telephone, and delivery of groceries.

There was some expansion of Liberty House after World War II. A branch was opened at Waikiki in 1949, and then branches in suburban Kahala and Kailua, but these were timid moves. When Sumner resisted Dillingham's pressure to build a Liberty House as the anchor store in the Ala Moana Shopping Center, it appeared that Amfac had turned its back on retailing as an avenue to growth.

The First Mainland Move

Reversal of this posture came when Smith hired laconic, lean E. A. Attebury from the Rhodes chain in the Pacific Northwest to come to Honolulu and take over management of the retail operation. Attebury smelled opportunity in the tourist boom of the 1950s and the coming of statehood. Accustomed to the placid growth rate of 3–4 percent in Oregon and Washington, he viewed the 8–10 percent being experienced in Hawaii as an occasion for expansion. With the development of a second unit at the Ala Moana Center, he had no difficulty reversing the management view. This was, he felt, an ideal site. He built there the high-ceilinged, airy, almost tropical prototype for subsequent Liberty Houses, and its imaginative displays became as profitable as any in bustling Hawaii. Under the new management the "upper store" was refurbished and Kahala and Kailua enlarged. At the same time Vern Elder, who was to advance with the growth of retailing, pressed the idea of establishing small, boutique-type shops in the burgeoning resort hotels on the neighboring Islands.

Attebury, a perfectionist as well as an expansionist, was the leader in the expression of discontent among the executive group in the mid-1960s. There was much to do in Hawaii and there were opportunities in retailing on the mainland, but nothing was being done. Amfac, he felt, was bogged down in a quagmire of loan covenants and caution. The dissension on the Board during the Weinberg period was discouraging, and he, too, considered resignation. The Walker-Gay philosophy was as welcome to him as the arrival of the miniskirt, or any other major stimulant, to sales. There was now an action-minded group to review his ambitions and a receptive Board to hear them.

While the senior Walker was fighting for space for civilian supplies aboard convoyed merchantmen during World War II, another retail man was saying: "Suddenly we realized it was a nation of young people, not necessarily in years, but in thinking." From this concept emerged the colorful, breezy, zesty Joseph Magnin chain of the postwar generation in the West. It took 25 years for Amfac to come up with parallel thinking. Then a union of the two companies became almost inevitable. It was consummated in 1969.

Mr. San Francisco

The junior Walker was in San Francisco when the deal was made, and Attebury and Gay invited him to join them and Cyril Magnin for a glass of champagne, celebrating the merger as though they had just won a world series. Magnin is the grandson of I. Magnin, the founder of the fashionable *haute couture* shops of San Francisco's Union Square, Los Angeles' Wilshire Boulevard, and other expensive watering holes of the West. Cyril's father, Joseph, left the family business in 1913 to found his own store across the street in San Francisco. The Joseph Magnin stores today are about as far removed from the somewhat grande-dame atmosphere of the other side of the family emporiums as Ethel Merman is from singing Handel's *Messiah*.

The deliberate, youthful characterization of the company's operations springs from Cyril Magnin's "sudden" realization and has proven to be good business. The chain now has 2,000 employees, over 40 outlets in the West, and is expansion-minded. Its President, Robert Berry, says he will "follow the sun" wherever it may lead.

Chairman Magnin is fond of a Kipling quote:

> They copied all they could follow
> But they couldn't copy my mind
> And I left them sweating and stealing
> A year and a half behind.

To keep that lead, youth and innovation have become the company's hallmark. Goods move exclusively by air freight. Cash registers are on the Uni-tote system, direct to the Brisbane computer center. There is special stationery for company correspondence, for example, a "J Memo" and "J Mail."

The corporate history is printed on a poster. The front

side shows a slender if busty blonde with full-blown lips, wearing a beret and the latest Joseph Magnin type shift and 3-inch clog heels. There is a particular style that identifies JM's drawings of women, and it is not all minis or maxis or whatever today's fad may be. The reverse side of the poster tells the company's story in JM's unique way. There are 35 uncaptioned, four-color photographs of JM people at work, models and salesgirls, buyers and artists. Although nowhere does it give names, you can identify President Berry at his desk in one and in another the friendly face of Chairman Magnin. Both seem proud although somewhat bemused by all they have created. The poster gives a brief history of the company. It emphasizes growth from within (it hires 50 or more college graduates each year for training and development) and its innovative and operating philosophy.

There is, of course, a *J Magazine*, usually three editions a year, with one devoted to travel prepared in a joint promotion with a carrier. Thus, an issue devoted to Tahiti, New Zealand, and Australia finds Pan Am as the featured partner. Pictured in full color on glossy stock are models, both male and female, wearing Magnin merchandise appropriate to the scene depicted, which can be cocktails at Quinn's in Papeete or boarding a Pan Am 747 in Sydney. The magazine thus provides an engaging, illustrated travel narrative which provides the opportunity to display upwards of 200 items of merchandise and to quote prices and relevant data, such as size ranges, but this is all low key.

Much thought is devoted to ways to intrigue customers. Five years were spent developing a special pattern for JM shopping bags and boxes "so graphic they can be spotted a mile or two away." Full-page institutional ads were taken to introduce these designs in spite of a general policy to avoid media advertising. In most cases JM favors such company-produced and controlled circulation publications as the *J Magazine*. Before the Christmas season of 1973 male customers received a little folder with space for noting female sizes in gloves, stockings, and such. The billing of 183,000 charge-account patrons provides another advertising opportunity. The "J Mailers" included with the bill are so sprightly it "makes paying a pleasure," one executive says with perhaps a trace of persiflage.

In San Francisco headquarters, looking out toward the Bay, there is a display factory which resembles the backstage of a theater, with paint and props, costumes and bijoux. While all window displays are prepared by teams dispatched from San Francisco, the individual store managers make their own local promotions. Nevada, for one reason or another, elects to salute Italy, and the State Line, Reno, and Las Vegas shops join in providing their customers with a lottery. The prize is a full 3-day trip "to nowhere" aboard an Italian cruise ship sailing from San Francisco. Opening the season at Palm Springs, JM sets up a fashion show of designer dresses for the benefit of crippled children with Dubonnet wine as a cosponsor and Mrs. Harry ("Bing" to you) Crosby as hostess.

Magnin was the first American establishment to represent the Italian house of Gucci. Four Gucci shops, one each in San Francisco, Denver, Las Vegas, and Honolulu, cheer Cyril Magnin's heart while pleasing the retailer in him with $50 shoes and $400 suede coats.

Still the main thrust is youth and leadership in fashion and fads. Buttons are "very 'in' now," I was told. Gloves are "out." Sunglasses are still hot items. Asking the manager of a new store in a massive shopping center well removed from San Jose who her customers were, I observed, "There is nobody around for miles." She replied, "Oh, they come all the way from San Francisco and Oakland, and they are all types. The other day a woman flew her own plane in from Reno to buy a couple of dresses. The next customer was a girl riding on the back of her boy friend's motorcycle. She had gotten cold, so she bought a fur coat."

In Las Vegas, one woman ordered special pockets sewn in her dresses. It later developed she used them in filching chips from the gambling tables. However, the manager there says her 47,000 resident customers discourage "chorus-girl stuff."

More Mainland Moves

Next came the 1969 acquisition of Rhodes, Attebury's previous company. Almost as old as Amfac, the Rhodes chain included a now-closed Portland store, the second oldest retail establishment in Oregon, which was founded in 1851 as Olds, Wortman, and King.

As young men, the Rhodes brothers had established themselves in a small Wisconsin town, where they bought out a storekeeper's inventory for $500 and rented his establishment for $5 a month. This was a Daniel Boone type of business with riverboat men and Indians as customers. The brothers ran a pawnshop (as Fred Harvey still does in Arizona) where the Winnebagos could pledge saddles and blankets for goods during the winter months. The Rhodeses sold out this first venture while still young and moved to the Northwest in 1889.

Tacoma had just become prominent as the new western terminal of the Northern Pacific Railway and, with $1,000 of capital, the Rhodes brothers set up a tea and coffee shop there, building their own fixtures. Their history is closely tied to that of Tacoma. During the gold rush the firm outfitted prospectors and even established a branch in Dyer, Alaska, to supply the miners. It is curious how apparently unrelated events fall into patterns as history's pages turn — Hackfeld in Sitka, the Rhodeses in Dyer, and Richardson buying an electrical supply outfit in Fairbanks. Guslander is now toying with the idea of hotels in Alaska to serve tourists and the prospective needs of businessmen brought there by oil discoveries and pipeline construction. In the case of the Rhodeses, however, Alaska was no bonanza. By the time its inventories arrived Dyer had become a ghost town. The brothers considered themselves lucky to break even, trading off their stock with the Indians for labor.

The Rhodes family sold out in 1925, and in 1933 the new owners brought in one John J. Riley to operate the chain. Under Riley, a great delegator, Rhodes began to assume the appearance of the structure acquired by Amfac. Initially embracing the Tacoma store, the Portland Olds and King establishment, and Oakland's Kahn's, it expanded to San Antonio and changed the name of all stores to Rhodes in 1960. New stores were built in Phoenix, Palo Alto, and Albuquerque in 1965.

The Albuquerque establishment is a reflection of the Rhodes operation. It is sparkling clean, its displays are crowded with goods, it appeals to the middle-income family (three-quarters of the Albuquerque market work for the government or government contractors), and it specializes in imaginative merchandising. When the city's zoo opened a new bear grotto, Rhodes brought in Liver Lips, the bear from Disneyland, for the dedication. By contrived chance, Liver Lips appeared to square-dance in the store as well, where there was a drawing for free trips to Disneyland. In another appeal to youth, there is a Lollipop Board of Directors to advise on youngsters' interests and stimulate such events as an earth-day hike to dispense 75,000 Rhodes-supplied ladybugs to control Albuquerque's aphids. A campaign led by the Rhodes Gaula Board to reduce the number of stray cats and dogs in the city won the Rhodes-organized group $1,500 (and Rhodes national publicity) in a civic affairs competition conducted by *Seventeen* magazine.

Attebury opposed the acquisition of his old company, fearing that the price was too high. Finally, it was Walker, with characteristic decision, who made the deal. He took the responsibility himself, closing the agreement in a 4-hour phone call with Portland. And were was he? In a motel room near Lake Tahoe. His California-Tahoe retreat overlooking the lake then had no telephone.

Shortly after the absorption of Rhodes, Amfac took another step in the Attebury campaign to become a major factor in retailing in the West. This was the acquisition of a small string of discount stores in the Bay area, known as Baz'ar. Renamed RhodesWAY Stores, revitalized in terms of fixtures and personnel, they were to reflect the bottom of the line in Amfac's retail structure as mass-merchandising outlets. They proved to be losers. With some sites upgraded and converted to Rhodes department stores and others sold, RhodesWAY was discontinued in 1973.

The Upper Store Moves Up

At the other end of the line results were different. It was Attebury's dream to duplicate the Ala Moana Liberty House in select mainland locations. That he pressed a worn heart too hard in doing it is one of those corporate disappointments that often appear in middle age. Attebury, still lean and well-conditioned, had to give up management responsibility and became a corporate consultant.

The group he left behind ·under the leadership of newly arrived Teller Weinmann, formerly President of Broadway Department Stores and now one of Amfac's two Executive Vice Presidents, carries on with his philosophy. "A store is a theater" is the belief and, as illustration, beauty parlors in the new Liberty Houses are arranged like amphitheaters with the chairs banked to permit TV viewing while hair is tended and dried. "There is a narrow line between merchandising and control." Too much dramatics, Amfac believes, is costly in a business where margins are thin, but glamour is lost in too austere administrative control. "The ultimate goal is to have three Christmases a year." So it is that Mother's Day and Yom Kippur are featured in Amfac merchandising. Rhodes in Oakland even offers free Alka-Seltzer to entice customers to shop on New Year's Day.

In a growing number of cases, a new JM store is a satellite adjoining a major new Liberty House. This is the case in Hayward, outside Oakland, and at Pearl Ridge and Kahala Mall, both outside Honolulu. Attebury's original "new" store in the Ala Moana Shopping Center is the prototype of these new Liberty House establishments. The sense of light and airiness recalls the Taj Mahal; the graphics, clear and incisive, never cute, lead shoppers where they want to go and tell them what they want to know.

It follows that subsequent administrations have had their ideas, too. The newer stores, while sticking with the basic Attebury design, surround a core, a shaft where several glass-walled boxes the size of elevator cabs move up and down displaying life-size mannequins wearing the latest fashions. The effect is theatrical, much as Ziegfeld might have presented his follies or as Las Vegas would introduce a chorus line. The stores are vibrant, and although they have many features in common they have an eye out for local tastes. The San Jose Liberty House, for example, serves teriyaki steak from Hawaii in its restaurant and plugs aloha shirts in its sportswear department. There are also enchiladas on the menu and mallard decoys displayed in the sporting goods section. Neither of these items could ever be found at the "upper store" in Honolulu.

The Retail Group offers more than goods. It runs cocktail

lounges, sells insurance and travel, operates beauty shops and shoeshine stands, styles men's hair, and rents books. Throughout the system you can find shirts selling for from $2.99 to $25.00 (plus a charge for monogramming).

If there is one characteristic of the retail business it is that there is always change. Styles in clothing appear and disappear. Magnin had a poor year in 1971 because buyers were confused on the outcome of the mini-maxi skirt controversy.

While they are very dissimilar in character, spanning as they do every major area of the retail market, including mail order, the Amfac stores share certain common policies. The customer is always right. He can return an item bought at Magnin's to Rhodes and get a refund. His Liberty House credit card will earn him a credit card in the other chains without further inquiry. They work as a total group in purchasing supplies such as paper, typewriters, and cash registers.

They are nonetheless separate enterprises when it comes to buying and pricing the merchandise to be offered for sale. Group headquarters doesn't interfere with the managers of the several chains but has comparisons made between divisional figures to be sure each buyer is doing his job at rock-bottom cost. The total purchases of the Group are made known to manufacturers who like to work with big-volume buyers. Very little merchandise is consigned to any one of the establishments though, again, as volume users they have opportunities to exchange items that don't move well.

Some impression of the scale of Amfac's retail operation can be gained from a visit to the 5-acre warehouse recently built in Dublin to service Rhodes and Liberty House operations in central California and the Northwest. Here, where security precautions (to prevent pilferage) remind one of the Pentagon war room, 16,000 packages weighing 326,000 pounds are handled in 4 days. The goods come by train to one or another of 19 spurs, as well as by truck and air. Two classes of merchandise are recognized: "middle" and "prestige." All articles are tagged with price and size here, the color of the thread employed being a code to guide the stores in determining the age of the goods.

Everybody Thinks Young

The management of the retail group is young, which pleases Cyril Magnin in particular. Robert Berry, Magnin President and former Vice President of Dallas's famed Neiman Marcus, is a zestful 50 who might have stepped out of one of his own displays. Sideburned, wide-tied, Gucci-shoed, and Napoleon-lapelled, he lets his salesmen know how they should dress.

The other merchandise executives follow the same style. They all dress in mod fashion, in sharp contrast to the Brooks Brothers pattern of Amfac 10 years ago. In fact, their zeal to lead changes in male fashions has communicated itself to the top floor of the Amfac Building, where Walker's shirts are almost as garish as Cox's scarf-sized ties.

As has been said, "Retailing is part theater, and that is the fun of it." Perhaps the most fun to come Amfac's way has been with its purchase of San Francisco's favorite store, City of Paris. The history of this establishment goes back to the gold rush, when a prominent hosiery manufacturer in Nimes, France, sensed opportunity in San Francisco and dispatched a bark there named *La Ville de Paris*. Anchored at the foot of Montgomery Street in 1850, it sold its cargo of silks, satins, laces, champagne, and cognac to the miners and their gaudy ladies across the beach. Thus began a tradition of dealing in luxuries that endures today. Finding the waterfront no place to display such finery, the Verdier family built a structure to house the City of Paris in 1851. This was the first of six locations, the last move being occasioned by the earthquake and fire of 1906.

In 1972 Countess Suzanne Verdier de Tessan, last of the family, determined to close the store. The building was old, San Francisco had moved to the suburbs, and this was the way of it. The popular White House, a block away, had folded years before. Her decision included closing its basement, Normandy Lane. Generations of San Franciscans had bought their Camembert and Chateau Lafite Rothschild there. The city's sophisticates, including sardonic *Chronicle* columnist Herb Caen, lamented the move. Some even cut up their credit cards in public to display their grief.

Thus when Amfac announced it would take over the location and agreed to continue the name and tradition, there was rejoicing from San Francisco's Pacific Heights to the swank estates of Woodside. The event was heralded by the Countess leading a parade of Citroens through downtown San Francisco to the store. There was a champagne party for the Mayor and other dignitaries. San Franciscans were gleeful when the public, some 3,000 of them, feeling jubilant about the revival of the old establishment, crashed the party. Still that was in a sense a tribute to the institution. You need an occasion to drink champagne in mid-afternoon.

The present building at Geary and Stockton has been in use since 1909. Its glass, lead-lined dome pictures *La Ville de Paris*, complete to the motto on the bow: "It may rock but never sink." Now "Liberty House at City of Paris" is in full swing as a theater of imaginative merchandising. Normandy Lane has been painted a plum color, inspired by springtime in France. Its menu offers "soups and entrées accompanied by our own brioches and croissants and wine by the half liter."

There are further plans for it. The building is old. Emerging on the back half of it is a new store capped by an office structure to house Amfac's Western Region offices. It is across the street from Joseph Magnin and Macy, down the block from I. Magnin, and a stone's throw from the big Emporium. In the manner of retailers, Amfac thinks that having all the competition around is just great. "This," the merchandisers say, "with the mass transit station to open just over there, is the best retail location in the West."

11

To Talk of Many Things

Amfac entered the distribution, as distinct from the retail, business in 1850 when Hackfeld opened the "upper store" and began supplying it, his chandlery, and the plantations with merchandise from inventories maintained on Queen Street. When, by 1853, he had opened branches on Kauai, Molokai, and Hawaii (all supplied from Queen Street), he had set the pattern for Amfac's Distribution Group as it functions today.

There were to be changes in detail, of course. Molokai closed, Hawaii opened, for example. New lines were added ranging from lumber bought through Pope and Talbot in 1851 to General Electric in 1944. More recently came the abandonment of other lines, such as food in 1952 and liquor in 1964; but in the prime of the distribution business there was a time when an Amfac employee could buy his every need from building materials to canned goods, automobiles to cigars, through the company and at a discount. There were months, old-timers recall, when some workers ended up owing the company more than they had earned.

Lost: 2,500 TV Sets

Major changes began in 1964 when Walker took over the Distribution Division with a mandate to make it profitable. One of the first men he picked to join him was John P. Richardson, elevated overnight from salesman to department head. There had recently been some shocking disclosures of mismanagement and inept control. For example, over $500,000 worth of television sets had literally disappeared, obviously pilfered with some collusion from warehousemen. Walker faced a quagmire of an organization with 24 department heads reporting to him. This end of the business was earning $300,000 a year before taxes, less than 1 percent on its investment.

There were heavy inventory commitments to a losing proposition in the retailing of electrical appliances, which also presented public relations problems. As G.E. representative in Hawaii, Amfac was a supplier to dealers with whom it competed in the retail market. This problem was paralleled by the experience with construction materials, in which Amfac was a builder competing with its contractor customers. Both areas were presenting Amfac with difficulties in achieving acceptable profit margins. Walker moved quickly to dispose of the retail appliance business. He made an arrangement with a well-established, successful Honolulu dealer to buy the operation over a period of time and gave him the respected Ramsay name to use at the retail level. He retained for Amfac the profitable role of distributor of all G.E. products (including

26) It was the prospects in retail trade and ship chandlery that attracted Hackfeld to Hawaii. After a year in the Islands, he opened an "upper store" somewhat removed from Queen Street; soon, and characteristically, he had a relative in charge of it. It was named for the nephew, B. F. Ehlers, and was so known until the end of World War I.

27) The new American owners called the "upper store" Liberty House, a name which now embraces a growing chain in Hawaii and the West. Here the initial unit of the chain is shown in the 1920s. Remodeled many times since, it remains on the site of the "upper store."

28) From these origins emerged the modern, uncluttered design that characterizes all Liberty House expansions. It began with this building in Honolulu's Ala Moana area. One of the world's largest shopping centers, Ala Moana was developed by Dillingham interests, long associated with Amfac.

(29) Each Amfac retail chain has its own style, directed to various retail appetites. Liberty Houses have a feeling of airiness and space, and there is ample display area with garments and goods readily available rather than buried in shelves and drawers as in the days of the "upper store." Depicted here is the 1974 Easter display at Ala Moana.

(30) Stores of the Rhodes division, which operates throughout the Southwest, also have a feeling of spaciousness, but where the atomsphere of the Liberty Houses is calm, at Rhodes it is busy. The Rhodes promotions—in marked contrast to the Easter scene depicted in Figure 29— are likely to feature a rock band or a dancing bear.

(31) Joseph Magnin reflects all that is youthful, zestful, and modern. Carefree color is its keynote. The mannequin at the left expresses the Magnin flair for imaginative appeal to the young in all of us.

(32) Shown is the first Joseph Magnin store to open in Tokyo. Note the European character of the figures and the costuming. Ten or more such boutiques are being planned throughout Japan.

(33) *Distribution of goods for resale followed shortly after the establishment of Ehlers' store. It became a major element in Hackfeld's business with the opening of plantation retail outlets on the neighboring Islands. As can be seen, the Wholesale Cash and Carry division was a busy place in 1929.*

(34) *Through the years, Distribution expanded to include the export of such Island products as pineapple and coffee. With the purchase of Henry May & Co., Amfac acquired the brand name Mayflower and used it, along with such exotic ads as that reproduced here, to promote sale of the coffee it milled along the Kona coast. In the 1960s Amfac abandoned both pineapple and coffee because of marketing problems.*

(35) *Recent expansion in the sale of pharmaceuticals on the mainland has generated volume and profit never approached by pineapple and coffee. Inventories of drugs are maintained at 32 branches in the continental United States.*

appliances) throughout the Islands. There was no emotional wrench in this disposition of the problem. After all, the business had been acquired only in 1944.

The Construction Materials Division was another matter. Amfac was the leading concern in the field in Hawaii, with $30 million in sales and $3.5 million in inventories. It had warehouses on all the Islands and a network of customers traditionally reliant on it for bonding, interim financing, and, ultimately, the provision and servicing of mortgages. There was also the fact that the various construction ventures of the company contributed substantially to the volume of the Division. While given no price advantage over outside buyers bidding on competitive projects, it permitted the development arm to have the knowledge that it was buying as favorably as anyone else. Finally, the distribution of construction materials was as old as Amfac itself. Recall that the first inventory of the *Wilhelmine* included, among other things, nails and chains.

Walker, after laying off 300 employees in the distribution setup by closing or consolidating the 24 departments into 3 and instituting security measures to end pilferage, had an interval, before becoming Executive Vice President, to evaluate the whole distribution concept. He was running it well, he felt, and yet it was not getting off the ground. The bright spots were the electrical and pharmaceutical supply departments and the importation and sale of glass. When events moved him into the Presidency, he put emotion and tradition aside and determined that construction materials should go. He was joined in this decision by Cox and Gay, who shared his determination to liquidate heavy capital commitments in low profit enterprises and shift the proceeds to areas promising higher earnings and growth. The problem became one of finding a purchaser of substance.

Wanted: Buyer for a 120-Year-Old Business

It soon developed there weren't any. The local competitors in the field wanted no part of it. They were having their own problems. One, in fact, had sold out to U.S. Plywood just before the Amfac decision was made. Though the Islands were being invaded by mainland capital, the interest was primarily in land, tourism, finance, and retail distribution. There wasn't another U.S. Plywood on the horizon.

A deal was finally reached with Telecheck, an apparently successful, obviously ambitious group of young men who had started out serving supermarkets in verifying the credit of customers paying by check. From this computer-oriented beginning, it had expanded into electronic accounting and programming services for all classes of business. Then it grew further. Its ventures ranged from plumbing contracting in Hawaii to the manufacture of snowmobiles in the Middle West. It was, in short, a nascent conglomerate in the day when conglomeration was the fashion.

Essentially, the Telecheck arrangement called for it to rent the physical facilities with an option to buy and to pay for the inventories and going concern value out of profits. A combination of bad luck and excess leveraging ensued. There was, first, a series of shipping strikes, followed by a series of prolonged strikes by West Coast and Hawaiian longshoremen. This not only tied up inventory but further slowed the pace of the construction industry in Hawaii, which was already catching its breath after a hotel and highway building boom. Telecheck was forced into reorganization and Amfac has the business back in its hands.

Walker does not seem displeased about getting it back. While some of the problems remain, he feels they are capable of solution through techniques learned in the expansion of distribution to the mainland. Drop shipments are being employed to reduce inventories; expenses are being trimmed through improved systems and reduced staff. The problem of selling to competitors of the Property Group has declined as Amfac has phased out of tract housing. He believes, in short, that the Construction Materials Division can be made to contribute equally with the other elements of the Distribution Group. So far it does.

Wanted: Green Eyeshade Companies

John Richardson, long-time manager of the Electrical Supply Department, now heads the Distribution Group. Relieved for a time of the problems of the Construction Materials Division, he was able to devote himself primarily to expansion. Backed by Walker's conviction that good profits were available in the distribution of certain lines, he was given the go-ahead to enlarge his activities in the wholesaling of electrical and pharmaceutical supplies on the mainland. Quiet-spoken Richardson, long a practitioner in the field, knows everyone in the business in the West. Like accountants, Chevrolet dealers, dentists, and appliance firms, distributors of these lines have their own conventions, their own trade journals, and a community of interest that sets them apart in fraternities.

Many of the firms in this type of trade are owned by individuals and are the product of the work of a lifetime. However successful, they are usually regional in nature, spanning an area no larger than an industrious proprietor can supervise and, in important matters, service personally. Those very characteristics make them attractive to Richardson and attract them to Amfac.

While determined to grow in the distribution field, Richardson wants no part of the problems of bigness. He says:

> This business is successful only if it is conducted on an eyeshade, crackerbarrel basis. For example, in the electrical supply game you've got to know your customer's problems so well you can help him in bidding on contracts and in the course of it sell him your lines. In the drug field the pharmacist has to know you so well that he can call you at home after hours in the certainty that you'll go down and open up the warehouse to get some rarely needed item to him in an emergency. The minute you get too big this intimacy is lost. So we want small companies and we want them to stay that way, growing with the communities they serve. This means keeping the owner on as manager along with the staff he has built through the years.

The owner, for his part, almost inevitably has personal problems that encourage him to sell to Amfac. The first of these is a desire to care for his people by providing them with an enterprise that will endure after his death or retirement. Another is that, as retirement approaches, he seeks an income source to replace the salary and profit derived from his efforts while active. Finally, and most important, he needs liquidity to pay estate taxes on his death. An exchange of his business for Amfac stock is an excellent means of accommodating these needs.

Attending conventions, dropping in on old friends, Richardson says he seeks out opportunities "like a fox in a henhouse." He is, in fact, welcome.

A case in point is Osborne Electric. Here is a vital, thriving business in the electrical supply field that was built by R. L. Osborne from the ground up in Las Vegas. When Amfac acquired it in 1972 its activities were centered around a new warehouse-office-storage yard complex in the industrial section of that city. (I had never, before visiting Osborne, known that the sun-fun city had industry.) The air-conditioned structure covering three-quarters of an acre is brand-new, houses 23 employees, and over 8,000 kinds of electrical gadgets. These include not only fuse boxes, floor plugs, lumeline tubes, and conduits but scores of items unfamiliar outside the trade. There are hot-line tools, insulation hoods, explosion-proof fittings, pier-type insulators, and double-span braces along with rolls of cable the diameter of a locomotive's wheel. The bulkiest of these items are stored in a fenced acre adjoining the warehouse. The more fragile and pilferable are kept under lock and key in rack-type steel shelving.

Half of Osborne's business is with electric utility companies and power distributors in a market area which extends south into Arizona and west into California. A large part is with the Atomic Energy Commission in connection with its underground nuclear tests. Irrigation pumps and motors are the third major source of Osborne's sales. Conventional construction needs account for only a small share of the business except when a new hotel casino, with all its demands for lighting everything from stages to slot machines, is being built. Then there is the need for special standby generators so that the occasional wind and rain storms that black out the area will not plunge the casinos, with all those chips and money around, into darkness. A measure of the scale of this business is found in the fact that Osborne provided over $500,000 of electrical products for the new International Hotel alone.

Why, then, would Osborne sell out when he had a fully competent successor in long-time friend and manager Thomas Logan? As usual, the personal considerations enumerated (complicated in this case by illness) were the decisive factors. Richardson knew Osborne, heard of his illness, sensed an opportunity, and worked out the acquisition.

In the case of Amfac Supply of Alaska, Valley Electric of

Ventura, California, and Edson Electric of Denver and Colorado Springs, which have also joined the Amfac fold, the pattern of individual control was present, and in each instance personal considerations were a determining factor in selling to Amfac.

The success of the Edson brothers in supplying electrical contractors was due to their personal experience in the field. They were so good, in fact, that they branched out to Arizona and soon each man set out on his own, one brother taking the Phoenix branch and the other brother, Jerry, keeping Denver and Colorado Springs. "Old Fox" Richardson found an additional Amfac appeal for Jerry, who has always wanted a chance to get ahead in a big corporation. Since the acquisition Amfac has sent him to a Harvard Business School summer course in Honolulu, let him survey the whole Amfac scene, and named him marketing manager for the group.

For somewhat similar reasons Western Drug Supply, which had 450 shareholders and dealt in six different marketing areas in the West, joined Amfac. A company founded in Sacramento in 1948, it began in a space about the size of a big living room and with three employees. Jack Rodda was not one of them but he was an initial investor. He joined the company as President 3 years later, and, as its principal shareholder and one of the most highly regarded men in his business, dominated the company. He says, "In this business you have to start out on a truck to become a good salesman." In the 10 years before joining Amfac his record showed phenomenal growth. Sales doubled and pretax profits tripled to the point where Western was serving 2,500 accounts in four states from 20 acres of warehouse space dispersed among them. It employed 400 people and inventoried 15,000 items, ranging from cocaine to wheelchairs and bismuth to novocaine.

Rodda, subject to the personal considerations that influence most of these sales, plus the desire of the remaining share-holders to gain liquidity and the promised opportunity for expansion with Amfac's resources behind them, happily re-sponded to Richardson's siren song. With Amfac's subsequent acquisition of Pacific Drug Distributors and its 20 branches in the South and Midwest, the whole pharmaceutical group has been consolidated in one organization, Amfac Drug Supply Co. Rodda got a little bonus from this merger, as he was named to head the expanded company.

Thus, Amfac's distribution business, once a matter of razor-thin margins, has been built into what is usually its second most profitable group in terms of return on investment. This has happened in the 5 years since the "violent reappraisal" of Amfac's destiny. Sales have tripled since 1968 and "contribu-tion" (Amfacese for earnings) has risen from $1,264,000 to $10,105,000. This is a faster rate of increase than that shown by any group.

While Richardson continues to search out additional oppor-tunities, he doesn't have to look too hard anymore. Walker says Richardson's knowledge is so thorough that with one glance at a firm's audited figures he can tell what Amfac can afford to offer. The problem, both agree, is to keep each constituent small, "attuned to the needs of its community."

This really introduces a basic question. How can Amfac abandon the wholesaler's role, so long a profitable collateral, in Hawaii, and expand it profitably on the mainland?

First, there is abandonment in Hawaii. The arrival of super-markets, buying on their own behalf, killed off most of Amfac's wholesaling in the food field. The arrival of mainland entre-preneurs with direct sources and their own established suppliers on the mainland took care of much of the rest. However, the new look being given to the Construction Materials Division seems to promise survival in that quarter.

Service Pays

Walker's and Richardson's experience in what has become the Distribution Group has convinced them of one thing. The place of the middleman remains essential in certain lines of endeavor. Two of these are drugs and electrical products, both well known to Amfac. Their common characteristic is service: the need for service by the pharmacist or the contractor on the spot. Where health is concerned, nobody is going to quibble about the cost of service. Where complex circuitry or environmental controls are involved, knowledgeable advice on alternative appliances and fixtures, as well as safety and availability of supply, is accepted as an element of cost.

A second characteristic common to the two types of enterprise is the vast inventory that each must maintain to provide service. In any one of the 89 warehouses, with 1,601,300 square feet of space, that Distribution now operates, 8,000 to 15,000 different items can be found. The pharmaceutical people must learn to describe the properties of the 500 or more new drugs that are developed each year.

A final service common to the two is presence "on the job." Most of Amfac's drug outlets are organized to make two or three deliveries a day to their pharmacist customers. The electrical people have specially trained engineers who sit in with contractors and help them work up their bids. This kind of cooperation resulted in successful bids for San Francisco's new Bank of America building and the Transamerica "pyramid." The latter complex is an engineer's monument, if painful to Bay viewers.

These essential qualities of service and the fact that "you must know the territory" have convinced Richardson never to act or look "big."

12

Land and Money, Hand in Hand

Amfac's Asset Management Group is the unlikely successor to the partners' early ventures in lending money, Isenberg advanced sums to his plantations, to B. F. Dillingham to buy rails for the Oahu railroad, to the coffee farmers of the Big Island, and to the rice growers of Hanalei and Kaneohe. When he and his cohorts did so it was to help build a plantation or win the agency for one, to give a hand to a business friend like Wilcox or a grower whose product they wished to process and sell. In short, lending money was not Amfac's business. It was done to further other ends. Today, lending money is very much Amfac's business and as much a part of its stock in trade as Arrow shirts, G.E. dynamos, and *mai tais*.

Mortgage Money

Evolution of the Asset Management Group has been relatively recent. It began with the servicing of mortgages as a logical means of attracting customers to the Construction Materials Division and employing Amfac's association with insurance companies, a major source of mortgage money. This modest activity, begun in 1953, had expanded by 1970 to a point where it engaged a dozen people servicing mortgages totaling $20 million. It was Paul Cassiday, recently out of Stanford, who made the Amfac mortgage and leasing business grow. An Island boy with a trace of Hawaiian blood and, in fact, "calabash kin" of the Pfluegers, it was logical that he should end up with Amfac; so logical that the night he was hired his wife asked him what his salary was. He had forgotten to inquire. The figure turned out to be $300 a month. Originally employed in the Insurance Department, he was transferred to a new subsidiary, Mortgage, Leasing and Finance Corp. It had been created to package odds and ends of lending and leasing in which Amfac had become involved through the sale of appliances, the installation of industrial equipment, and the servicing of mortgages for John Hancock. On taking over, the modest margins generated by the business concerned him, as he could see many better ways to have money make money.

Cassiday prevailed on the management to expand the financial activity to include leasing of physical assets through an arrangement with the U.S. Leasing Corp. of San Francisco. Under this agreement Amfac set up an 80-percent-owned subsidiary to operate in Hawaii, with the other 20 percent being paid the California firm to train Amfac personnel in the business, assist in its management, and help enlist customers for it. While originally the principal items leased to Island corporations were automotive and construction equipment, the intervening years have seen Cassiday rent everything to his clients from airplanes to pizza cookers.

In the mid-1960s the fiscal problems of the parent led to strictures being imposed on what became the Financial Group.

Capitalized for only $500,000 to begin with, the right to call on the parent for further sums was severely limited, confined, in fact, to $1.5 million. This right was cut in half in the stringencies of 1966. As earlier noted, this led Howard Hamamoto, Cassiday's ambitious number 2 man, to quit and join the Bank of Hawaii as a Vice President. Cassiday was about to follow him when Gay arrived on the scene and displayed both understanding and enthusiasm for some of his ideas.

High Horizons

Of all the dramatic growth at Amfac, nothing has been more spectacular in the business sense than that of this endeavor. With Gay's support and guidance and Cassiday's leadership, the once moribund mortgage service-leasing enterprise has blossomed into one of the biggest financial institutions in the western United States. This has been achieved through acquisition, internal generation of funds, and enterprising construction financing.

Amfac's first acquisition was Metropolitan Mortgage Corp. of Los Angeles, a firm servicing about $150 million in mortgages (seven times the Amfac portfolio at the time) and employing about 40 people. Metropolitan Mortgage is, as are the distribution companies acquired by Richardson, the product of one man's energy and application. It was founded on a shoestring in 1948 by Robert Alshuler. Initially, he worked by phone out of his own home and his wife had to keep the children quiet while he talked so that prospects wouldn't know he couldn't afford an office. That didn't last long. Today, Alshuler describes his business as "creating and selling loans." He doesn't wait for somebody to come in and ask for money. He and his people ferret out opportunities for contractors and developers whether they be in tracts, shopping centers, industrial parks, or high-rise construction. Having created the need for a loan, they then place it with one or more of the 24 Eastern and Midwestern financial institutions with which they work. These range from the Chase Manhattan Bank's Real Estate Investment Trust and the State Farm Life Insurance Co. to the Lutheran Church Pension Fund.

Alshuler continues to head his old enterprise and has taken on the added responsibility for another, even larger and more recent, acquisition in the same field. Commonwealth, Inc., of Portland, Oregon, was founded in 1911; it was later acquired by GAC, which, facing the need for liquidity, put Commonwealth along with other subsidiaries on the market in 1972. It is a big company with 259 employees servicing 33,000 mortgages having a value of over $500 million. Its purchase, coupled with the mortgage business already in hand, makes Amfac Mortgage Corp. (which was organized to embrace all such activities) the twenty-sixth largest such business in the United States.

Commonwealth has been even more diverse than Alshuler in "creating" loans. Operating from 18 branches throughout the Western states, the company is a land developer as well as a broker. It is, in fact, the largest such in Oregon, deriving from 15 to 20 percent of its profit from that activity. It is also a home builder, often erecting as many as 100 homes in a tract for its own account and as many as 400 in joint ventures with contractors. Currently, its major development is a 282-acre Portland project called Greenway. Unlike Alshuler, Commonwealth borrows from the public, using debentures to raise cash to fund mortgages. It is also distinctive in that it will guarantee the sale of a current home at a price fixed by independent appraisers to induce the owner to purchase a new one—with a Commonwealth mortgage, naturally.

There is something about Commonwealth that recalls the old saw about the packing house that uses every part of the pig but the squeal. Commonwealth has its own escrow and property subsidiaries, pays the property taxes for its thousands of mortgagees, and even has its own collection agency.

Up the Ladder

This abundance of mainland activity forced a reluctant Cassiday to move to Los Angeles. He had deferred it for some time because he prefers life in Hawaii, but he finally consented because, staying in Honolulu, he felt he was "sort of a cap on the top of the bottle." In transferring, he permitted others to move up a rung. His old associate, Hamamoto, succeeded him in the Presidency of the Island operation. Cassiday found himself moving up, as well, when his activity was given group status and he was named a Senior Vice President of Amfac.

Before leaving Honolulu, Cassiday had engineered two expansions of the area under his command. One was the move of Amfac Financial into the business of specialized development of property. Condominium ownership of apartments is popular in Hawaii, which was one of the first states to adopt enabling legislation. Building costs have soared in the Islands, and Amfac sensed the opportunity in buying up modern but older structures operating on a rental basis, which the owners, having gained the tax advantage 'of accelerated depreciation, were often looking to sell. Converting the buildings into condominiums, says Cassiday, is "like buying at wholesale and selling at retail." This procedure has been so successful that Hamamoto intends to have one undertaking of this sort in the works at all times.

Notwithstanding high building costs, Cassiday and Hamamoto decided to start a condominium of their own in a joint venture with seasoned realtor salesmen. This building, in an excellent location within walking distance of downtown Honolulu and a major shopping center, was marred only by its proximity to cemeteries. Even so, it was so successful that the original buyers of a $30,000 apartment with only a $5,000 down payment could have sold out for $40,000 when the building was completed. While Amfac Financial had no part in such windfalls, it did profit from financing the project, its share of the developers' earnings, and the mortgages generated.

Cassiday's second area of expansion was to develop the Amfac "Thrift Plan." The concept of paying higher interest rates for larger amounts left with a depository for a fixed period of time is not new, but as presented by Amfac in Hawaii it jolted the savings fraternity. Here was a company, in which the community had as much confidence as in the federal government, offering to pay 7 percent on sums over $1,000 left with it for 3 years. Gay and Cassiday hoped to raise $5 million to $10 million in this fashion and so to gain independence for further growth without relying on the parent organization. The response was overwhelming: before they could shut off the advertising and reduce the inducements, over $38 million had been deposited. One man alone put in $1 million. From being the stepchild with little call on the resources of the parent, the finance operation has emerged in 8 years as the fat cat of the corporate groups. It alone has no need to call on Amfac capital, so it does not compete with the other groups for Amfac funds. It generates all its own requirements. Its assets and profits are listed separately from those of the parent in financial statements, as is customary with financial, as distinct from conventional, business operations. They are, of course, reflected in the ultimate Amfac earnings per share. Its contribution, multiplying five times in as many years, reflects a growth second only to that of Distribution.

A Marriage of Convenience

The decision to improve Kaanapali and the demand for housing on Amfac lands adjoining burgeoning Honolulu led to the organization of a Property Development Department in the early 1960s. That fledgling staff embarked on what has become a principal Amfac activity: the conversion of land to higher and better uses. There is, however, little resemblance between the semiprofessional, Hawaii-oriented efforts of 10 years ago and the skilled, widespread land management practiced today.

Slim, almost boyish R. Gregg Anderson was induced to join Amfac by Eichelberger and Walker in 1967. He was charged with the formation of what was for a time the Property Group. Anderson had a background in southern California real estate and 5 years' experience operating his own development company. In the 6 years he headed the group, before returning to his own business, his acquaintance with the personalities and the perplexities of the business throughout the West was to stand Amfac in good stead. On his departure, with the financial arm ever more deeply involved in property development, the merger of the two activities under Cassiday became a logical move.

Awash in Land

Problems abounded in property. Kaanapali, in the Isenberg tradition, had been developed with hard cash, and the low rentals offered to induce building on the property were not offsetting expenses. In fact, the lease of the most spectacular site to contractors who built a hotel there and then sold it to Sheraton was almost a giveaway. A second tenant, with a vague concept involving the sale of condominium apartment units, had, in effect, been subsidized by Amfac. A third developer, the Royal Lahaina Corporation, a consortium of golf-course architect Robert Trent Jones, golf pro Jimmy Hines, and West Coast investors including entrepreneur J. C. Earle, was in trouble.

On Oahu a three-way arrangement between Amfac, its landlord, the Bishop Estate, and a tract developer was serving to increase rentals paid to the estate and making a profit for the builder but doing little for Amfac. There was talk of a new office building in Honolulu. On Kauai a $3 million shopping center, built also for cash, was proving a losing proposition.

In the course of the development of Kaanapali, Amfac principals had become acquainted with a San Francisco builder, who encouraged them to join him in acquiring a 1,000-acre country club near Napa, California, called Silverado. Beautifully situated among rolling hills and oak trees and with a magnificent golf course, Silverado nevertheless faced a score of problems and presented another land development situation in which the costs of Amfac were "sunk"—deep.

Hired to solve these problems, Anderson was given an even broader charter when Amfac entered the Walker-Cox-Gay period. Anderson was encouraged to look for development possibilities not only on company-owned land but in general either in Hawaii or on the mainland. He first set about restructuring the Amfac posture wherever possible. At Kaanapali there was little he could do about the Sheraton lease. Subsequently Lyle Guslander (this was before he sold out to Amfac) was induced to buy the Royal Lahaina Hotel venture. This establishment had a checkered financial career, including a recapture of the golf course by Amfac in 1963 and the simultaneous purchase of most of the original interests by J. C. Earle. Anderson began to solicit new tenants for Kaanapali at realistic rentals, building further condominiums at more marketable prices, and creating an "executive" (par 3) golf course for duffers who had been complaining about the difficulties of the Robert Trent Jones "championship" layout.

The ingenuity displayed by Anderson at Kaanapali has been reflected in a unique shopping center, Whalers Village. Capitalizing on the historic association of the Lahaina area with the whaling fleet of Hackfeld's day, this center is in effect an open-air museum exhibiting relics from the time of Melville's *Moby Dick*. Thought was given to building a pool large enough to display a live whale until the cost of transporting and caring for one of the leviathans was explored. Instead, there is a whale-sized pool, but only the skeleton of one of the mammoths is on display.

While the credit is not all due to Anderson—the growing tourist boom, the natural beauties of the site, the excellent physical plan, and the very passage of time were all working in his favor—Kaanapali is now out of the woods. Under his administration the cash-flow problems were reversed and, in his words, "From now on, it is nothing but a money machine." One evidence of this is found in the recent agreement to sell 8 acres there for $1 million an acre. There are 1,400 acres in the Kaanapali plan, making it larger than Waikiki. The company has another 15,000 acres nearby now being farmed in sugar or lying idle. It would be foolish to assume that all of the unplanned acres are worth $1 million each, but in time there will be sales at perhaps even higher prices.

On Oahu, Anderson revised the agreement with the Bishop Estate so that it would bypass the builder, whose construction business was experiencing difficulties, and put Amfac into a new role as tract developer. This proved to be a sage and profitable move (Amfac has now sold over 3,125 single-family homes). It also led the way to the development of a major shopping center, Pearl Ridge, and an attendant town-house complex. In the area in which this building goes on, the state is constructing a 50,000-seat stadium for sports-minded Oahu. Amfac has the lease on 222 acres surrounding that site and plans to develop them for commercial and apartment uses.

Finally, the Kauai shopping center was sold off.

Getting Off the Ground

It is a measure of Anderson's sense of the "present value of the dollar" that he brought Amfac Center, the office complex in Honolulu in which Amfac has its headquarters, into being without using any cash. He brought in a Northwest engineer and contractor, Richard H. Hadley, as a 40 percent joint venture partner. Using his own staff, long experienced in the design of high-rise office buildings, Hadley worked up plans for two 20-story towers, no corporate monuments but pleasant in their simple appearance. Amfac contributed the land, on which the old courthouse stood, for the remaining 60 percent. Jointly, they operated a Center Properties organization to get the first building up and the space leased. The cost per square foot resulting from the arrangement was so favorable that unusually low rentals for new office space in downtown Honolulu could be offered. As a consequence, the tower was rented before it was built, leading the partners to go ahead immediately with the second one. They had earlier thought of it on a "perhaps" basis for some future time. In the no-nonsense approach that characterized the whole venture, the second tower was built from the same plans as the first one, lending a certain symmetry to the Center while saving over $500,000 in design costs. To conclude the undertaking, Amfac sold its interest for $6 million to a private investor, Maurice Smith. This terminated Amfac ownership of the old courthouse site after over a century.

The company occupies the upper floors of the first tower, and the development will continue to be known as Amfac Center. A small cluster of shops on the ground level connecting the two structures includes restaurants, boutiques, and a JM's and generates enough traffic to give the complex a certain swinging air.

This is modified on the side of the block facing Fort Street Mall, where a gate from the old Hackfeld building and a graft from a tree that graced the courthouse garden preserve its memory. There, also, a distinctive fountain plays. Built by the Walker family in memory of H. Alexander Walker, it marks a path he walked nearly every working day for 40 years.

As Table 1 in Chapter 7, which shows Amfac's major land holdings in Hawaii, suggests, there will be opportunities in the future for both resort and recreational development on company-owned property. The limitations here are two. The first is the growth of travel to the Islands and the policy of the local government regarding its limitation. The second is the state's policy toward the conversion of agricultural land to urban purposes.

As this is written, the state continues to encourage travel to Hawaii. The current annual government appropriation for the semiprivate Hawaii Visitors Bureau is $1.7 million. The private sector contributes $569,000, of which $17,392 comes from various Amfac sources.

The state's position on the conversion of agricultural land to resort and urban uses is less clear. To date, Amfac has been able to develop all the land it required for these purposes with one exception: the property adjoining Lihue on Kauai, where the issue is not connected with agriculture but with the extension of the airport to accept trans-Pacific jets on direct flights, bypassing Honolulu.

In the future the company should encounter no difficulty in converting its properties on the neighboring Islands to different uses. Attention focuses on Oahu, where there has been an outcry about the loss of prime agricultural land to urbanization. To the extent that this concerns the environment, it is, in a sense, right. The loss of acres of green sugar and pineapple, which spread now like a vast lawn beneath Oahu's mountain ranges, will sacrifice some of the Island's beauty. The degree of loss, however, depends on how the subsequent development is done. Some of the tracts that have replaced sugarcane land are frightful scars worse than the "slurbs" of Los Angeles. Other farming areas have been diverted to housing with grace and, as their landscaping has emerged, have regained much of the tranquil beauty of times past. Castle & Cooke has done it with its Mililani Town, Lewers & Cooke with its Pacific Palisades, and Amfac with Pearl Ridge.

To the extent that the prophets of doom base their arguments on the economic theory that the loss of an acre of cane or pineapple land means the irretrievable loss of jobs and income to the state, they are talking hogwash. Hawaii has produced and always will produce all the sugar and pineapple it can sell profitably. There is ample land on the neighboring Islands to do it. The true limitations arise in Washington's regulation of the sugar price on the one hand and in the outcome of bargaining sessions between the ILWU and the plantation owners on the other.

California, Here We Come

In the West, Anderson engaged in the more exciting game of searching out opportunities for the acquisition and development of raw land, primarily for single-family housing. In this area his successors are in competition with a score of major operators. Everyone knows where the principal ownerships lie and which may be for sale. The game is to find the purchase formula that will fit the owner's needs, usually dictated by tax and estate considerations, and still leave a margin for a developer's profit. The principal success in this respect to date occurred with the purchase of 1,400 acres outside San Diego from a real-estate investment trust. It was bought on a "subject to" basis (that is, the purchase would be consummated only if engineering, title search, zoning, and such aspects proved out). This basis gives the buyer, in effect, a free option for a period of time. In this case, all points proved out and, most importantly, the requisite zoning was acquired during the option period. Without so much as turning a spade of earth, it was then sold for a profit.

This, of course, is the ultimate realization of every developer's dream. Wisely, Amfac has not insisted that a repeat performance be included in every annual profit goal; but a quiet sort of prowling around continues as a basic element in Cassiday's program.

A part of that program is the development of the Silverado property. Bought by Amfac in 1965, when the Isenberg concept of paying cash prevailed, Silverado is an example of "sunk" costs, as real-estate men say. There are all those dollars in the ground that can be recovered only through sales. Belief in the "present value of the dollar" analysis in real-estate acquisition never would have permitted the purchase of Silverado. Although smaller and with less potential for expansion than Kaanapali, it may be the better known of the two. The development of the 700 acres peripheral to the golf courses (Amfac added a second course) is under way, and 400 condominium units at an average price of $50,000 each have been sold in the past 5 years.

Other mainland ventures have presented problems too.

There was the purchase of a developer of mobile home sites. After several years of experimentation it was concluded that, notwithstanding the tremendous popularity of this form of housing in the West, the profit margins were not there.

Months were spent in trying to work out a satisfactory project in redevelopment with the federal and local governments in California. The beach front at Santa Monica and the Bunker Hill area of downtown Los Angeles are examples. Both got buried in red tape. As a consequence, Amfac has turned away from redevelopment to town-house construction in resort centers such as Palm Springs. It also searches out long-term, planned community projects, as in its joint venture on former Crocker family land adjoining Brisbane down the peninsula from San Francisco.

The Name of the Game

In relying on people like Hadley, another policy emerges: don't try to employ in-house capability. Cassiday has no engineers, planners, carpenters, or plumbers on his payroll. He is supported only by a small staff in California and young, aggressive Earl Stoner in Hawaii. They, in turn, have project managers for each current development. To the extent needed, they work with consultants on retainer or job out construction work to contractors and their subcontractors. Thus the staff is small, intimate, and fast-moving.

The question arises, "Why is all property development not centralized under the Asset Management Group?" Agriculture is developing land in Australia, Retail is building a department store–office building complex in San Francisco, and, as will be seen in Chapter 13, Hospitality is undertaking development in many areas, none more conspicuous than at the new Dallas/Fort Worth Airport. It will also be seen that the new

Food Group has cleared 8,000 acres in Washington for agricultural use. The answer is this: When the other groups get into activity with land and structures it is as a tool, only one of the many elements essential to the generation of their final product. In the case of Asset Management, land, money, and structures are its product, and its tools are ingenuity, imagination, and negotiating skill.

13

Western Hospitality Goes Aloha

Amfac's expansion into certain endeavors, like retailing, has been the logical evolution of a traditional business. Other developments, such as the processing of food, have been carefully plotted by company analysts; but entry into the "hospitality" field was, in many respects, forced upon it as a consequence of its decision to undertake the Kaanapali project on its own. There came a point where Amfac had a beautiful golf course and some graded ocean-front hotel sites, of 10 acres each, awaiting tenants where only brooding algarroba thickets stood before. Three hotels and a sprinkling of condominiums paying lackluster rents existed, their presence in effect being subsidized to get Kaanapali off the ground. Reviewing the yearly rental receipts, about $300,000 in 1966, it became evident that others were making money but Amfac wasn't.

At the head of the line, nearest the cash register, were the contractors. Then came the tenants, like Sheraton. Labor was doing all right, too. Kaanapali provided a battleground for the state's two leading labor unions. Rutledge of the Teamsters was entrenched with Sheraton and Hilton on Oahu and therefore in a position to organize their expansion on the neighboring Islands. These Islands, however, were the stronghold of Harry Bridges' ILWU, which, in its control of Pioneer Mill's sugar workers, dominated the labor market around Kaanapali. Women from the plantation villages were to be the source for hotel workers. Thus, as the battle joined, each union promised to get the better contracts, and so higher wages, for its members.

Then there were the tour operators and taxicab drivers, the airlines and the laundries, the insurance agents and the hula dancers, all making money off Amfac's investment. Standing back, hungering for some share in these rewards, Amfac concluded that it must find a place further up the line. Not being very gifted as hula dancers, that meant, to the executive group, getting into the hospitality field.

This is an oversimplification. Walker was under an injunction from his Board to diversify. It was a position he enthusiastically supported. The one chance in Hawaii, in the absence of natural resources, in the face of the decline of pineapple, and with quota limits on sugar production, was in the growing tourist travel to the state. Further, Gay and, later, Cox, in searching the national scene, reached the conclusion—shared by many others—that the hospitality business would provide one of the great opportunities of the 1970s. Increased leisure time, the growth of industrial pension plans coupled with larger social security benefits, rising income levels, increased mobility by auto and air, all encouraged participation. So the decision was made.

The Fred Harvey Legend

In surveying mainland companies already operating in the field, Amfac management identified a number of possible acquisitions. However, it was Director Hoffman, who died shortly thereafter, who suggested what seemed a natural: the legend of the West, the Fred Harvey organization.

Recalling that half the people in the country are under 25, it might be well to go back in time a bit and tell something of Fred Harvey for those too young to have ridden a train through the Southwest. He was an Englishman who, in the tradition of Dick Whittington, arrived in New York at the age of 15 with no cat but $2 in his pocket. At the same time that he was advancing in the restaurant business from busboy to proprietor in a New Orleans restaurant, he was working his way westward to seek opportunity. He served later as a clerk on the first mail car to operate west of the Mississippi. He became the owner of several properties in Kansas, so he knew the territory. Observing the lack of opportunity for passengers to take decent meals during the long railroad hauls of the West, the ex-restaurateur suggested to his employers that they set up dining rooms along the rights-of-way at logical stopping points. He was turned down, but when he took the idea to the then Burlington and Santa Fe it won quick acceptance. He established the first of the Harvey Houses on the second floor of a little red-brick depot in Topeka, Kansas, in 1876. Thus a century-old business was born.

The pattern of Harvey's service became a tradition of the West. At their peak there were 70 Harvey Houses, some of them hotels as well, spaced along the Santa Fe tracks which had been surveyed by camel-borne engineers only a few years before. He aged his bourbon in Deming, New Mexico, where he judged the humidity to be just about right. His waitresses, the Harvey Girls of film and fiction, were young women recruited with an eye for looks and personality and a stern regard for morality. Eventually there were to be 20,000 of them.

Each restaurant had a basket at the entrance where guests were required to deposit their weapons. Although a 13-course meal cost only 75 cents, Harvey was painstaking in his insistence on elegance in cookery and napery. Daggett Harvey, his grandson and current Amfac Board member, displays in his Chicago office relics of these early days, Irish linen and English silver; but lost are the songs the waiters sang to greet debarking passengers, along with the kitchen odors of solid Western food in preparation.

Harvey early began to stock novelties and gifts in counters adjoining his restaurants and was to become a major outlet for Indian artifacts in a Southwest that was only then being opened up to palefaces. Harvey's hobby was Indian art, and his collection, now housed in the Hurd Museum in Phoenix, includes baskets, beadwork, and silver jewelry. It was valued at over $600,000 when the family donated it to the Harvey Foundation, and it is regarded as the best collection of American Indian craftsmanship in existence.

After the Santa Fe closed the railside Harvey Houses in the interest of speedier passenger schedules, Harvey operated the dining cars on such luxurious transcontinental trains as the *Super Chief* for a time. The few remaining trains are being phased out by Amtrak, and the Santa Fe association is a memory but for a slender thread at the Grand Canyon. When the railroad ran a spur there in 1904, it called on Harvey to provide the food and lodging needs of tourists at the Canyon's rim. He leased land from the Santa Fe and built the El Tovar Hotel, overlooking the chasm, and thus opened America's greatest natural spectacle to the public.

When the Canyon was embraced by the National Park System in 1918, Harvey's long-standing association with the Park Service began. In time, it extended to hotels in the Sequoia and Kings Canyon Parks in the high Sierras and Mount Rainier in Washington, all since sold. The elite Furnace Creek Inn in Death Valley continues in the system.

Prior to its acquisition by Amfac in 1968, Harvey, with its major feeding operations suspended, sought other means to generate earnings. Some restaurants, such as the one in Cleveland's depot, with heavy, nonrailroad-oriented traffic, were continued. New sites were sought, which led to the purchase of the Spinning Wheel, a tearoom sort of operation outside Chicago. Another was the food service concession in the glamorous new Music Center in Los Angeles. There, among other things, Harvey operates an elegant top-floor restaurant overlooking the city's complex of freeways. In this establishment the founding Harvey would be proud to read the menu and fondle the cutlery.

In its search for new business, the Harvey organization logically tried other forms of feeding travelers. Restaurant concessions were won all the way from the Las Vegas and Ontario airports to Chicago and Grand Rapids, Michigan. A system of highways, called "tollways," serves Chicago, and there are seven Harvey establishments dotted along them with the inevitable gift shop as part of the scene.

Still the Harvey problem was more basic than the substitution of restaurants for those lost along the Santa Fe. For nearly 100 years that railroad had, in effect, been providing Harvey not only with customers but with much of the capital required in its business. All Harvey supplies were freighted free. It was the Santa Fe that built the stations that housed the restaurants.

The working capital shortage that followed the end of the

Santa Fe association presented the family-owned firm with a major problem. Even as it was turning down the lights at all railroad restaurants, save Cleveland, Chicago, and Los Angeles, it was making a public offering of the company's stock. The result was to put 36 percent of its ownership in nonfamily hands, but that did not solve its basic troubles. Thus, when Hoffman came up with the suggestion that Amfac consider Harvey, its situation resembled in many respects that of other Amfac acquisitions. It was a family-controlled institution, its owners needed liquidity, and the business needed Amfac's resources. The deal was made in June 1968. Immediately Harvey's President, Leslie Scott, ex-Dean of the Michigan State Hotel School, was put in charge of Silverado and the Beachcomber Hotel, then being planned for Waikiki, and urged to consider a hotel for Kaanapali. These arrangements turned out to be short-lived, as the Harvey management was engulfed in the purchase the following year of Guslander's Island Holidays.

The Great Gulch

No discussion of Harvey would be complete without comment on the Grand Canyon operation, which remains its major profit generator and a basic contributor to Amfac earnings. The Canyon has become America's greatest natural tourist attraction. Over 3 million people a year visit the grand gorge and marvel at its colored sculpture and shudder at the recollection of the collision of two sightseeing transcontinental flights that crashed in midair in 1956 and plunged more than 100 people to their deaths. The stories of the area, from the first attempts to ride the rapids of the Colorado River, 4,000 to 5,500 feet below, to the celebrated visit of President "Teddy" Roosevelt in the days when conservation and ecology were little-known words, are legion. Roosevelt, an outdoorsman and naturalist, urged the abandonment of the copper and asbestos mines, with names like "Lost Orphan" and "Last Chance," and the adoption of the Canyon as a national park. Perhaps the best-remembered remark about the Canyon is attributed to stone-faced General John J. Pershing, who toured it after World War I. Impatient with the recurrent quarrels of Europe, he observed, "It would make a good boundary between France and Germany."

Adjacent to the El Tovar Hotel is the Hopi Trading House, where Indians (often, in fact, University of Arizona graduates) perform their traditional rain dances. More recently, Harvey has built the Bright Angel Lodge, the Yavapai Lodge, the Grand Canyon Auto Lodge, and other structures, which have expanded the number of rooms in the Park to over 700.

At the bottom of the Canyon, usually reached by mule back, is the Phantom Ranch—a cluster of cottages for the overnight visitor. So popular is this trip that you have to book an animal in the spring to ride in the peak summer months. Notwithstanding an impressive Amfac passport, I couldn't rent one to go down on a Memorial Day weekend. This was not too distressing when I heard tales of scraped shins on canyon walls, heart attacks suffered by men my age, and occasional broken legs from jumping off during the descent. A squad of "emergency mules" is held in reserve to get troubled riders out. Visualize an "emergency mule" in a hard hat, painted red, pitons in his saddlebags, a climber's rope looped around the pommel of his saddle, ever alert while munching hay at the Canyon's rim.

While breakfast is no longer the steak and eggs, hash and wheat cakes, climaxed with apple pie and coffee, that the original Harvey offered, food in the Park is excellent and cheap. It comes with amazing promptness considering that Harvey serves 6,500 meals on a busy summer day.

Not the least of the problems faced in conducting operations in the Grand Canyon area is the maintenance of a coordinated program with the National Park Service. Although the association is cordial and has a 56-year history, the objectives of the two groups are not always the same. The Park Service sees the Canyon as a place for people of whatever description and as a wildlife and botanical reserve not to be disturbed by further construction. There are conservationists who would have the Service force Amfac to tear down El Tovar and other structures along the Canyon's rim to permit reflective contemplation by back packers and others with an outdoor bent. Amfac sees it as a resort to be oriented to hotel guests. While it is reconciled to the fact that few more hotel rooms can be built there, it is concerned about providing more public recreational facilities and dormitory space for hotel help.

Sedate Fred Harvey hired matrons to shepherd his young women and personally complimented each waitress who stayed on the job, unmarried, for 6 months. He would have had some problems with today's young women at the park. As they do at many colleges, they share the same dormitories with young men also employed there. Amfac's concern is less with the social aspects of this communal life than with the fact that the dormitories are so overcrowded that often, when one occupant is on duty, someone must use his bed to get some sleep.

Water is another problem. Pumped across a vast plateau that separates the north rim from the south rim, where Amfac is, there is enough of it for hotel needs. The government built the line and charges Amfac and other users in the Park $2.45 per 1,000 gallons. To discourage the eruption of motels and campsites at the Park's boundary, they charge $6 per

(36) Distribution of electrical products on the mainland has also had a dramatic growth. Here, too, the maintenance of inventories of as many as 8,000 different items at each location is a basic part of the business. So warehouses, such as the one pictured here, are essential to Amfac Electric Supply Co.

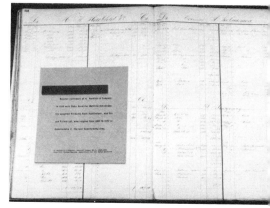

(37) For nearly 100 years Hackfeld's and his successors' primary concern with credit was in extending it to customers. The sums were substantial when large-scale operations were involved. Debt was avoided until after World War II. Now debt is deliberately employed as one source of capital used to expand the scope of Amfac.

(38) The Asset Management Group uses debt to finance construction of projects such as Camelot, a Honolulu condominium apartment building. Designed for singles and couples, its facilities are directed to recreation and the youthful life.

(39) This 1880 photograph shows passengers awaiting the train at the Santa Fe station in Topeka, Kansas, where travelers could eat in the Fred Harvey dining room. At their peak, there were 70 Harvey Houses along the Santa Fe tracks.

(40) These waitresses, the original "Harvey Girls," became a legend of the West, where, it was said, "They made the desert bloom." Fred Harvey carefully selected them for character, provided them with chaperons, and personally complimented each girl who remained unmarried for 6 months.

(41) In sharp contrast to the days of the Harvey Houses is this scene at the Coco Palms Resort on Kauai. One of a chain of Amfac resorts on each of the major Islands, Coco Palms has established a tradition of its own: torches are lit at nightfall and a loin-clothed Hawaiian youth blows a conch shell to signal that dinner is ready.

(42) For generations the magnificent beach at Kaanapali, Maui, was screened from the public by thickets of algarroba. Behind Black Rock, at the left, Amfac's Pioneer Mill Co. penned cattle and stored molasses, and, further inland, it grew sugar. In 1960 master planning of 1,000 acres in the area was begun.

(43) Shown here is a portion of the Kaanapali resort today. The beach tower, with attendant cottages, is Amfac's Royal Lahaina. Where the molasses tanks and cattle pens stood is a portion of the championship golf course, one of the many features of the resort. On Black Rock itself, with a commanding view of the Pacific and the neighboring Islands, is the Sheraton Maui. Kaanapali's development, now approaching 400 acres, is a function of the Asset Management Group. Operation of the Royal Lahaina and another Amfac hotel further down the beach is under the Hospitality Group.

(44) Amfac's Lamb-Weston, headquartered in Portland, Oregon, processes potatoes in plants throughout the Northwest. They are sold by the carload as frozen french fries. Here the potatoes emerge after having been cut to shape by the Lamb Water Gun Knife. This unique device forces them through a tube that encases a crossword-puzzle-shaped set of knives which are adjusted to the desired sizes. The potatoes are pushed through the blades by water.

(45) Cattle are an Amfac business in Colorado as well as in Australia. In this photograph animals destined for the Wilhelm Foods' Denver slaughterhouse enter one of two feed lots capable of finishing 100,000 head per year.

(46) In 1972, Amfac acquired Pacific Pearl Seafoods, a small shellfish company with two processing plants at Kodiak, Alaska. It plans to expand its markets if its sources of raw product continue to improve under the sound biological conservation practices it supports. Potato, beef, and seafood processing are the province of the Food Group.

1,000 gallons to outsiders. This penalty on those who seek to house the hordes that Harvey must turn away does not make for a happy neighborhood. The laments can be heard as far away as Washington's 18th and F Streets, where the Interior Department stands.

Clean across the Old Mojave

Harvey was many things when Amfac took over. There was the Victor Hugo Inn, one of the leading restaurants along the southern California coast, and the Ranch House at Valencia, California, where the Newhall Co. is building one of the first viable new towns in America. There were other airport operations, Palm Springs, Albuquerque, Lincoln, Nebraska, and Lansing, Michigan, among them. There was the chain of ever-present gift shops selling everything from beaded Indian jewelry to *Playboy* magazine.

Most of all, there was a tradition of the West, best reflected in the Cameron Trading Post. Located at the southwest entrance to the vast Navajo Indian Reservation that flanks the Grand Canyon, this is the principal meeting place for the tribe. It offers more than a conventional motel, clean dining room, and welcome to motorists driving through the isolated desert area. It is a place to see the Indian way of life while buying their silverwork, rugs, Chimango blankets, baskets, or a long-dead scorpion embedded in plastic. Here, also, the tribesmen pledge their jewelry, saddles, or other possessions to buy black felt hats, beads to be strung, and food to be eaten during the cold winters. Pledged jewelry is held 6 months, and if it is not redeemed it goes into Harvey gift shops across the country, where it is carefully identified as genuine. Once accustomed to the differences, it is easy to distinguish this jewelry from the more or less production-line silver and stone bracelets and baubles usually identified as Indian.

A bit of doggerel reflects Harvey's traditional place in the West:

> Harvey Houses, don't you savvy,
>   clean across the old Mojave,
> On the Santa Fe they string 'em,
>   like a string of Indian beads,
> We all couldn't eat without 'em,
>   but the slickest thing about 'em
> Is the Harvey skirts,
>   that hustle up the feeds.

Harvey people provided Amfac with more than managers and accountants. There are old-timers throughout the structure who helped contribute to its history. Larry Bridges runs a vestige of the old Harvey Houses at the Albuquerque Airport, where the waitresses wear the flowing gowns of the pioneer days and Indian kachinas (rain-bringers) adorn the walls. At the Canyon, Chef Marquez and his assistant, Gomez, recall the old days when they worked for Daggett Harvey's father, serving such famous people as Franklin Roosevelt and, more recently, John Wayne and Senator Barry Goldwater. The latter, when a Phoenix businessman, used the El Tovar as a personal retreat and also as a conference center for the executives of his department store.

There is Trammel Bowman, part Indian, who speaks the Hopi and Navajo dialects and purchases their goods for sale at the Cameron Trading Post and the gift shops throughout the system. Another old-timer is Jay Bozo, a trail foreman and muleteer, now retired on his own ranch and enjoying the proceeds of modeling for the "Marlboro Country" cigarette ads. Pete Lombardi, once a dining-car steward, would swing his way through a swaying diner singing operatic arias in Italian

and claiming to speak 13 languages while denying any knowledge of English. Then came the day when a foreign traveler
pointed to a menu item and asked, in a language Lombardi
really didn't know, what it was. Pete was heard to yell, with
operatic intensity, "It's fish, goddamnit."

Feeling the Way

Apart from the Harvey acquisition, it was somewhat surprising
that Amfac's first entry into the hospitality field on its own
behalf was not at Kaanapali. However, the company held a
lease at Waikiki on an area somewhat removed from the
beach but in the line of the pedestrian traffic generated by
that tourist target. Liberty House occupied the spot, and the
lease, which expired in 40 years, if renewed, seemed to provide an excellent opportunity. A high-rise hotel could go up
there, with an enlarged and modernized Liberty House occupy-
ing the bulk of the ground floor. Haste in making a decision
was dictated by the impending activation of a new zoning
ordinance, which required a greatly increased number of
parking spaces and reduced the footage that could be built
on the property. The lease was extended to 75 years. Plans
for a structure, necessarily awkward because it had to accommodate Liberty House and an inhospitable traffic pattern,
were completed and the building got under way before the
zoning deadline. Amfac was not alone in this race. Everyone
with property at Waikiki who had any intention of building
a hotel rushed to meet the same year-end date. As a result,
there were a great many more rooms than needed at the
beach in 1971, and few new hotels have been erected there
since the cutoff date.

Before the Amfac hotel was finished, the company sold a
half interest in it to United Air Lines in the expectation that

passengers from that largest of Island air carriers would help fill it. That United itself would become attracted by the hospitality field was not then apparent to either party; but with a change in management United announced a few months later its acquisition of the worldwide Western International Hotels chain. So it was that Harvey, upon joining Amfac, found itself not only with its own hospitality operations but also confronted with the construction of a hotel at Waikiki, the operating problems of Silverado, and the opportunity to build at Kaanapali.

Burns, the ex-sugar man who had been put in charge of the Harvey Division and engineered its relocation to headquarters in Brisbane, soon began to sense some of Harvey's problems. They were of a character that doesn't show up on the balance sheet or the profit and loss statements in the course of a negotiation. Among these was the fact that the once-proud Harvey name had become abused. The tollway restaurants in Chicago made no use of it; in fact, they corrupted it with a tentfold reading, "Ma Harvey recommends." The only trace of it on the menu of many restaurants in the chain was a Fred Harvey sandwich or salad. Nowhere was the restaurant itself identified as Harvey's. The last of the Harvey Girls is a 60-year-old at the Albuquerque Airport; she wears the flowing gown of the wagon days rather than the black-and-white outfit of Santa Fe times. The only black-and-white gowns long associated with Harvey are being worn by the Navajo waitresses in the remote Cameron Trading Post.

Apart from the fragmented restaurant operation, the aging company's other surviving undertakings were showing doubtful results. Attempts at industrial feeding, that is, serving factory or university cafeterias and the like, had proved a marginal and highly competitive business at best. A related activity and a logical successor to the Harvey tradition, in-flight feeding, the preparation on the ground of meals to be served aloft, presented its problems, too.

Harvey had gotten into this business in several locations, Grand Rapids, Albuquerque, and Las Vegas among them; yet here again its inadequate capitalization had prevented it from becoming a power in the field. The only reason the airlines don't do this for themselves everywhere (most now do so at major terminals) is that they can preserve precious capital by having someone else do it on less-frequented runs and cut further corners by introducing competitive bidding— Marriott versus Harvey, for example.

In Las Vegas, however, Harvey came up with a real college try and put in the $750,000 of Amfac money needed for a proper installation. An in-flight feeding facility is enormously complicated. To provide the three meals each day for United Air Lines alone (and six other carriers also serve Vegas) with its various classes of service and different types of aircraft, each with its own design of food bins and tableware, requires the preparation of 260 different types of servings daily. Then there is the liquor, which has to be guarded from pilferers with much counting and signing in and out and which requires the preparation of 4,500 pounds of ice cubes per day. While the facility provides a silver-washing and -polishing machine the plates must be scraped manually into garbage bins. It is amazing how much people don't eat. The unused rolls, potatoes, cake, and butter would feed a city, but public health authorities require that they be destroyed.

Hawaiian Hospitality

While absorbing the Harvey acquisition, Amfac was negotiating with Lyle Guslander, the owner of Island Holidays, the leading chain of neighboring Island hotels. "Gus" certainly ranks among the top two or three of the self-made men in postwar Hawaii, and he could probably outmatch any of them with the liquidity of his assets. His association with Amfac goes back a long way.

After a stint as manager of the cottages that made up the old Niumalu Hotel, where Hilton's Hawaiian Village now stands, Gus shifted over to Matson to run the Moana-SurfRider. But he was no corporate man and Matson at the time was a very complex corporation. Gus spotted opportunity in a 24-room Kauai hotel: opportunity, perhaps, to make a little money and set up a retirement Shangri-la for himself on his favorite Island. The working capital came in the form of a loan from mainland friends. It wasn't much—the rent was only $600 a month—but Gus did get an option to buy the shacky little hotel for $175,000 and lease a whole coconut grove surrounding it. At the time he didn't have $1,750 but the option was to become the basis for his fortune. It was quite a site for someone with vision. Tall palms reflecting their fronds in the canals, once used to barge sugar, lace the property and give it a Gauguin-like quality. To one side is the lazy Wailua River, where Isenberg and the Rices picnicked a century ago, and across the road is a beach.

If Gus needed help to achieve his vision, he went to the right place when he hired a petite blond fireball named Grace Buscher (who later became his wife) and installed her as manager. The rest is Island business history. Once an astrologer's assistant, Grace had a knack of foreseeing the future of tourist travel to Kauai. She also had a knack for keeping costs down, setting a good table, and using the romantic setting as a backdrop for the sort of drama most Island visitors expect and don't usually get. She initiated the sunset torchlighting ceremony now copied in many resort hotels. When she and Gus began enlarging Coco Palms they used huge clamshells for washbasins, lined the walls with imitation tapa, the native fabric beaten from mulberry bark, and decorated the rooms with tikis, the wooden figures that depict the many native gods.

During this period, when Gus started expanding Coco Palms, bought Maui Palms on Kahului Harbor, and left Matson, he began to dream about an Island-wide chain. At this time he also began to need credit badly. I asked him how he happened to sell to Amfac when there were other contenders. "Oh," he said, "I needed $25,000 desperately some years back and I went to Conch Smith and he let me have it. I paid it back but soon needed $40,000. I paid that back, but it wasn't long before I needed $100,000 and he let me have that. We've been close for a long time." The junior Walker recalls staying at Coco Palms the first week Gus took over. Amfac helped in other ways as well. It was in the liquor business when Gus started out and it stocked his bars; its construction materials business could help when it came time to expand; and it also sold kitchen and bar fixtures.

By the time Island Holidays had become big and prosperous Kaanapali was having its troubles with the Royal Lahaina, the elegant low-rise hotel that was spilling red ink over the manicured green of the lawns and golf course. Gus bought it for over $3 million, paying in Guslander fashion: some cash, some paper, some IOUs in the form of free room rent for the heirs of J. C. Earle, and, some say, a few Confederate bonds. Anyway, he got it. "All the place needed was business," Gus says in explaining the financial turnaround that followed his take-over. A high-rise building now abuts the languorous Royal Lahaina lobby, and, although some of the elegance has disappeared, business is booming.

By the time his negotiations with Amfac began, Gus had built his 24-room Coco Palms into a 200-room keystone to an arc of hotels that spans all the major Islands. Their sites commingle sand and sun, the primary tourist objectives, with the travelers' secondary interest, a romantic, historic setting.

On the beach near Coco Palms, Gus recently opened the Kauai BeachBoy, which provides a modern, popularly priced 250 rooms for the "forgotten guy in the back of the bus." Further around the Island on the sandy beaches of Poipu, which have the same exposure and climate as Waikiki, he converted the historic Knudsen home to a cottage-type hotel. The Knudsen name you will recall as Isenberg's introduction to Kauai.

Here "Kanuka," as the Hawaiians called second-generation Eric Knudsen, once spun his yarns of *menehunes*, the dwarfs that Hawaiians believed did their work and played their pranks unseen. He also told of the prowess of Hawaiian gods of his mountain home at Kokee and the great Alakai swamp that hangs like an apron from the hips of Mt. Waialeale, the wettest spot on earth. Gus's guests can no longer hear Kanuka's voice, but his tales have been collected into a book and make engrossing reading in this setting. Adjoining Waiohai Gus has built the Poipu Beach Hotel as a more conventional companion. Between the two hotels a tennis club and an additional 350 rooms are planned.

A Waikiki hotel is a must to any neighboring Island operator, since almost every first-time visitor wants to spend some days in that much-vaunted location. At Waikiki Gus operates the Holiday Isle, a block removed from the beach on bustling Lewers Street, where he opened a restaurant, Shipwreck Kelly's. Its nautical decor, borrowed in part from Don the Beachcomber's and Trader Vic's, is a madhouse of binnacles, ropes, pulleys, and ships' lanterns.

The Royal Lahaina on Maui, close to the old Island capital and whaling town of Lahaina, gives guests a feeling of participation in Island history. So does the King Kamehameha on

Hawaii, which overlooks not only the weighing-in spot for the Kona coast's marlin fishing fleet but also Mokuaikaua Church, established by the first "company" of New England missionaries when they arrived in the Islands in 1820. The King Kamehameha, a 140-room unit built in Gus's less opulent days and showing it, will be torn down to make way for a 460-room replacement that will make optimum use of the magnificent site.

The final establishment in Gus's chain when he sold out was still being built. It is the Keauhou Beach with 315 rooms. It was the first hotel to go up on the Bishop Estate development of a new resort some 10 miles down the Kona coast from the King Kamehameha. It reflects Gus's prosperity (some of his earlier hotels were built on the egg-crate principle) and is sumptuously done. It also reflects the collective good judgment of his group in knowing what makes the best resort hotel in Hawaii in terms of visitor satisfaction on the one hand and operation and profit on the other. His organization at the time included Grace Buscher; his brother-in-law to be, Frank Lippman, an engineer-builder who, like Hadley, gets a lot of structure for his dollars; George H. Shipman, his money man; Ron Barr, then manager of the Royal Lahaina and dean among Gus's hotel men; and Myrtle Lee, now President of Island Holidays.

Gus hired Myrtle Lee, a Chinese woman, out of Hilo High School years ago to become a reservations clerk. For years now, she has headed an organization of over 100 people devoted solely to filling his hotels. With a computerized reservation system and offices in New York, Chicago, Seattle, Los Angeles, and San Francisco, she has quite a domain. As if she had nothing else to do, she makes periodic swings throughout the country and the Pacific, presenting to travel agents and convention group managers live Hawaiian entertainment, slide shows, and a strong personal appeal and incentive for them to settle on Hawaii as a destination, with Island Holidays as their host. In this connection, not because he liked it but because a neighboring Island hotel operator needs to be in the transportation business to funnel travelers to his hotels, Gus got into that business as well. He now runs the second largest operation in the state, Hawaiian Discovery Tours.

When Gus and his associates sold out for 367,500 shares of Amfac stock (then quoted at 50) in July 1969, some 50,000 shares of it went to Myrtle Lee, to whom he had no formal obligation, in acknowledgment of her many contributions. The 367,500 shares was a compromise figure which Gus accepted because Grace, whom he married at that time, thought it a favorable combination under the horoscope. The Guslanders have since given $1 million to the University of Hawaii to establish a professorship in its hotel management school.

In the year between the acquisition of Harvey and that of Island Holidays, Harvey, with Les Scott in the lead, had just enough chance to acquaint itself with the opportunities presented by the new association. Finalizing the plans for the Waikiki Beachcomber, choosing a hotel site at Kaanapali, encouraging the purchase of the first of a planned string of airport hotels (the Airport Marina in Los Angeles) and the revitalization of a faltering management of the clubhouse and condominiums at Silverado were all in the Harvey mill when the Island Holidays deal was consummated. Thus was introduced, as the ancient Hawaiians said, "red in the clouds at sunset," or trouble.

Changes Come Fast

Island Holidays, with its vital performance record and promising future, introduced a conflict in the philosophy of running the hospitality business. The academic but activist Scott was given, for the first time since joining Harvey, the opportunity to move with adequate working capital and credit. He was, nevertheless, a stranger to the powers in Honolulu. On the other hand, there was Guslander, who had it made and made it himself, and knew them well. He had doubts about some of the National Park operations and, to prove that he was not pulling any punches, the economics of the Amfac-inspired Waikiki Beachcomber. It was inevitable that Guslander would get the nod and have the hospitality field turned over to him.

The conflict didn't end there. Gus, who would prefer to be known as an ex-bellboy than as an alumnus of the Cornell Hotel School, laid a heavy hand on the Harvey structure. Employees with 30 years' service were brought out from Chicago to Brisbane and, after sitting on their hands a while, given early retirement. Fred Harvey started using Chase and Sanborn coffee a century ago and his reputation for good coffee became a sort of trademark. Gus, a coffee drinker too, threw it out in favor of his own brand. The most unkind cut of all came when, deciding the Sequoia and Kings Canyon National Park operations could not be made profitable, he sold them off. His reasons were good: the short season and the inadequacy of the hotel structures. Since Harvey had bought them only a few years before, this was a blow not only to relations with the Park System but to pride in business judgments as well.

Relentless Guslander, who probably has spent more passenger hours flying between the Hawaiian Islands than some commercial pilots on the route, couldn't bring that kind of personal supervision into play with Harvey. He had difficulty in expanding his control as far east as Cleveland. He spotted good men in critical places, Bruce Curtis from American Airlines to the Grand Canyon, for example; but his relations with others deteriorated to a point where he had to spend half his time in Brisbane to pull mainland hospitality operations together.

Even as some aspects of Harvey were disintegrating, others were growing. A newly built airport hotel in San Francisco was bought and renamed the Airport Marina. A new low-rise hotel, conference- and convention-oriented and extremely well air-conditioned to meet the extremes of Fresno weather, has been built near the airport of that California valley city. There is a big airport hotel open now in Albuquerque to complement the airport restaurant. Recently completed is a 600-room establishment in the Dallas/Fort Worth Airport complex, which promises to be in the Texas style in every sense of the phrase. An Airport Marina Hotel in Las Vegas is next.

The job of re-creating the Harvey image, salvaging the remnants of its management, and expanding the concepts of airport hotels and Shipwreck Kelly's restaurants now seems well under way. The big need is people and Gus is out to get them. He has a saying: "You don't train hotel men; you steal them."

Meanwhile, he has developed some priorities to govern mainland undertakings. First, he sees the need for more hotels and surveys the opportunities from Fairbanks to Atlanta. Next, he thinks there is room for more restaurants like Shipwreck Kelly's. Although its decoration is nautical, the menu is strictly traveling salesmen—steak, chops, potatoes, and pie. So too are the waitresses. Miniskirted and white-booted, they are a far cry from the Harvey Girls. Some say Guslander owns more white boots than did the Marquis de Sade. In any case, the formula is working well in the airport hotels. Gus has used it in the Spinning Wheel in Chicago's suburbs, giving that teahouse-type establishment a swingers' wing. Finally, while he is dubious about other National Park operations, he is enthusiastic over those 3 million people a year at the Grand Canyon. "The trouble is that they don't come in the off-season," he says. The solution he sees is not in more hotel rooms, which the Park Service would oppose, but in convention and conference facilities to draw business and professional meetings in the fall and winter months.

Guslander, always in motion, never misses an opportunity to sell. He finds his recreation in cooking, using that pleasure to help him sell, too. When in Hawaii he goes to Kauai every weekend to a place he and his wife have at Wailua. Every Friday and Saturday night 16 guests from his Kauai hotels are selected to join them as he prepares Chateaubriand, beans, and frozen mangoes flambé over passion fruit sherbet. While the guests usually are prominent repeat visitors, travel agents, writers, and the like, he has played host to Frank Sinatra, Bing Crosby, King Leopold, and the former Lynda Bird Johnson. They counted recently, and at these weekend dinners they have served over 1,500 guests.

I asked Gus what was the biggest problem facing a hotel man in Hawaii today, expecting some answer related to seasonality, overbooking, or the competitive practices of the big chains, maybe even labor unions. But his answer was "sand." He went on, "They leave their towels on it to wash away when the tide comes in. They track it through the lobby. They stretch out on sofas without washing it off. When they wash it off they don't do it at the taps outside; they do it in the showers and clog the plumbing." Pausing, he reflected, then added, "There is nothing more trouble than sand."

Hearing this, I concluded it was this sort of common sense applied to his business that has put Gus where he is. He admires Hanko Walker and probably continues to work because of his pleasure in the association. In expressing this admiration he is, as in all things, very explicit. Thus it is that, somewhat to Hanko's embarrassment, one airport hotel has a cocktail area called the "Henry Walker" lounge.

There remains a question of how long Hanko can keep Gus content with the corporate life, with its environment of memoranda, 5-year plans, "contribution," and conferences. All those Amfac dividends and the opportunity to cook on a Kauai beach every night may move Gus out to pasture. One hopes not. Amfac wouldn't be as much fun or as profitable without him.

14

Make Mine Beef and Potatoes

Amfac has always been close to the food business, though it was not too successful as a processor and marketer of pineapple and coffee. With the coming of the supermarket chains to Hawaii, it abandoned its distribution of a full line of food products to retail establishments. It continues as the Island's largest producer of sugar. Walker and Cox, in their analysis of the possibilities in diversification, found they headed a company which traditionally had dealt in food but had only a small role in that basic and growing segment of American commercial life.

It was evident to them that changes in eating habits were occurring. The number of meals taken out has increased from 20 to 30 percent in the last 20 years. Instead of eating three times a day, Americans are snacking four, five, and even six times a day. Fast-food operations are taking over the bulk of the restaurant business. Young people, freed from the house by the automobile, are packing the kids in the back to eat at McDonald's or munch their way through a meal at a drive-in movie. At home, TV dinners or pizzas are the custom.

The idea of starting up a food production operation in Hawaii, unless it involved an exotic item like mangoes or macadamia nuts, was unthinkable. Also, these products would not meet Amfac's needs either from the standpoint of time (most tree crops are so slow to mature) or of volume. Walker and Cox wanted something that would increase sales and "contribution" promptly. The timing requirements also ruled out the possibility of starting out fresh on the mainland as a producer or processor. For that matter, the sugar-oriented management would have had problems in staffing such an undertaking, much less marketing its production. All criteria pointed to the acquisition of an existing company with a potential for growth in the changing patterns of American feeding habits. So the search was on.

Lamb-Weston Story

This line of reasoning, within the parameters already set up by Walker (growth should be in the West and in a line of endeavor in which the management had some experience), suggested a processor or a grower-processor for the fast-food market. Setting aside the farmer-owned cooperatives, not too many organizations meet this description. Quick to come to their attention was the family-owned Lamb-Weston Co., a frozen french fries producer headquartered in Portland with plants in Oregon, Washington, and Idaho. But Cox, who was handling the negotiation, found that F. Gilbert Lamb, the controlling shareholder and family spokesman, was not ready to sell. Determined to get into the field, Cox turned to a smaller competitor, Prosser, and made the acquisition, bringing in as well a 20,000-acre tract of prospective farmland along the banks of the Columbia River.

Several months later Cox, finding himself in the Northwest and still wishing he had been able to acquire the larger, more aggressive Lamb-Weston, decided to give it another try. This time "Gib" Lamb seemed favorably inclined and the lawyer in Cox tenaciously set about working out an agreement, with special consideration to the Lambs' tax problems. Prosser had to be sold lest Amfac encounter antitrust questions. Some of the Amfac stock to be exchanged with the Lambs had to be sold through a public offering. The farmland acquired in the Prosser deal was retained and put into cultivation to supply a new plant being built by Lamb-Weston in nearby Hermiston, Oregon. Cox stitched it all together in 1971, selling Prosser to Twin City Foods and putting 238,080 shares of Lamb's Amfac stock in the packaged offering of new Amfac shares along with the holdings of the Hoffman heirs.

Thus Amfac had the nucleus for its sixth group, Food. It was to be built around the capabilities of John L. Baxter, Jr., President of Lamb-Weston. More of him later, but first a look at his company and its history.

While Hackfeld wasn't poor, the founders of many of the companies that have joined his venture seem to have been. Gib Lamb is no exception. His father was a modest fruit broker in the town of Milton Freewater, Oregon. Gib's job, while still in his teens, was to ride the caboose of freight trains carrying carloads of apples consigned by his father to dealers throughout the country and oversee their distribution. This was in 1933 and apples weren't selling very well even when offered by bankrupt stockbrokers on Wall Street corners;

so the senior Lamb sent a shipment to England with Gib convoying it. When he arrived there he learned that his father had been killed in an auto accident. On his return home, 18-year-old Gib and his 16-year-old brother, Reese, started picking up the pieces. By 1938, Clarence Birdseye having led the way, the freezing of food was beginning to win favor. The brothers leased an apple storage warehouse and converted one room to a cold-storage plant, where they froze strawberries, marketing them through a cooperative called Norpac, still prominent in the Northwest.

This change-over from fresh to frozen products was the first of several moves that led to the Lamb brothers' success. The next was World War II and the action of the War Production Board in limiting the use of tin. Faced with an increased demand for frozen products, the Lambs talked York, a manufacturer of cold-storage equipment, into leasing them a $50,000 freezing tunnel. Their net worth at the time was $10,000, but they had a contract with Campbell Soup, which had previously shipped peas in tin, to freeze part of their crop. During the war this business expanded and the list of customers grew to include such names as Smith Canning and Heinz. The Lambs abandoned the fresh fruit business and concentrated entirely on the freezing of peas. Then a fire destroyed their plant, leaving them with $300,000 of insurance proceeds and the rentals from a warehouse.

Then came a pause in the Lamb-Weston story. While vacationing in Alaska, Gib happened on an old issue of *Fortune* containing an article describing Clarence Streit's movement, "Union Now," and its goal of a federation of North Atlantic nations. He was so moved by it that he went to Washington and volunteered his time to help the cause. He served for a year, but finding that he was being used increasingly as a fund raiser he became disillusioned and returned to Oregon.

In 1950 the Lambs saw an opportunity to get back into the freezing business, and this became the third turning point in the Lamb-Weston story. Using their insurance money, they bought at auction a cooperative pea cannery plant in Weston, Oregon, that had gone bankrupt and converted it to a freezing operation. They changed the corporate name from F. G. Lamb & Co. to Lamb-Weston to appease the local growers who had invested in the plant. They processed their first pack in 1951. Though Lamb-Weston finally packed about 10 percent of the country's frozen peas, Amfac found the operation unprofitable and later sold this plant.

The Potato Purchase

Since this is potato country, Gib turned his inventive mind from peas to the possibility of freezing potatoes. The first company to do so, the Snow Flake Canning Co. in Maine, had long since proved the marketability of the product, so the problem was not so much if it could be done as how best to do it. Processing potatoes is a business of moving water and applying heat. It is also a wasteful one. Peels alone account for 26 percent of the weight of a potato. Damaged raw material can run from 10 to 80 percent of the crop, depending on the state at which it is harvested. On the average, 50 percent of the raw material is lost through some form of damage or defect and can only be converted to cattle feed. Handling methods thus became the principal objective of Gib Lamb's study.

The other problem was to find a means of slicing the potatoes into french fry sections of the greatest length and with the greatest recovery. The desirability of this from the production point of view is obvious but length is also an asset in the marketplace. Most fast-food operators serve french fries in a container of some sort, usually a bag or sack. At wholesale, french fries are bought by weight. Long french fries fill up a sack with less weight than short ones and so command a premium.

Such considerations led to the development of the Lamb Water Gun Knife and with it the next turning point in the fortunes of the company. Gib Lamb is a tinkerer if not an inventor. One night, while experimenting with dehydration, an idea struck him, and in 24 hours he had developed his gun. This implement feeds potatoes into a long tube under intense water pressure and forces them through a grill of knife-sharp blades that slice them into lengths of precisely equal widths. The blades, being adjustable, can be set to slice potatoes of different sizes, and the use of water minimizes the damage.

Convinced he had the answer to his problems, Lamb built the largest frozen potato processing plant in the world at American Falls, Idaho. With 9 acres under the roof, he produced in such volume that he became too important a part of the total sales of Norpac. Members of the co-op feared Lamb-Weston domination of their affairs. There is some evidence that there was a subtle sabotage of Lamb-Weston potato sales in the 1960s as a consequence.

Mass Marketing

Lamb-Weston recognized the need for a different means of marketing the product. Gib invited Ed Watson, a former Vice President of Pict-Sweet Frozen Foods and a member of his Board, to come out of retirement and manage the company with the specific responsibility for establishing its own marketing organization. Watson built well. Within a short time Lamb-Weston was marketing heavily along the East Coast and felt the need for an Eastern production facility. Thus in 1965 it acquired the Snow Flake Canning Co. and with it its President, John L. Baxter, Jr. (which proved to be a more important event than buying the cannery).

As the frozen potato business grew, Lamb-Weston continued to expand. Purchase of a new but defunct plant in Quincy, Washington, in the northwest corner of the Columbia basin, introduced it in 1967 to the superior quality of the potatoes grown there. In 1968 a fire destroyed the Snow Flake factory in Maine. This facility was not replaced. Despite a long-standing reputation, Maine potatoes do not match the quality of Idaho's and Idaho's yields do not match those of the Columbia basin. Baxter was brought to Portland, and Lamb acquired a second plant in the basin, in Connell, Washington, with the insurance money. As an aside, $5 million was spent to triple its production and install two new processes paralleling patents held by McDonald's, the hamburger people. The resulting contention delayed Lamb-Weston from becoming a McDonald's supplier for some years.

The posture of Lamb-Weston when Cox prevailed upon the Lambs to join up was that of a vegetable processor with $55 million in sales. It packed over 300 million pounds of frozen potatoes, 80 percent of which were frozen french fries, constituting nearly $50 million of those sales. Two-thirds of its potatoes were distributed under the Lamb-Weston label. Equally as important as the physical facilities acquired with Lamb-Weston was the fact that Amfac gained a proven marketing organization, an ingenious research department, and a skilled executive in the food field.

Watson had built, and Baxter had refined, a marketing structure under a single vice president. Under regional managers operating out of Portland, there are nine district managers in distribution centers throughout the country. They in turn direct the energies of about 70 food service brokers, all of whom maintain frozen-food warehouse facilities as a service to their customers. Two-thirds of all Lamb-Weston products are sold east of the Mississippi, and most go into fast-food outlets. To further develop that market, the company operates three mobile test kitchens that move from city to city, where brokers schedule them for demonstrations with prospects. Appropriately, for a frozen-food salesman, one of these units is operated by Charlie Johnson, a full-blooded Eskimo.

Research, while directed to frozen-food products, is permitted to range beyond vegetables. There is a garage in Portland, darkened now and converted to growing mushrooms. Vice President and Research Director Bruce H. Morgan thinks he can get good yields using a new compost made from lumber wastes and can harvest the mushrooms mechanically. A further interest is aquaculture—the controlled production of fish and crustaceans under special conditions of water temperature and plankton population—which led to the purchase of a small Alaskan shellfish cannery and a 110-foot crab boat for it to operate.

Other new products are frozen fruit turnovers, processed at the rate of 22 a minute, and two styles of onion rings. One is extruded from chopped onions and shaped to represent the familiar onion ring. The application of the extrusion principle to food opens wide fields for further research. There are many uses for extruded protein, fish or animal. Shaped attractively, perhaps preseasoned, in portions sized for fast-food feeding, airline meals, and TV dinners, extruded protein could find a multitude of markets.

Further Foods

Finally, in the merger Amfac got Jack Baxter, who is their kind of guy. He is poised, organized, and a model administrator, and his family has been in the food business for generations. His great-grandfather packed corn for the Union Army in the Civil War. Baxter himself has been in the business since his graduation from Bowdoin. A trim, fast-moving 54, he succeeded Watson as Executive Vice President of Lamb-Weston in 1967. Tapped by Walker and Cox to head Amfac's new Food Group, he has been named an Executive Vice President and is confident of meeting the standards imposed on him, a growth rate of 10 percent or more a year. He knows it will not be easy and realizes that he can only achieve it through acquisitions, avoiding any field that is becoming obsolete, such as, he says, "the oatmeal business." Here is how he puts it:

> Of course, we are going to look for diversification. Our current business is commodity-oriented in that the raw materials of potato and fat represent 64 percent of our finished product cost and labor only 17 percent. There is low input of specific skills or proprietary information. Finally, we are totally carbohydrate and should diversify into proteins.
>
> In considering acquisitions, we still have to look closely at profitability and management. A high-return company in the food industry will demand a high multiple, which means we will be looking mostly at companies having returns lower than Amfac goals. This means we will be constantly faced with sort of semi-turnabout situations. I'm not going to tell you today what we are going to do because I don't know.

Since being named Chairman of the Food Group, Baxter has removed himself from the flow of Lamb-Weston administrative details. His first acquisition, Wilhelm Foods of Denver, resulted from the fact that per-capita beef consumption has increased from 55 to 113 pounds in 36 years.

David Wilhelm is a fit 50, a Chicago Cudahy, a Yale graduate, and a much-decorated World War II fighter pilot. He has strong convictions about meat packing. He argues, compellingly, that most packing plants are in the wrong places. With five partners, he set out in the early 1960s to prove it. They acted on his conviction that it was pointless to take feed to cattle; instead, move the cattle to where the feed is, and that is always near water. A second conviction was compatible: slaughter when the cattle are ready, not when the packer is. Two feed lots, capable of supporting up to 70,000 animals, were established in Colorado in support of these views. Next was the construction of a packing plant in Denver with holding facilities for animals brought in from the feed lots so that their slaughter could be conducted as a conveyor-type operation when they were ready.

Cattle in the feed lots have been financed by selling units to investors seeking a profit on resale and tax deferment. A service fee for administration and care of the animals is charged, and accurate accounts of the costs of each unit, as well as the final return on the sale to a meat packer, are kept. At the conclusion of the cycle, shareholders are given their share of the proceeds or losses. The investor's loss is limited by contract to a fixed amount per head.

The next expansion of the Food Group, also into proteins, was the acquisition of what is now Pacific Pearl Seafoods, with two floating processing plants for crab and shrimp at Kodiak Island in Alaska. A new shore-based processing plant is being constructed adjacent to the floating plants to increase the production capabilities of Pacific Pearl Seafoods. The company, which has a firm position in the quality crab and shrimp markets, was established by Ivar Wendt, who continues to supervise the entire operation.

Speculation on the future of the Food Group introduces the larger question of "Whither Amfac?"

15

Whither Amfac?

L et us consider Amfac's record since Walker, Cox, and Gay got the company moving again:

Earnings per Share (Restated)

1967	1968	1969	1970	1971	1972	1973
$0.85	$1.28	$1.52	$1.71	$1.92	$2.16	$2.36

Though the corporate cookie is said to crumble that way, dollars do not always reflect the full degree of corporate accomplishment. In the case of Amfac there have been some major achievements that are evidenced only in part by these figures. They have yet to reflect their full impact.

Restructured Amfac

The first achievement is the assembly of people. Ten years ago 11 men were listed as principal officers of the company; of these, only Walker remains now. While illness and retirement account for some of the changes, the figure also reflects a general reorganization of the executive force as well as the multiplication of responsibilities that has attended the company's rapid growth. Today 18 principal officers are listed, 2 of them Executive Vice Presidents and 7 of them Senior Vice Presidents, where there was only 1 Senior Vice President in 1964. The change among the Directors has also been dramatic. Only 3 of the 17 who are now in service sat on the Board 10 years ago. This is a Board, remember, which saw Gaylord Wilcox serve for 50 years and Walter Dillingham for 45.

This realignment has not been confined to the corporate stratosphere. Below the vice-presidential level there has been constant redeployment and reassignment as men were tested and proved or found wanting. Nowhere has this been more conspicuous than in the controller's department. There D'Arcambal has created a structure to help him pull the financial analysis and reporting function of the six diverse groups into a coherent whole that provides headquarters with reliable and comparable figures promptly.

Another great change not fully evidenced in reported earnings is the redeployment of resources. That is the business

TABLE 1 *Contribution of Groups as Percentage of Amfac Total*

Group	1969	1970	1971	1972	1973
Agriculture	11	6	4	8	21
Distribution	6	7	9	14	15
Retail	31	31	31	28	—
Asset Management	20	30	28	27	33
Hospitality	14	9	12	12	10
Food	18	14	16	18	19
Discontinued and other operations	—	3	—	−7	2

of getting out of assets with a low return on investment and into areas with better margins and growth potentials.

While the figures in Table 1 suggest some trends, the point to be made is that they are no more than weather vanes indicating shifting directions that may not be reflected in profits for years to come. The details behind them are important also in assisting management to identify problems early, permitting prompt correction. To date the response has been fast. Witness the abandonment of the operation in Uruguay and the RhodesWAY stores.

Less easy to quantify is the other diversification, the geographic one. One of the Islands' leading banks, First Hawaiian, recently put out a brochure titled "Hawaii—The Most Vulnerable State in the Nation." It is basically an appeal for Congress to do something to keep the supply lines to and from Hawaii open in the face of labor disputes involving overseas shipping. This position undoubtedly has the support of the business community and probably the bulk of the consumers, certainly those who are not members of the seafaring and longshoremen's unions. Whether this appeal is effective or falls on deaf ears in Washington is another question.

The very fact that this substantial and knowledgeable institution would put its name to a pamphlet with that title underscores the significance of Amfac's shift of the bulk of its activities to the mainland. Two-thirds of its sales and employees are now there. That this leaves the remainder of its business in Hawaii still vulnerable is not to be argued. A smaller share in the Islands might be desirable, but a point has already been reached where the geographic diversification permits an averaging process to function. As evidence there is the year 1972, when Hawaii was plagued with a series of shipping strikes. Amfac was nevertheless able to achieve all its profit and growth goals.

The final factor at play, the one that will take the longest time to manifest itself in earnings per share, is the evolution of the planning function. At various times the company has moved before the winds; at others it has had some pretty exotic double-dome thinking given to its future plans. Today, while completely committed to the need for planning, the best template is still being tested. For several years decentralized 5-year plans were required of every group and processed through the Operations and Financial Review Committee. It then developed that these plans, to be updated annually, were often out of date in months. Mistaken views, competitive developments, and new opportunities required their early modification.

Plotting the Future

A sort of a studious judgment has now been imposed by corporate headquarters on all such projections. This is more than the intuitive type of decision making Isenberg used. From experience and the cross-fertilization of ideas there is a consensus at the top, a feeling for the way the company should go. Despite Walker's conviction that growth should be in the West and in the lines of business the company knows best, this top-level intent is flexible. Berry is allowed to "follow the sun," which rises in the East, and Baxter gets into the frozen-fish business, which is a far cry from sugar, which Amfac knows best.

The following discussion of the groups' objectives is based on conversations with their leaders, as well as some hints dropped at headquarters and the clairvoyance of the writer.

Retail will pause for several years to digest the expansion of Liberty House to the mainland and the conversion of certain of the RhodesWAY mass-merchandising sites to full-fledged Rhodes department stores. This period of analysis in regard to its aims will not prevent growth of JM's boutiques, which will continue to "follow the sun," nor will it preclude further expansion, over the long term, through acquisition of another major retail chain. Thus, though Amfac still likes the retail business, it will not be quite as aggressive with its expansion in the years immediately ahead.

Distribution will continue to be on the prowl for new opportunities while modifying some past patterns of operation. In Hawaii the Construction Materials Division will be run on an even more austere basis. On the other hand, Richardson sees a major new opportunity for distribution in Hawaii and on the mainland in providing equipment, such as pumps and filters, solvents and cleaners, that will be in increasing demand as legislation designed to protect the ecology and the environment finds widespread enforcement.

Agriculture will expand sugar production in Hawaii to the extent that land availability and sugar quotas permit. Offsetting influences include the ever-increasing cost of labor and the inroads on cane land to provide housing for Honolulu. Papaya production on the Island of Hawaii, being extended now to 750 acres, can prove a modestly profitable sideline for this group. There is ample land for further expansion in this fruit, as the papaya tree is a fast grower and finds lava soils, which are inhospitable to other crops, congenial. However, the real potential for the Agriculture Group may be in western Australia. Here the prospects are limited only by the market. While wool is a somewhat mercurial commodity, the rapidly growing world demand for protein, particularly in the form of beef, presages long-term growth there.

Asset Management, with its independent resources, will continue to flourish, its pace regulated only by its ability to absorb acquisitions and meld new managements into its control structure. The horizons here are wide indeed. Amfac, as noted earlier, has access to lands that are excellently situated in Hawaii. It can be expected to develop them at a rate dictated by the growth in tourism to the Islands and the growth of urban Honolulu. Travel to Hawaii is expected to double in the next 10 years and Honolulu will grow with it, if at a more modest rate. The only thing that might interfere with this, other than a major economic downturn, is the imposition of government measures to limit growth. Though seriously debated, such restraints do not seem likely to be adopted. There may be difficulties in getting all the zoning Amfac would like adjoining Honolulu because of the emotional opposition to urbanizing prime agricultural land. On the mainland its recently announced joint venture on Crocker lands near Brisbane, California, will occupy it for many years, as will the development of more town houses in resort centers. There is no directive that this activity achieve the 10 percent or more growth goals set for the company as a whole. Walker and Cox recognize the dangers in pressing precarious land development too hard. On the other hand, the talented young staff under Cassiday may be expected to come up from time to time with a coup like San Diego (see Chapter 12).

Hospitality, facing no land limitations in Hawaii, should grow with the number of travelers to the state. There is, however, this qualification: the Japanese visitors coming to Hawaii in increasing numbers will probably want to stay in hotels that are being bought up or built by Japanese interests. On the mainland this group expresses satisfaction with its airport-oriented establishments and is actively expanding them. There is a feeling that opportunities also exist in commercial hotels in downtown locations, but Guslander is not, like some of the major chains, a real estate operator wheeling and dealing in hotels. His dedication is to the hospitality field and consequently hotel operation is his business. The expansion of the

Shipwreck Kelly's restaurants into a national network is a different matter and is presently on a back and very low burner as far as the Operations and Financial Review Committee is concerned.

The newest group, Food, is prospering and promises to develop with the changing eating habits and the growing emphasis on convenience feeding in the United States. Owing to beef shortages, the demand for fresh meat was so great that the full potential of marketing it in frozen and extruded forms remained untested. For some time to come the seafood venture will explore production methods and marketing techniques for protein from the sea. While there is no prospect for dramatic growth in this group in the immediate future, it does not have to contend with any restrictions, as sugar has.

The prospects for the six areas of Amfac activity vary, then, from a walk to a gallop. The average of the lot, Walker and Cox are confident, will continue to generate at least a 10 percent increase in Amfac earnings each year. They visualize, however, that in the future there will be greater reliance on internal growth and improvement than on acquisition.

Half a Century of Walkers

For nearly 50 years the Walker family has been associated with Amfac. H. Alexander ("Sandy") Walker, who joined the company as its Corporate Secretary in 1927 at $750 a month, was no kin of the missionary *kamaaina* Alexander family; rather, he said because he was the youngest of 11 children, his family just ran out of names. His father, John S. Walker, was a Scotsman who came to the Islands after getting mountain fever guiding Mormon parties through the Rockies and the fabled Donner Pass. He worked briefly for the Hackfelds in the 1850s, then married the Lahaina-born daughter of a ship chandler from Australia named McIntyre. Sandy Walker was first and last a sugar man. In his youth "King Cane" ruled

Hawaii and was its prime topic of conversation. Everyone watched the yields and earnings of the many plantations with the attention that they now pay to the Dow Jones averages. Sugar stocks were given to children at birth, served the thrifty in lieu of savings accounts, and were often part of a dowry.

After attending Harvard briefly, Sandy served with the Red Cross during World War I, doing relief work in Siberia. On his return he joined the HSPA, specializing in labor matters while gaining a knowledge of the research work of its experimental station and an acquaintanceship with each of the plantations on the four sugar-growing Islands. He then went to work for American Factors, as it was then known, and after 6 years he was catapulted into the Presidency when his predecessor was killed in a yachting accident.

That was in 1933, when Congress began passing New Deal legislation to cure every economic ailment, including that of sugar. In 1934 Walker began a series of trips to Washington that were to make him and his wife habitués of the Mayflower Hotel and the F Street and Chevy Chase Clubs. The first legislation governing sugar, the Jones-Costigan Sugar Act, which Hawaii opposed, was declared unconstitutional. The subsequent law, which Walker helped frame, was passed in 1938 and has endured, despite frequent amendments, until the present uncertainties arose.

In the course of these long years in Washington the Walkers made many friends. Among them were such distinguished figures as John Foster Dulles, Ambassador Ellsworth Bunker, and publisher Henry Luce. After Dulles became Secretary of State, whenever he was in Hawaii he would stay at the Walkers' ocean-front retreat, Muliwai, to rest and work in privacy.

The Walkers' Honolulu home, where ancient palms tower over gardens jeweled with orchids, has long-time Amfac associations. It was built by George Rodiek before his World War I troubles began. It was then bought by a Wilcox of the Kauai clan and was subsequently sold to the Walkers.

During World War II the Walkers' long-time friend, Delos Emmons, returned to Honolulu as a lieutenant general and as military governor and Army commander under another old friend, Admiral Chester W. Nimitz. Although Walker was given to working in his shirtsleeves and was once seen serving as a swamper when one of his truck drivers needed help with an awkward load, he was also very much at the top of Hawaii's social pyramid.

On retirement, Walker continued as Chairman of the Board during the early tribulations of his successors. But he was no longer even a Director when his son, Hanko, began to surface in the executive suite; nor was either of them on the Board when Hanko was named Executive Vice President.

Hanko had all the advantages available to children of influential parents. There are childhood pictures of him visiting with Shirley Temple and with the great Hawaiian swimmer, Duke Kahanamoku. He was an avid reader as a boy and still is. He took tennis, riding, and golf lessons. In 1937 his parents brought him to Washington to learn his way around and meet some of their friends. This was followed by St. Paul's, Harvard, and the Navy. That tour, culminating in his marriage, was marked by a bachelor dinner staged for him by Admiral Nimitz. Not bad for a lieutenant junior grade! He had met his wife, Nancy, on a blind date through a fellow naval officer. She continued as a New York social worker while he took business courses at Columbia.

When he elected to return to the Islands, his father did everything he could to dispel the appearance of nepotism. The son started as a $200-a-month trainee and diligently studied the affairs of every department of the company. He was working as a driver's assistant when the truck drivers of the Wholesale Division asked him to join them in their usual lunchtime haunt. It was a big question of policy whether he should join them in their noontime beer as well. He did. There are those who are retired now and have no need to toady who say, "Henry has earned everything he has gotten."

After his father's death Hanko took over as head of the family. His sisters vie for the pleasure of sitting next to him at dinner in their mother's home. His friends range from men with *kamaaina* names like Charles Spalding, Peter Dillingham, and Zadoc Brown to Jack Lord, of TV's "Hawaii 5-0" fame, with whom he has shared the honor of being "Hawaii's salesman of the year."

Like his father, who for 17 years headed a charity supporting Hawaii's many victims of Hansen's disease, Hanko is generous in both public and private affairs. Everyone in the Islands knows that he headed the United Way drive. Few know of his financial generosity with some of the less affluent in his family.

Fond of mechanics and automobiles since boyhood, he has made one concession to executive status. At Conch Smith's orders, he gave up racing sports cars. In Hawaii he drives a BMW and in California a Porsche. There is a rumor making the rounds of a 100-mile-per-hour speeding ticket on an Oregon freeway last year.

Fate of the Dynasty

From all the plans and the thinking of the group chairmen, certain common characteristics appear. They suggest that the Amfac of the future will continue to be concerned with the provision of goods and services for people. These will range from sugar, potatoes, beef, and seafood to articles of clothing and virtually everything used in the home. It will offer shelter in many forms: apartments, town houses, single-family dwellings, and accommodations for businessmen and tourists. More recreational facilities—tennis and golf clubs, discotheques, and dining rooms—are a certainty. Financial activity will expand to embrace more than thrift accounts, mortgages, and consumer loans. Another area of expansion will be in getting goods to people who serve people, such things as dynamos, lumber, plumbing supplies, and roofing materials.

The backdrop for all this will be, appropriately, the Pacific basin. A theme common to all of it will be the zestful, the youthful. There will be even more colorful Joseph Magnin displays. Distribution will sell more electrical and health care products. Asset Management will be developing housing for the young marrieds and, with its mortgages, help them along. It is the young who seek the quick, prepared foods in McDonald's and the TV dinners where the meat, fish, and sugar will go. The resorts and hotels will be designed to appeal to the young in all of us.

On a recent visit to Europe I took the occasion to make a detour to Bremen to see if any evidence remained of Hackfeld's dynasty. The countryside is little changed from his and Isenberg's time. The brick and white-stuccoed farmhouses date from the eighteenth century. Fat sows graze the same flat land the Amfac founders knew, and white seabirds still float along the languid Weser. In Bremen, tomato soup flavored with gin continues to be a favorite dish. Of the Hackfeld business structure nothing remains.

I met the distinguished grandson of J. C. Pflueger, named Heinrich after Hackfeld. His business as an agent for food processors is in no way related to his grandfather's enterprise. His son, a successful insurance man, has no intention of continuing his father's current activities. I also met Dr. Pruser, head of the historical museum there, who had written a paper some 30 years ago on Paul Isenberg. It was, however, as much concerned with Isenberg's antecedents as his business prowess.

The only remaining physical evidence of the Hackfeld-Isenberg legacy is two charitable enterprises; one, carrying the Hackfeld name, is a dormitory for orphaned students; the other, the Paul Isenberg Foundation, is a reform school for boys on the outskirts of the city. In addition, downtown Bremen's conspicuous Lutheran Church has bronze doors donated by the Hackfelds, which survived the bombings and fires of World War II. Beyond those, nothing is left except memories. I find that there are more Hagens, Pfluegers, Isenbergs, and Rodieks scattered across the United States than in Bremen. The wealth so carefully nurtured is dissipated among them, nowhere concentrated in an enduring enterprise.

Whether we are witnessing, in 1974, the revitalization of an old regime or the inauguration of a new one remains to be seen. That may not be established for another 125 years. What is evident is that the profile of Amfac's history resembles an hourglass. There was, at the beginning, an enterprise that ranged much of the globe, however modestly. Then there was a time, at the waist of the glass, when its affairs were confined to miniscule Hawaii. Now, Amfac returns to the suns and seas of its origins as it straddles most of the United States and all the reaches of the broad Pacific that nourished Hackfeld's dynasty.

Bibliography

The following sources provided the bulk of the information and background employed in the text:

Adler, J. *Claus Spreckels: The Sugar King in Hawaii,* Honolulu, 1966.
Alexander, M. *William Patterson Alexander,* Honolulu, 1934.
Alexander, W. D. *Brief Account of the Hawaiian Government Survey,* Honolulu, 1899.
Allen, G. *Hawaii's War Years,* Honolulu, 1950.
Amfac, "Minutes of the Board of Directors," 1919–1974.
Baldwin, A. *Memoir of Henry Perrine Baldwin,* Cleveland, 1915.
Chinen, J. *Great Mahele,* Honolulu, 1958.
Clavell, J. *Taipan,* New York, 1966.
Cook, J. *Voyage to the Pacific Ocean, 1776–1780,* London, 1784.
Damon, E. *Koamalu,* Honolulu, 1931.
Daws, G. *Shoal of Time,* New York, 1969.
Friend, seaman's newspaper, Honolulu, 1843–1950.
Fuchs, L. *Hawaii Pono: A Social History,* New York, 1961.
H. Hackfeld & Co. "Minutes of the Board of Directors," 1898–1918.
Hawaiian Gazette, Honolulu, 1865–1918.
Hawaiian Star, Honolulu, 1828–1925.
Hawaiian Sugar Planters' Association. *Proceedings,* Honolulu, 1904–1971 (annual).
Hobbs, J. *Hawaii: A Pageant of the Soil,* Stanford, 1933.
Horman, B. "Germans in Hawaii," master's thesis, University of Hawaii, 1931.
Horowitz, R., and J. Finn. *Public Land Policy in Hawaii: Major Landowners,* Honolulu, 1967.

Indices of Awards Made by the Board of Commissioners to Quiet Land Titles in the Hawaiian Islands, Honolulu, 1929.

Jarves, J. *History of the Sandwich Islands,* London, 1843.

Judd, G. P., IV. *Dr. Judd: Hawaii's Friend,* Honolulu, 1960.

Judd, Laura. *Honolulu, 1828-1861,* New York, 1880.

Kuykendall, R. S. *The Hawaiian Kingdom,* 3 vols., Honolulu, 1938-1967.

Lord, W. *Day of Infamy,* New York, 1957.

"Mahele Book," State Archives, Honolulu.

Pacific Commercial Advertiser (now *Honolulu Advertiser*), Honolulu, 1882-

"Population Estimates and Censuses of Hawaii 1778-1850," *Hawaii Historical Review,* Honolulu, 1963.

Simonds, W. A. *Kamaaina: A Century in Hawaii,* Honolulu, 1949.

Spoehr, F. M. *White Falcon: The House of Godeffroy and Its Commercial and Scientific Role in the Pacific,* Palo Alto, Calif., 1963.

Thrum, T. G. (ed.). *Hawaiian Almanac and Annual: A Handbook of Information on Matters Relating to the Hawaiian Islands . . .,* vol. 1, Honolulu, 1875 (published 1925-1935 as *Hawaiian Annual* and since 1943 as *Thrum's Hawaiian Annual and Standard Guide*).

Twain, M. *Letters from the Sandwich Islands,* San Francisco, 1937.

Chief Executive Officers
and Principal Partners
of Amfac and Its Predecessors

Name	Role	Dates
Heinrich Hackfeld	Founder and Manager	1849[1]
J. C. Pflueger	Admitted as Partner	1853
	Managing Partner	1861-1871[2]
J. C. Glade	Managing Partner	1871-1883
H. W. Schmidt	Managing Partner	1883-1889
P. I. Isenberg	Managing Partner	1889-1898[3]
P. I. Isenberg	President	1898-1903
J. F. Hackfeld	Vice President	1898-1903
J. F. Hackfeld	President	1903-1917[4]
H. A. Isenberg	Vice President and Manager	1903-1906
W. A. Pfotenhauer	Vice President and Manager	1906-1913
George Rodiek	Vice President and Manager	1913-1918
J. F. C. Hagens	President	1918
George Sherman	President	1918-1919[5]
J. F. C. Hagens	General Manager	1918-1919
A. W. T. Bottomley	President	1919-1933
H. Alexander Walker, Sr.	President	1933-1950

Name	Role	Dates
H. P. Faye	President	1950–1952
Emmett Solomon	President	1952–1953
G. W. Sumner	President	1953–1959
C. Hutton Smith	President	1959–1964
Harold C Eichelberger	President	1964–1967
Henry A. Walker, Jr.	President	1967–1973
Henry A. Walker, Jr.	Chairman and Chief Executive Officer	1974[6]
Gilbert E. Cox	President and Chief Operating Officer	1974

[1]Continued as the nominal head of the firm (after returning to Bremen in 1861) until 1881. He then became a silent partner and sold out his interest in 1886.

[2]Left Hawaii in 1881 but continued to serve the firm from Bremen until his death in 1883.

[3]H. Hackfeld & Co. was formed December 24, 1897, but the election of officers did not take place until early 1898.

[4]In this period J. F. Hackfeld introduced the concept of a nominal President with affairs being run by a manager in Honolulu.

[5]Sherman was nominated by the Alien Property Custodian to preside during the course of the transition. Subsequently, he became Chairman of the Board, but he was never a force in directing the affairs of the company.

[6]The concept of a Chief Executive Officer sharing responsibilities with a Chief Operating Officer is a growing one among American corporations. With the 1974 appointment of E. Laurence Gay as Vice Chairman and Chief Finance and Administrative Officer, Amfac has further broadened the concept.

A Glossary of Hawaiian Terms

In the Islands the same names are often used for more than one place. Those listed are identified here as used in the text.

Aiea (eye-a'ah) Once a plantation, now largely urbanized.

Calabash kin Frequent adoptions by Hawaiians led those of different blood lines to eat from the same calabash.

Ewa (eh'vah) A district and plantation west of Pearl Harbor recently acquired by Amfac.

Great Mahele (mah-hay'lay) The redistribution of the land between the chiefs, the king, and the government, begun in 1846 by Kamehameha III. By 1850 foreigners could own land outright.

Hana (ha'nah) A district in southeastern Maui, once a plantation and now a ranch and resort.

Hanamaulu (ha-nah-ma-oo'lou) A district adjoining and now part of Lihue Plantation on Kauai.

Haole (hah'oh-lay) A member of the white race.

Hawaii (ha-y'ee) The southernmost and largest Island of the chain bearing the same name.

255

Heeia (hay-ay-ee'ah) A point on the windward coast north of Honolulu, once a sugar plantation.

Hilo (he'low, as in sew) Principal city and port of Hawaii.

Honolulu (hoe-no-lou'lou) The state capital on the south shore of Oahu.

Hui (who'ee) A syndicate or partnership.

Kaahumanu (kah-ah-who-ma'nu) Favorite wife of Kamehameha I, who succeeded him as monarch and abandoned the native gods and taboos.

Kaanapali (kah-ah-nah-pah'lee) Resort adjoining Lahaina developed by Amfac.

Kahului (kah-who-lou'ee) A principal business center on the north coast of Maui and the Island's only port.

Kailua (ky-lou'ah) Resort and sport fishing port on the southwest coast of Hawaii.

Kalakaua (kah-lah-cow'ah) King of the Islands from 1874 to 1891; known as the Merry Monarch.

Kamaaina (kah-mah'eye-nah) A long-time resident of Hawaii.

Kamehameha (kay-may-ha-may'ha) The name of five kings of the Islands. Kamehameha I reigned 1810–1819; Kamehameha II, 1819–1824; Kamehameha III (also known as Kauikeaouli), 1825–1854; Kamehameha IV (also called Lot), 1854–1863; and Kamehameha V, 1863–1872. King Kamehameha is the name of an Amfac hotel in Kailua-Kona.

Kanaka (kah-knack'ah) A native Hawaiian.

Kauai (cow-eye'ee) Northernmost Island of the chain.

Keauhou (cay'ah-hoe) Resort south of Kona developed by the Bishop Estate and site of an Amfac hotel.

Kekaha (kay-kah'ha) A district and an Amfac plantation on western Kauai.

Kilauea (key-lah-way'ah) A district on northern Kauai.

Kipahulu (key-pa-who'lou) A district and a former plantation on eastern Maui.

Koamalu (koh-ah-ma'lou) The Rice family home in Lihue, Kauai.

Koloa (koh-low'ah) A district, site of the oldest plantation in the Islands, now part of McBryde Sugar Co.

Kona (ko'nah) A district on southwest Hawaii where Hackfeld & Co. failed in sugar but experimented with many crops.

Koolau (koh-oh-low´, as in cow) A mountain range on Oahu.

Kukui (coo-coo´ee) A nut whose oil was used by natives for lighting as well as for medicine.

Lahaina (la-high´nah) Seaport and resort area; also headquarters for Amfac's Pioneer Mill on western Maui.

Lanai (la-nigh´ee) An Island west of Maui.

Lihue (lee-who´ee) Largest community on Kauai and headquarters for Amfac's Lihue Plantation.

Lilikoi (lee-lee´coy) Passion fruit and the name of a defunct plantation.

Liliuokalani (lee-lee-ooh´oh-kah-lah´nee) Queen of the Islands from 1891 to 1893, when she was dethroned; she was the last reigning monarch.

Luna (loo´nah) A foreman of a plantation.

Lunalilo (lou-nah-lee´low) King of the Islands from 1873 to 1874.

Mai tai Hawaii's exotic drink.

Manoa (ma-no´ah) A valley in residential Honolulu.

Maui (mow´ee) Second largest Island and second most southerly in the chain.

Menehune (may-nay-who´nee) A mythical Polynesian dwarf.

Molokai (mo-loh-kah´ee) A ranching Island just southeast of Oahu.

Nawiliwili (nah-wee´lee-wee´lee) A valley on Kauai and the name of its principal port.

Oahu (oh-ah´who) The second most northerly Island and home for 85 percent of the population of the chain. Also the name of Amfac's largest plantation.

Olaa (oh-lah´ah) A district on Hawaii adjoining Hilo and the name first given to the Amfac plantation now known as Puna.

Pahoa (pa-hoe´ah) A district south of Puna once planted to sugar.

Pepeekeo (pay-pay-a-kay´o) A district on the northeast coast of Hawaii and the name of a plantation once in the Hackfeld group.

Poi (poy, as in boy) Taro paste, a staple in the diet. Also the name given dogs which were cooked over heated stones and eaten with poi.

Poipu (poy´poo) A resort development on the southern coast of Kauai, near Koloa, where Amfac has hotels.

Puna (poo´nah) See Olaa.

Taro (tare′o)   A tuber, the source of poi.

Waiahole (y-ah-hole′ee)   A valley on the northern coast of Oahu from which a ditch provides Amfac's Oahu Sugar Co. with irrigation water.

Waialeale (y-ah′lay-ah′lay)   The mountain that dominates and is encircled by Kauai.

Wailua (y-lou′ah)   A river, east of Lihue, where the Rices picnicked and Amfac hotels stand today.

Waianae (y′ah-nigh)   A district and site of a former Amfac plantation on western Oahu.

Waimanalo (y-mah-nah′low)   A town on eastern Oahu, once the site of a sugar plantation.

Waimea (y-may′ah)   A district on southern Kauai.

Waipahu (y-pa′who)   Headquarters for Amfac's Oahu Sugar Co. adjoining Pearl Harbor; also a town.

Index

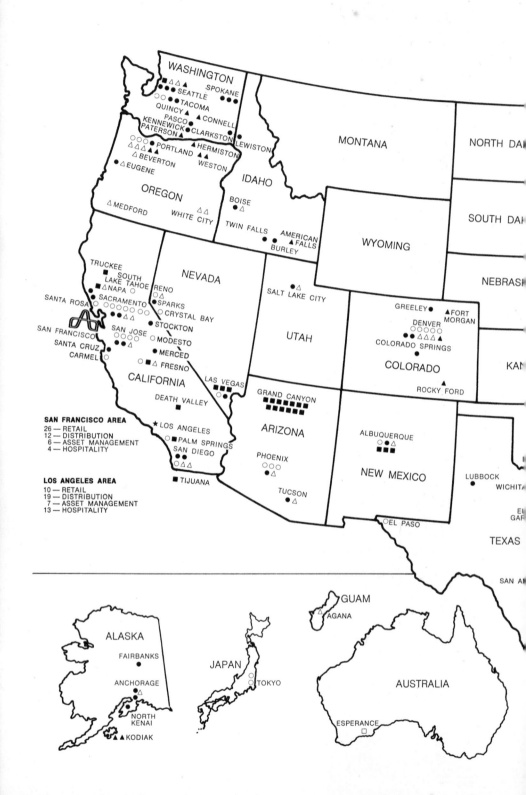